THE NEW INTERNATIONAL ECONOMY

THE NEW INTERNATIONAL ECONOMY

Edited by Harry Makler, Alberto Martinelli & Neil Smelser

 SAGE Studies in International Sociology **26**
sponsored by the International Sociological Association/ISA

For information address

SAGE Publications Inc, 275 South Beverly Drive,
Beverly Hills, California 90212

SAGE Publications Ltd, 28 Banner Street, London EC1Y 8QE

British Library Cataloguing in Publication Data

The New international economy.
  1. International business enterprises
  I. Makler, Harry M.
  II. Martinelli, Alberto
  III. Smelser, Neil J.
  338.8'8   ND2755.5   81-52746

ISBN 0-8039-9792-2

CONTENTS

III INTERNATIONAL AND NATIONAL FINANCE

IV POLITICAL AND SOCIAL THEMES

PREFACE

This volume is a collective product of the Research Committee on Economy and Society of the International Sociological Association (ISA). More concretely, it is a collection of papers presented at a conference of the committee, entitled 'The Social and Political Challenges of the New Economy in Comparative Perspective,' held in Bellagio from 24 to 28 April 1979.

The research committee itself crystallized within the ISA as a merger of two independently formed ad hoc research groups. The first, a group on economy and society, was organized and sustained under the leadership of Alberto Martinelli and Neil Smelser during the 1970s. The second, a group on entrepreneurship, industrial leadership and development, was carried through the same period under the leadership of Fernando Cardoso and Harry Makler. At the initiative of the Executive Council of the ISA the two groups merged in 1976 and were given formal approval as a research committee within the ISA in 1978. At the present time the Executive Committee of the research committee is Fernando Cardoso, Neil Smelser (co-chair), Alberto Martinelli, Luciano Martins (co-vice chairman), Harry Makler (executive secretary) and Arnaud Sales (treasurer).

The measure of the research committee is broader than the focus of the volume — encompassing the vast interplay between the economy and all social and cultural institutions — but the strategy of the organizing group of the Bellagio conference was to focus on ramifications of contemporary capitalist development, because of the centrality of this subject in contemporary scholarship as well as its importance for the survival of contemporary civilization.

The committee is grateful to the Ford Foundation for providing funds to finance the Bellagio conference, and to the Rockefeller Foundation for making its Bellagio Study and Conference Center and staff available to us on a virtually no-cost basis. We should also like to thank the publications committee of the ISA for approving and accepting this volume into the sociology series.

HMM
AM
NJS

1

INTRODUCTION

Harry M. Makler
University of Toronto, Canada

Alberto Martinelli
University of Milan, Italy

Neil J. Smelser
University of California, Berkeley, USA

ISSUES IN THE ANALYSIS OF
THE INTERNATIONAL ECONOMY
AND ITS IMPACT

As the twentieth century draws towards a close, we see three great
threats facing the people of the planet earth. The first is the threat
of a nuclear holocaust, which could bring death to millions or
billions and destroy civilization as the world knows it. The second
is the threat of ruination of the earth's environment, whether by ex-
hausting its key resources through unregulated economic activity or
unregulated population growth, or by poisoning its waters and atmosphere and, through them, its people. And the third is the threat
of repeated and disastrous economic crises, breakdown and conflicts stemming from a new and distinctive world economic situation that appears to have evolved beyond humanity's current
capacity to control either that economic situation or its political
and social ramifications; we refer to this situation as the new international economy.

We see these threats not as independent, but as a related family
of threats. The threat of environmental ruination is unintelligible
without the understanding of the growth of industrial capitalism,

its competition within itself and with the socialist economies, and the spread of both systems to the Third World. And the threat of nuclear war is rendered intelligible only by grasping its main causes, among which international economic competition and the breakdown of the world economy are paramount. Toward the end of the essay we shall speculate further on the interconnections among the different classes of crises facing the world. But in this introductory essay, and in the volume as a whole, we shall concentrate principally on the international economy. In the first section (initially prepared by Alberto Martinelli) we shall lay out the broad historical phases of the development of the world economy; following that (in a section initially drafted by Harry Makler), we shall characterize its financial dimensions; third, we shall comment on the broad world context of the international economic order, indicating what parts of that context appear to have been rendered perhaps obsolete by it; and finally, we shall say a few words on the rationale for the organization of the remainder of the volume, and identify the nature of each author's contribution (Neil Smelser prepared the initial draft of this section, and also co-ordinated the other drafts).

By the term 'international economy' we refer to a patterned system of economic relations among national economies and other types of politico-economic organizations such as corporations and financial institutions. While each of these agencies can be studied on its own, we stress that the unit of analysis on which we focus is the system as a whole, which stands above and cannot be reduced to any of its component parts. Furthermore, we focus on the distinctive problems of the integration of the international system and on its distinctive conflicts and contradictions. These problems of integration, conflict and contradiction are, in part, 'economic' problems, but they are political and social as well. The organization of production and exchange on a world scale implies a new international division of labor, new relations among classes and other groups, new bases of conflict and new power relations among states no less than it implies a new organization of firms and markets.

BROAD HISTORICAL PHASES IN THE DEVELOPMENT OF THE WORLD ECONOMY

Without implying any inherent evolutionary tendency, we can identify a few major phases of development of the world economy: first, the transition from feudalism to capitalism; second, the stage of competitive capitalism; third, the stage of imperialism; and, fourth, the stage of transnational capitalism in the context of international bifurcation and polarization of the 'capitalist' and 'communist' blocs of nations. In tracing these phases we concentrate on the modes of integration of the world economy and on the relations among firms, markets and states, emphasizing that these relations imply both integration and conflict, planning and breakdown.

The long transition from feudalism to capitalism, stretching from the sixteenth century to the Industrial Revolution of the eighteenth and early nineteenth centuries, witnessed both the emergence of a world trade system at the international level and the development of distinctive cultural, legal and social-structural arrangements that were conducive for the implementation of capitalist economies and societies. The principal lines of development during this transition were the freeing of labor from feudal restrictions, the accumulation of merchant and financial capital, and the growth of international markets.[1]

As a kind of culmination to this transition, the world economy entered the stage of competitive capitalism, which dominated throughout the nineteenth century, and might be said to have reached its culmination in the great world economic crisis of 1873-96. This phase was characterized by the gradual implementation of an interdependent world economy. During this period the major integrative mechanisms were the principles of the free competitive market, combined with economic and political intervention on the part of nation-states, especially Britain, in periods of instability. Under these conditions, world commerce, which had expanded only slowly during the mercantilist era, accelerated dramatically in the middle decades of the nineteenth century, then slowed toward the end of the century.[2] Politically, the period brought 'the hundred years peace,' policed by the free trade-oriented, maritime power of Great Britain, coupled with an international and cosmopolitan financial class, who resisted, at least temporarily, the growing tendencies toward national power politics.[3]

The two great intellectual diagnoses of this phase of capitalist development were those of the classical economic thinkers (from Adam Smith to John Stuart Mill) and of Karl Marx. While opposed in many respects, these diagnoses shared certain common themes. Both the classical school and Marx regarded the capitalist system as a distinctive system, integrated by exchange in national and world markets; both regarded capitalism as possessing the capacity to bypass or destroy feudal constraints on the free movement of the factors of production; and both stressed the powerful drives toward economic growth in the capitalist system. And, in different ways, both understated the role of the state in the national and world capitalist economy. For the classical economists, the international market emerged as a harmonious summation of a huge number of free transactions among rational economic agents. The market itself was the central — and automatic — integrating mechanism. By contrast, state action would fragment world markets, support narrow class interests rather than the general welfare, and promote conflict rather than cooperation in the world economy. As a result of these assumptions, the classical economists did not see the integration of the world economic system as a political problem. Neither did Marx, but for an opposite reason: he thought that no conscious effort by political actors could prevent the collapse of the whole system. Marx analyzed the major contradictions of capitalism — the contradiction between the growing socialization of the means of production and the increasingly centralized private appropriation of profits, the contradiction between the organized character of the firm and the anarchy of the market — in almost exclusively economic and sociological terms. Intra-bourgeois competition over profits and inter-class conflict over the control of the production process were stressed, with little regard to the growth of and rivalries among nation-states. And, on the whole, the internationalization of capitalism meant the spreading of class conflict from the advanced industrial countries to the rest of the world.

In retrospect it is possible to recognize that the role of the state in the nineteenth-century international economy was more significant than either set of authors acknowledged. During the middle of the century — between the 1840s and 1870s — the world economy revolved around Great Britain. The first to industrialize, Britain's large, open economy developed ties with the rest of the world, particularly in areas of recent settlement, which built their railroads with British capital and British goods and exported their agricultural products to the 'workshop of the world.' In a process later described as 'the imperialism of free trade,'[4] Britain dominated world markets for manufactured goods with its products and encouraged peripheral states to specialize in production and exportation of primary products to Britain. It is true that the British government played little direct role in trade and capital export. Nevertheless, British military power — particularly maritime power — helped maintain British access to world markets. Britain's national colonial policy played a role helpful to British capital domination. Her colonial control over India impeded and sometimes destroyed indigenous Indian textile manufacturers and thus contributed to Lancashire's rise and consolidation of control over the cotton textile manufacture.[5] And as the nineteenth century wore on, the British-dominated international monetary system came to be more dependent on British access to Indian gold and protected markets in the Empire.[6] Even the policy of laissez-faire implied a definite state presence, since with that policy the state provided a legal and institutional framework that left political decisions to capitalists and gave freedom of movement to labor and other resources.

The link between the state and capitalist development became increasingly evident in the transition to the third phase, imperialism, which covered the turbulent period between the world economic crisis of 1873-96 and the Second World War. It is characterized by increasing concentration of industrial and financial capital; the increasing closeness of interest between those trusts that held economic power and the nation-states that wielded political-military power; the colonial partition of the non-industrialized areas of the world by the industrial powers; and a growing rivalry in international relations. While notable overall for its distinctive model of capital concentration and politico-economic domination in the form of imperialism, the phase is also marked by notable discontinuities — the acceleration of the movement of both people and money around the turn of the century; the progressive change from economic competition toward political-military confrontation prior to and cumulating in the First World War; the precarious restoration of the imperial order in the 1920s; the economic collapse in the Great Depression of the 1930s; and the second great political collapse in the Second World War.

Economic and social thinkers in the early twentieth century, both liberal and Marxist, did not fail to diagnose the imperialist developments; and the writings of Hobson, Hilferding, O. Bauer, Luxemburg, Bucharin, Lenin and Schumpeter superseded those of the classical economic theorists of Marx and Engels.[7] The main drift of the Marxist diagnosis — found both in writers of this period and in subsequent works — was to identify new kinds of contradictions not stressed by Marx and distinctive to the imperialist period. The first contradiction noted was between the internationalization of economic life and the increasing nationalism of nationally based bourgeois groups. The second contradiction was between the largely international process of capital circulation on the one hand and the nationally based processes of consensus-creation, political legitimization and the social reproduction of capital. This implies that, although market interdependence and capital internationalization may reduce the direct role of the state in the capitalist economy, the state must continue to sustain the basic socio-political conditions necessary for that economy. The implication of the first contradiction is that differences in the timing and sequence of industrial development in different nation-states led local, emerging bourgeois classes to rely on the political and military power of states to facilitate their competition with other, established capitalists elsewhere. For example, state tariffs, adopted by industrial 'latecomers,' were at first designed to overcome the disadvantage of national capital in the international market, but now became the source of high profits for powerful domestic groups, who sought the protection of the state not only to meet foreign competition but also to extend their protected markets and secure sources of raw materials. The liberal ideal of peaceful coexistence among independent states was transformed into the imperialist ideology, stressing the role of the state in curbing labor demands at home and pursuing policies of conquest and rivalry abroad. In this view, imperialism was an adaptation to these fundamental and inherent contradictions.

Liberal analyses of imperialism also emphasized the alliance between the state and capital in the late-developing countries. Economic factors do play a role in these interpretations, as illustrated by the interpretation of the German tariff of 1879 as a 'marriage of iron and rye.'[8] Prospective economic competition may also have played a role; European governments entered the scramble for colonies, especially in Africa, not so much because they were certain that economic advantages would accrue (as often as not they did not), but because they were attempting to prevent their rivals from acquiring the opportunity for prospective gains. Yet other factors are given more prominence in the non-Marxist tradition. Liberal writers on imperialism have stressed the persistence of struggles for power in world politics, above and beyond the economic interests of the contending actors. Following Schumpeter, they have emphasized the tendency of imperial states to extend their empires in an attempt to protect their 'turbulent frontiers,' or their power and prestige.[9]

The collapse of the international economy in the Second World War was so complete that many Marxists regarded the prospects for the continuation of capitalism as remote, and many liberals, including Keynes, felt that a return to a free international economy and to liberal economic policies was unlikely. Yet, again in retrospect, these diagnoses underestimated the resiliency of capitalism, and it is possible to view the postwar decades as a movement to a new phase, defined as the phase of transnational capitalism, characterized by continued competition but in the context of the hegemony of the United States.

When this phase of world economic development began and where it is going are subjects of great uncertainty and debate. Scholars even disagree whether or not the postwar period is anything qualitatively new. Some, mainly Marxists, see the period as a continuation of imperialism, citing such features as the growth of capital concentration and direct foreign investments. Others, mainly liberals, see the period as a kind of restoration of the free competitive world of the nineteenth century, with the United States assuming the dominating and monitoring role that Britain previously played. Both these views highlight genuine continuities, but both appear to miss certain distinctive characteristics of the most recent era. For example, it is true that the transnational corporations are the heirs of the cartels and trusts of an earlier era, but transnationals develop very different relations to the states of their home and host countries than did cartels and trusts, as well as very different relations to the international workforce they employ.[10] Furthermore, there are distinctive features of the world political order that must be taken into consideration; in particular, in so far as the American economy enjoys general hegemony, it does so in the context of the intense economic and political competition with the Soviet bloc, which operates in some degree as a separate world economy. Furthermore, serious economic and political threats to domination have arisen within each sphere — from Western Europe and Japan in one, and from China in the other. And the political role of the decolonized Third World is clearly less passive than in the imperialist era.

The main new features in the internationalization process are the increased importance of international trade within nearly all sectors of the economy (including the private service sectors) and the rise of transnational corporations, which are distinguished by direct investments abroad and the internationalization of entrepreneurship and technology. Whatever indicators are selected,[11] they show that international interdependence has increased significantly since 1945, certainly reversing the trend of the first half of the century, and in some cases accelerating faster than comparable trends in the nineteenth century. World commerce more than quintupled between 1950 and 1971; the annual rate of its growth was more than 7 percent in the 1950s and about 10 percent in the 1960s, often less than the rate (from a lower base) in the mid-nineteenth century but remarkable when compared with the interwar decline.[12]

The trends in capital flow are even more dramatic. Much of this increase in the 1950s and 1960s was due to investments of transnational corporations based in the United States, but short-term capital movements also played an important role. More recently, long-term direct investments by other advanced industrial countries have also increased rapidly. Another measure of the same process is the increasing internationalization of production. In the 1960s, the gross national product expanded by about 4 percent a year in most industrial countries, while imports and exports have increased by 8 to 10 percent, and production by subsidiaries abroad increased by 10 to 12 percent.

Among the political and technological factors that have facilitated this kind of expansion and the internationalization of industry and capital are the formation of an integrated economic sphere (with American dominance), the reconstruction of the international monetary system, the liberalization of trade, the development of advanced technologies permitting significant economies of scale, and the tremendous development in transportation and communications. The 1950s witnessed significant liberalization of import controls, the lowering of tariffs and the gradual return to convertibility beginning with the Bretton Woods agreements. The opening of the system accelerated in the 1960s, with a more nearly complete return to convertibility after 1958, several rounds of further tariff cuts through GATT agreements (for example, the Kennedy Round), and the development of regional trading areas, such as the European Economic Community, which was launched in 1957. These trends were paralleled by liberalizations in domestic economies, as direct discrimination regulations over the prices and quantities of commodities and factors of production gave way to lesser measures aimed at influencing aggregate demand.[13] Beginning in the 1960s, however, especially in Japan and France, there appeared the reverse trend to return to more detailed state interventions into the domestic economy; this tendency spread to other industrialized countries in the 1970s, when most of them experienced scarcities of basic factors of production such as oil and low-cost labor.

Beginning in the 1970s, this remarkable combination of economic and political arrangements began to show signs of weakness if not outright disintegration. The international monetary system became much more turbulent, beginning with the devaluation of the dollar in 1970. Protectionism in external economic relations increased in part because of competition between advanced and newly industrialized countries. World trade and foreign direct investments continue to grow at high rates, but the major industrial countries seem incapable of guaranteeing sustained rates of growth and employment with controlled rates of inflation; the 1970s became the decades of 'stagflation.' Communications and transportation continue to advance, but the capacity of productive organizations to exploit economies of scale has been thrown into doubt. Finally, the dominance of the United States has been challenged and eroded to some degree by both oil-producing countries and their industrialized partners.

The ultimate significance of the most recent changes, however, is the subject of debate and different interpretations. Marxist observers such as Mandel and Amin interpret the weakening of the American economic position in the late 1960s and early 1970s as pointing the way to a new condition of intra-capitalist rivalry.[14] At the same time, non-Marxist scholars like Gilpin have drawn analogies between the position of Great Britain in the late nineteenth century and that of the United States in recent decades; according to this view, the United States has been overinvesting abroad, and providing its technological expertise to the rest of the world at too low a price, thus undermining its own industrial strength.[15] Other phenomena cited as evidence for the 'declining hegemony' thesis are the declining proportion of world production accounted for by the United States, that country's inability to prevent large increases in oil prices imposed by formerly impotent oil-producing countries, and the recurrent crises of the dollar during the past decade.

The view that American dominance — and, with it, the present international order — will collapse has been challenged by those claiming that recent events imply not an inter-capitalist rivalry and significant shifts in power among advanced capitalist countries, but only a 'readjustment' — a persisting American hegemony, possibly accompanied by a more active role of other advanced industrial countries in the regulation and governance of the international system. In addition, while it might be argued that America as a nation-state may be in the process of some erosion, most of the transnational corporations nevertheless continue to be based in the United States, and through their influence the American presence continues to be felt.

Regardless of how one weighs the evidence — in favor of continued hegemony or of divisive rivalry — the debate suggests clearly that the integration of the world economic system under American leadership is more problematic now than it was during the 1950s and 1960s. As a result, strategies followed by other states — particularly by Japan and Germany and other European states — are likely to have a significant impact on the evolution of the system as a whole. The advanced industrial states will not easily be able to compartmentalize their policies as clearly as before, since strategies of association and dissociation in trade, energy and monetary policies may have decisive effects on the system as a whole.[16] The existence of greater economic and financial competition among the industrial powers, moreover, also raises the question of whether the basis of their political-military alliances may not be eroded as well. In any event, to the degree that the international world economy can no longer be regarded as generally being subsumed under the policies and strategies of the United States, its integration, regulation and stability become correspondingly more complicated and problematical.

THE SPECIAL PLACE OF
FINANCIAL INSTITUTIONS IN
THE NEW INTERNATIONAL ECONOMY*

While most students of the development of the world economy have acknowledged that increasingly complex patterns of banking and other financial arrangements invariably accompany — indeed, are thought to be a condition for — the growth of complex patterns of resource allocation, production and marketing, it has been less widely appreciated how powerful banks and other financial institutions can be in actively influencing the growth of a developing economy and affecting the very nature of the developmental process. By the allocation of surplus capital from savers and investors toward different kinds of economic activities, financial institutions have served as a mechanism for social control, favoring desirable countries, or sectors of an economy, and simultaneously discouraging or marginalizing others.

A number of economic historians have pointed out the non-neutrality of banking networks with respect to economic development. Cameron,[17] for example, outlined a comparative framework within which to analyze the development of existing financial structures of various countries. His conclusion is that the fundamental dynamics of economic development lie outside of the banking network, but its structure can either facilitate or hinder socioeconomic development. Gerschenkron[18] presents a similar framework, suggesting that banks play a key role at certain 'stages' of the development process, but his specification of these stages is not very precise. Patrick[19] follows these leads by asking whether and when a financial system can be a growth-inducing sector. On the one hand, the financial sector can be 'demand-following', so that 'as the economy grows it generates additional and new demands for these (financial) services, which bring about a supply response in the growth of the financial system.'[20] On the other hand, finance may play an inducing or 'supply-leading' role by effecting the transfer of resources from a source of surplus to deficit and/or sectors of the economy. Other observers, notably McKinnon[21] and Shaw,[22] have identified more specific internal mechanisms for financing

* We appreciate the collaboration of Wendy Barker in the preparation of this section. Ms Barker, currently a graduate student in the sociology department at Yale University, intends to do doctoral research on this topic.

economic development, such as interest rates and their effect on domestic savings and financial markets.

These formulations — as well as a number of empirical studies — indicate that banking networks have often played more than merely a 'passive and permissive' role. But perhaps the most decisive evidence of banking institutions' potential for active intervention is found in the history of the international economy during the period following the Second World War. In 1944 representatives from the industrialized nations of the world met at Bretton Woods, New Hampshire, to develop a host of new institutional arrangements to oversee and regulate international economic relations. That year marked the creation of what was to become the first publicly managed international monetary order. Prior to this time, economic development was financed by private foreign investment, and international trade was characterized by highly competitive monetary depreciation. The 1930s witnessed the collapse of the international monetary system through severe competition and the erection of trade barriers, which were themselves a response to the economic hardship occasioned by the Great Depression. Also contributing to the collapse was a history of international lending extended with little concern for the borrower's uses of the funds, which had resulted in turn in widespread default. To restore international economic stability, and to prevent further implementation of economic policies directed at protecting domestic markets, the representatives of the world's developed countries negotiated plans to design a consciously managed international monetary order: the Bretton Woods system.

The main institutions created to direct this new international monetary order were the International Monetary Fund (IMF) and the World Bank Group. The IMF Articles of Agreement imposed a system of fixed exchange rates which required all countries to establish parity of their currencies against gold, and to maintain exchange rates within 1 percent (plus or minus) of parity. Any alteration of these ratios required the IMF 'seal of approval.' To facilitate international trade, domestic currencies were officially made convertible.

Not only were these institutions designed to regulate and ensure the flow of private capital and the internationalization of production, but they also symbolized the alignment of advanced capitalist nations against the threat of international communism. The Bretton Woods institutions were designed by the 'liberal-democratic' nations (especially the United States and the United Kingdom). Although the socialist bloc (the Soviet Union in particular) participated in the negotiations they declined membership in the fund when it was inaugurated. In the main the industrially advanced nations adopted a 'modernization' perspective which led them to believe that the causes of the backwardness of the 'less-developed countries' were the internal remnants of traditional society that could be abolished by massive doses of foreign aid and investment.

There was yet another, perhaps even more important, reason for imposing this kind of monetary order at this particular moment in history. The Second World War had devastated the European economies, and this had disrupted many of the major markets for American goods. The enormous deficits in the balances of payments of the European countries signified the destruction of their productive capacity and threatened to generate a condition of continuing economic instability and political chaos. The IMF's designated responsibility was to advance loans to countries in these kinds of predicament. From a capital fund it could issue short-term (three- to five-year) loans. Its capital reserves would be composed of contributions from member countries in gold and in their respective currencies. The size of the loan was to be dependent upon a country's 'quota' in the fund. The first 25 percent of the quota could be drawn with 'no strings attached.' However, above this percentage greater restrictions could be applied. Through a 'Letter of Intent' the IMF could and can prescribe the adoption of certain monetary policies to restore order to the borrowing country's economy. These policies usually are deflationary, involving currency devaluations, wage cuts and strict reductions on governmental spending.

The International Bank for Reconstruction and Development (IBRD), the leading member of the World Bank Group, was also originally designed to facilitate postwar economic recovery. This role, however, proved to be secondary, as the world banking institutions turned their attention to addressing the aspiring interests of many developing countries and to retaining political influence over these potential allies in the Cold War. The World Bank, rather, concentrated in advancing funds to the less developed countries for specific development projects. To fulfill this obligation a number of different institutions have been created; these constitute the World Bank Group. The most important of these is the IBRD, which has moved towards issuing long-term (15-25 year) loans to governments at commercial rates for specified development projects. The International Development Association (IDA) administers 'soft-term' loans to less developed countries with very low gross national products, loans that carry at a nominal service charge rate for a period of up to 50 years. And the International Finance Corporation (IFC) specializes in stimulating the private sector of developing countries.

More than 50 percent of the World Bank Group's capital is supplied by the highly industrialized countries. These countries also tend to dominate the decisions concerning what countries receive loans and for what purposes. In practice, both the motives and the effectiveness of the operations of the Group's activities have been questionable. The activities supported by long-term loans are primarily developing projects requiring advanced technology and/or elaborate economic infrastructures, both of which, once begun, require sustained imports of equipment and know-how. The proliferation from such 'growth-inducing' projects to many societal members has yet to materialize. In effect, the activities of the World Bank Group tend to encourage uneven economic development in the world. More often than not the World Bank, in making decisions to lend, takes its 'cue' from the IMF on what countries are economically and politically 'good risks.' Many countries that receive World Bank loans are also receiving IMF financing for balance of payment deficits, and must also comply with the 'conditional' economic policies that accompany it. A recent report in the *New York Times*[23] outlined the effects of IMF recommendations that were attached to a loan to Jamaica. It reported that despite — or perhaps because of — the IMF's policy recommendations, in the past year real wages had fallen by more than one-third, consumption was down, malnutrition seemed to be rising, and economic growth was negative for the fifth consecutive year.

Some observers have argued that the world's official banking institutions have created a new form of economic dependency. To paraphrase Dos Santos,[24] foreign financing has become a necessity. Because of their dependence, many less developed countries (IDCs) have been unable to diversify exports or gain control over the means of production for their own economic base. Since they must in consequence import goods that are not produced internally in order to industrialize, the result is great deficits in their balance of payments. In this way a vicious circle is created. Foreign capital must be borrowed simply to serve the growing deficit, to secure a better position in the world trade, and to make strides toward some kind of development. The internal economic ramifications are likely to be regressive; the banking systems in LDCs favor private and official borrowers who absorb the limited finance available at low rates of interest. Small farmers and indigenous 'traditional' workers are bypassed as the bulk of bank credit goes to elaborate infrastructure projects, industries based on the export of primary products, large international corporations or government 'white elephants' (for example, Brasilia).

To return to other aspects of the fortunes of the Bretton Woods arrangements, it became apparent that the international monetary order invested at those meetings was not functioning as anticipated. The main problem was that the IMF's modest reserves (initially $8.8 million) were insufficient to deal with Europe's huge balance of payments deficit. At this time the United States, the only 'unscathed' country after the war, stepped in to fill this deficiency. The international monetary system thus came under more or less unilateral American management. The World Bank lost much of its international character and became virtually an 'American' institution, for the United States supplied most of IBRD's loanable funds and served as the principal market for the Bank's sale of securities with which it raised capital. The United States was the largest shareholder, which gave her the voting majority in the decision-making process. The European nations accepted American leadership, since they needed the strength of the dollar to assist in the rebuilding of domestic production. In 1947, therefore, the dollar became the world's currency and the United States its central banker. The combination of America's economic and military strength, the fixed relationship of the dollar to gold, and the commitment of the United States government to convert dollars into gold made the dollar by far the strongest major international currency.

During the next decade the United States encouraged an outflow of dollars under the Marshall Plan and the European Recovery Plan to provide liquidity for the international economy. American interests were vitally involved in this flow, for European recovery meant a widening market for American exports. Subsequently, in the 1960s, the United States developed a number of 'development banks' and aid agencies, which actively influenced the economic policies of affected countries. In 1961 the Inter-American Development Bank (IDB) began its operations, which, like the World Bank, extended long-term and soft loans. The Agency for International Development (AID) also increased its level of lending at this time. The latter agency openly discussed and attempted to influence the economic policies of borrowing countries, and, in addition, relied on political criteria in selecting borrowers. The Export-Import Bank, although created before the war, was inactive until afterwards; its main activity was to increase markets for American exports by issuing credit to buyers of American goods.

During this period the role of the private banking network was largely confined to providing long-term financing through the sale of bonds and short-term loans to 'creditworthy' clients. Gradually, however, in response to a growing demand for banking services by transnational corporations in the 1950s and 1960s, private banks began branching out to channel funds for transnational operations. For example, in 1965 there were only 13 United States banks abroad with assets of $9.1 billion, compared with 125 with assets of $124 billion in 1974.[25] During the same period the international activities of private American banks grew faster than domestic activities; in 1964 the Chase Manhattan Bank's foreign earnings accounted for only 14 percent of its total profits, whereas in 1974 the corresponding figure was 49 percent.[26] Thus, up to this point there was a rather strict division of labor between the public and banking institutions, but both spheres revealed America's financial hegemony, which paralleled its dominance in the international economy generally.

The system of encouraging foreign holdings of United States dollars was made possible if other countries ran a balance of payment deficit to the United States. But, moving into the 1960s, this pattern began to change. The Japanese and many European economies had revived, and their foreign dollar holdings began to exceed United States gold reserves for the first time. The United States deficit was difficult to control because of the enormous capital outflows involved in military and foreign aid programs. The weakness of the dollar was becoming more and more evident. Realizing that the United States could no longer play such a leading role as international money manager, the European community and others initiated a number of moves toward collective management. European central banks moved toward greater international cooperation; the Group of Ten[27] was formed to constitute 'money managers' for the exchange of banking information as well as proposals for negotiating monetary reform.

The 1960s also witnessed the growth of the 'Euromarket,' which consists of the Eurocurrency and Eurobond markets. These private markets have dominated in the 1970s, while bilateral and multilateral forms of financing have diminished in importance. The Euromarket first made its appearance in the 1950s. Its origin has been traced to the deposit of American dollars by the Soviet Union and other East European countries into London and Paris central banks, instead of United States banks, mainly for political reasons.[28] The Eurocurrency market (sometimes termed the Eurodollar market as well, since most deposits and loans are in United States dollars), consists of a number of banks that operate out of London and, more recently, Caribbean and Middle East financial markets and accept and make loans in different currencies. The Eurocurrency market has a competitive advantage; it pays high interest rates on deposits and lower rates on loans, and operates with fewer reserve requirements than most banks. The Eurobond market is of limited importance as a source of capital for developing economies.

In these ways a new system of multilateral management — consisting of networks of monetary 'elites' — surfaced to internationalize banking, to attempt to restore stability, and, in the process, to replace American leadership. The result of these developments is a relative loss of United States financial domination and its diminishing ability to impose its will on other countries. The growth of other strong economies — especially West Germany and Japan, but also 'emerging' strong economies such as Taiwan, Korea and Hong Kong — has correspondingly decreased the world's reliance on the United States, especially in terms of trade.

In addition to the challenges from emerging strong economies, American dominance was brought under pressure from demands on the part of the newly developing countries — mainly through such forums as UNCTAD. These countries expressed dissatisfaction with a system that shaped their economies without their participation in the inner circle of management. Their concerns included their vulnerability in terms of trade, their continuing dependence on the developed nations, and their limited capacity to develop themselves. These kinds of grievances became 'packaged' in what was to become a demand for a New International Economic Order (NIEO).

The United States entered the 1970s with high inflation and unemployment and an escalating balance of payments deficit, which had been aggravated by an outflow of dollars and the enormous military expenditures during the Vietnamese war. On 15 August 1971 President Nixon declared that the United States would no longer abide by the ground rules of the Bretton Woods international monetary system; foreign dollar holdings would no longer be convertible into gold, and a temporary trade barrier (10 percent surcharge on dutiable imports) would be erected. This marked the collapse of the Bretton Woods system of par values and stable exchanges, and the beginning of the situation of uncertainty, currency instability and floating exchanges that has persisted until this time. By 1973 all major currencies were floating, with 2½ percent (plus or minus) of parity.

In 1973 another crisis struck the world economy. The Arab oil-producing nations declared an embargo on oil to the United States and the Netherlands, and initiated general reductions in oil production. Within a year the price of oil had quadrupled — from $2.50 per barrel of Persian Gulf oil in early 1973 to $11.65 per barrel in 1974. The crisis in oil produced four major effects almost immediately: (1) a major disequilibrium in international payments on current accounts between the oil-exporting and the oil-importing countries; (2) heightened inflationary pressures in oil-consuming countries; (3) a recession in the oil-importing countries; and (4) a problem of recycling surplus oil funds (estimated at $70 billion in 1974) that could not be absorbed into the economies of the relatively underdeveloped oil-exporting countries.

The 'petrodollar' crisis was eased to some degree by the initiative of the international private banks. Their willingness to act as financial intermediaries in recycling Arab oil surplus dollars enabled the world economy to continue functioning and to avert a major international financial crisis after 1973. Since the middle 1960s, in any event, these private banking networks had been making more and more loans, mainly through the growing Euromarket. This trend served to restructure the formal division of financial labor that had existed between the public and private financial sectors of the international system.

A number of factors lie behind this trend. From the economic point of view, the climate of the international economy has been uncertain and gloomy, because of the rising oil prices and spiraling inflation; long-term loans of foreign investment capital have been in relatively short demand in developed countries, as these economies seek to protect their domestic markets and their short-term earnings. In the developing countries, however, there is ample demand for these kinds of loans. In Brazil, for example, the state's power and stability rests on an unbroken momentum of rapid industrial growth. But there are few and weak security exchanges in Brazil through which stocks and bonds can be issued to obtain capital needed for investment. Commercial banks supply some domestic firms with capital, but this is mainly short-term working capital if the firms are not affiliated with the 'dynamic' industrial sector. This presses businesses to develop connections with outside financial agencies to obtain long-term capital, or else to align themselves with new economic ventures. On the supply side, United States private banks have faced a problem of excess liquidity, occasioned mainly by the gigantic deposits made by the oil-producing countries. On the demand side, developing countries have been experiencing great balance of payment deficits. The major industrialized countries have been relatively able to cope with higher prices of oil and related products because of ability to sell sophisticated and expensive capital goods to the oil-exporting countries and because they accumulated great reserves of dollars from the deposits of oil-producing countries; the less developed countries lack these abilities and resources, and are therefore cast into weak trading positions.

Increasing demands on the IMF for greater loan assistance to meet balance of payment service schedules has strained the IMF's limited pool of financial resources, which are still mobilized through the sale of bonds in private capital markets and by repayments of loans. In the financial climate of the 1970s both the sale of bonds and the ability of governments to repay loans has decreased significantly. Private transnational banks have moved in to assume this mandated role of the IMF since it has been apparent from the early 1970s that it cannot fulfill that role.

One further innovation that has accompanied this 'privatization' of international finance is 'consortia banking.' Consortias developed in response to the need for recycling surplus capital accumulated from the oil price increases, to spread the risks of making large loans, and to 'hedge' and speculate against exchange rate increases. The IMF and the World Bank have supported and welcomed private syndicated bank activities. For example, the IMF guarantees loans administered by private banks who assemble financial 'packages' for viable investment opportunities. In addition, the public institutions 'co-finance' loans by private ones.[29]

Other data reinforce the picture of increased participation of private banks. In 1967 only 5½ percent of the external financing of the less developed countries was provided by the private sector; by 1976 this proportion had risen to almost 50 percent.[30] The Morgan Guaranty Trust Company of New York has estimated that United States banks have provided two-thirds of the $60 billion loaned by private banks to the non-oil-exporting less developed countries.[31] These loans have been concentrated in a small number of less developed countries. According to the United States Federal Reserve Board, by the middle of 1976 Argentina, Brazil, Peru, Mexico and Indonesia had received nearly $32 billion from American private banks; of this amount Brazil and Mexico alone received $19 billion. In Brazil the percentage share of official capital (i.e. from public financial institutions) has declined from 74 percent in 1967 to 42 percent in 1975, while the rate of private borrowing has increased from 26 to 58 percent in the same period.[32]

These selected countries have been deemed 'creditworthy' clientele because of their development potential, rich natural resources, relatively stable political atmosphere, labor laws and willingness to denationalize industry. Only in the last decade have private banks established separate departments designed to evaluate the 'creditworthiness' of potential loans recipients and the commercial viability of major development projects. The assembling of financial packages in support of these projects is rapidly becoming an essential part of any large bank's repertoire. Terms on such loans are harsher than loans advanced by other public financial institutions, but private loans are more readily available through the Euromarket. The effects are much the same, however. Private loans further deepen the dependence of less developed countries on foreign capital. Because of the restrictions on the use of these funds, their deployment often fails to confront the long-term problems related to the structure and the international terms of trade. The growing debt burden — termed the 'debt trap' — inhibits equitable socioeconomic development. For example, it has been estimated that 40 percent of Brazil's estimated export earnings of $12 billion has gone to servicing that country's foreign debt alone.[33] Further analysis of Brazil's debt, however, suggests that the problem is not so much the magnitude of outstanding debt but the stringent terms of borrowing. The debt structure has been concentrated in short-term securities. Brazilian firms appear often to have borrowed internationally in order to supplement domestic credits; most of these financial credits have had maturities of less than one year.

The present trend of capital flows reduces the nationally based businessmen to a status of intermediaries for foreign capital; this works against their accumulation of capital. Rates of interest set artificially low are frequently below the rate of decline in the value of currency through inflation; this has the effect of discouraging saving and encouraging lending. The combination of these conditions establishes a kind of 'debt trap.' Recycling has vastly increased the capital available to creditworthy clientele. This credit is extended in a kind of 'private-public' way, with the private banking sector extending the capital and the IMF the 'conditions' of lending, including demands for changes in domestic economic policies. The IMF acts as a kind of central credit agency, setting the standard by which other sources of funds may be obtained — including such institutions as the World Bank, regional developmental organizations, bilateral government-to-government loans, and private sources. Furthermore, it appears that the IMF does not limit its role to imposing conservative economic policies on the less developed countries; its policies clearly have political implications as well. For example, President Allende of Chile was, on several occasions, unable to secure funds because of this unwillingness to accept the conditions that the IMF sought to impose; yet after the coup in September 1973, Chile was able to secure IMF approval for loans.

Looking at the postwar financial history as a whole, we can observe a considerable alteration in the international 'division of labor' among public and private, and number of structural changes, national sources of capital and shifts in the balance of international financial power. Yet, regarding the decades from the standpoint of the less developed countries, there has been a certain continuity of economic dependency on the suppliers of capital. In a variety of ways the lenders have succeeded in attaching 'strings' relating to types and directions of investment, monetary policy, fiscal policy and trade policy, and in these ways intruding on the capacity of the less-developed countries to determine their own course of economic development.

THE NEW INTERNATIONAL
ECONOMY IN
POLITICAL AND SOCIAL CONTEXT

Up to this point we have made an effort to sketch the broad economic and financial dimensions of the new international economy. It remains in this introductory essay to offer a few speculative comments on the context in which this economy has developed. By 'context' we mean the military, political, ideological and social arrangements onto which this new economy has been grafted. These arrangements, we suggest, were fashioned at a different phase of economic and political development of the world, and may or may not be appropriate to the new patterns of production, trade and finance in the late twentieth century. At the very least, the new internationalism of the economy creates adjustment problems for these arrangements; at the very most, it renders them obsolete. Keeping this general notion of context in mind, we offer the following points for reflection.

1. Prior to the rise of transnational productive and financial institutions to their present level of prominence, economies functioned primarily within the boundaries of the nation-state. Within any given state various economic sectors (for example agricultural, mining, industrial, service) could be regarded as dynamic vs. stagnant, modern vs. traditional, or central vs. marginal to the economy: the resulting picture was a kind of national stratification of the economy. Similarly, at the international level economic stratification was to be calculated in terms of developed vs underdeveloped or rich vs poor nations. While international factors (trade between industrial and primary-product nations, capital flows) contributed to these kinds of stratification, the primary point of reference was the nation-state.

To some extent these statements still hold true; the story of any given economy continues to be the shifting pattern of certain dynamic industries undermining and displacing less dynamic ones, and production and stratification can still be calculated on a national basis. But the internationalization of production and finance has cut across these bases of stratification with a new principle. The displacement and marginalization is orchestrated by direct foreign economic intervention, and the stratification is more often one involving internationally based industries and financial institutions than involving domestic ones. So while it is still possible to speak of leading and lagging industries as well as rich and poor states, the point of reference is not only to other states but to international and to some extent stateless organizations. In these ways a new principle of national and international stratification has intruded on the old.

2. The facts just observed carry great implications for the power of the state (as well as its importance as a unit of analysis). In the 1950s Kuznets could argue that nation-states are the appropriate unit for the analysis of economic activity; his case, furthermore, rested on the argument that it is mainly the state that influences the fortunes of economic life. Nation-states set the 'institutional conditions within which economic activities are pursued, the boundaries within which markets operate and within which human resources are relatively free to handle material capital assets and claims to them.' Furthermore, the sovereign government of the state is 'the overriding authority that resolves conflicts generated by growth and screens institutional innovations, sanctioning those believed essential and barring others.'[34] There is reason to believe that such assessments are growing progressively less accurate. One of the dramatic ways to illustrate the change is to point out that, of the 100 largest economic units in the world, only half are nation-states, the others multinational companies of various sorts. Furthermore, the rate of growth of the multi-nationals has been so spectacular that the proportion is likely to change further in favor of the internationals.[35]

This kind of development poses problems for the autonomy and sovereignty of the state in both home and host countries. From the home state, regulation becomes difficult on two grounds — first, because of the far-flung nature of the operations of transnational organizations, making it difficult to monitor those operations; and, second, because of the economic power and political influence enjoyed by those corporations in relation to the determination of the policies of the home state. For the host state the main problem created — besides the fundamental impact of foreigners investing in one's own land — concerns its inability to regulate that impact. Transnational corporations are large, disruptive of the lesser centers of power in the host countries, and likely to buy up local firms; and they generally pose problems of corporate or financial domination for the host countries. Furthermore, when opportunities present themselves, not only one but many transnationals are likely to invade the host country in order to exploit those opportunities.

The problem of the relationship between host governments and transnational organizations, however, is not simply one of domination. Once transnationals have penetrated, host governments are likely to want them, mainly because they are dependent on the level of economic activity brought to the country for their own prosperity. Host governments tend to strike up symbiotic agreements with transnationals, and both often conspire to act as a coalition to maintain conditions of economic stability so that both the host government and the transnationals can continue to profit from that symbiosis.[36] In these ways, the notion of the state as sovereign has become further eroded.

3. By the same token, the main ideological buttress to the nation-state — nationalism — has receded in relevance, because it has become progressively more misdirected with respect to the loci of economic and political forces in the contemporary world, which are increasingly international in character. Nowhere is this more evident than in Western Europe, since the development of the EEC and other international establishments, and the increasing role of Western Europe, as a *system* of economies in the world economy. Dutch, Danish — even French and German nationalism — may continue to have an audible voice; but with respect to the respective fates of those nations, the concrete manifestation of those sentiments — the state — is weaker as an agency. It is one of the ironies of contemporary Western European politics that the periodic political campaigns are waged primarily in the context of a nationalist rhetoric — involving the implicit assertion that the nation has control of its own economic affairs — when the international economic and political realities render that assumption progressively unrealistic. At the same time, various kinds of 'transnational' ideologies, such as the ideology of capitalist free enterprise and the ideology of international communism, have themselves diminished as rallying cries for unified political action, as the political unity of the political blocs based on these ideologies has grown more fragile. In this connection, we might suggest that among the many complex causes contributing to the surprising emergence of various sub-national ethnic and nationalist movements — Scottish, Welsh, Basque, Quebecois and others — are a kind of mirrored reflection of the decline of the viability of nationalism as a politically unifying force, a decline occasioned moreover, by the

economic and political internationalization. 'Irrational' in one sense — that the 'sub-nations' advocated by adherents would be even more impotent internationally than the nations of which they are now a part — these movements may nevertheless operate in part to fill a kind of void of political integration that has arisen with the overshadowing of the nation-state and nationalism.[37]

4. The movement toward internationalization appears to make more problematic, if not actually to weaken, certain other traditional bases for political integration and political action. Nation-based capitalist economies — as well as other economies, in a variety of different ways — have evolved class systems appropriate to their development; and, despite some efforts to internationalize these class relations, most of the conflicts among classes (capitalist, workers, petty-bourgeoisie, for example) have occurred at the national level, and those conflicts have been mediated in a variety of ways by national governments. The increasing internationalization of the economy has also clouded this picture in a number of ways. On the one hand, workers' organizations in home countries — in particular, the United States, which is the home country for most of the giant transnationals — have assumed a stance of opposition to these corporations, on grounds that the export of technology to low-wage areas constitutes a threat to their own employment and to the American balance of trade; implicitly, at least, this creates a momentary alliance with non-transnational elements of the business classes, who themselves feel threatened with competition generated by the internationally operating enterprises.[38] On the side of the solidarity of labor, the fact that transnational corporations hire multiple types of labor in multiple countries, and that communication among these fragments of their workforces is inhibited by geographical and cultural distance, greatly weakens the potential for united worker action against the transnationals themselves, as well as their political unification for other purposes. So while the internationalization of the economy makes for a truer internationalization of class relations and class conflict, the fact remains that the possibilities for political mobilization in this arena, particularly on the part of workers, is extremely difficult.[39]

5. In a development somewhat unrelated to the trends towards internationalization — but definitely affecting the power of nation-states directly — we refer to the vast changes in the technology of warfare in the past several decades, including the development of nuclear weapons and sophisticated delivery

systems, as well as the tendency for these technological improvements to proliferate irregularly among nations. While not under-emphasizing either the probability of a nuclear conflict — particularly as proliferation proceeds — we would stress that, overall, the middle range to large military operation on the part of nation-states has been ruled out as difficult if not unacceptable, because of the threat of the generalization of such an operation into a nuclear disaster. In this way the politico-military terms of conflict have been further dichotomized; nations find themselves relying either on the threat of nuclear conflict (or incursions that may escalate to it) or on lesser operations, such as mischievous disruption, importing 'volunteers' from a non-superpower ally into a domestic conflict and the like.

6. To characterize these trends at their most general level, it appears that certain traditional sanctions available to international actors have receded in significance, and others have come to greater prominence. Those that have been overshadowed have been the exercise of political power by individual nation-states (over their own and others' economic fortunes, in particular), the exercise of political power by individual nation-states, and the appeal to nationalistic and supra-nationalistic ideologies as a basis for mobilization. Those that have assumed greater salience are economic and financial sanctions, wielded internationally by consortia of state, corporate and financial agents (OECD, OPEC, the consortia of IMF and private banking networks, for example). The ultimate irony associated with this shift, however, is that the world's capacity to regulate, control, or prevent the exercise of these international economic and financial forces has at least not kept pace with the growing strength of these forces, and has probably deteriorated. It is that irony that accounts for the continuing atmosphere of uncertainty, instability and crisis that has come to be normal on the international scene.

THE ORGANIZATION OF THE VOLUME

Each of the essays in this book takes up one or more of the themes touched in this overview of the historical, economic and financial aspects of the new international order and expands and deepens those themes. The four essays in Part I attempt, in different ways, to fathom the character of the recent 'internationalization' and 'transnationalization' of the world economy, and to assess the significance of these developments in various ways. In chapter 2 Charles Albert-Michalet advances the theme that transnational corporations have effected a fundamental alteration in international exchange, involving the replacement of exchange through trade by a system of exchange through transfer of technology, organization, capital and merchandise. So important have been these changes, Michalet argues, that existing theories of international exchange, based on the assumption that trade and financial exchange take place among nation-states, is becoming progressively less relevant to the analysis of the world economy.

The essays by Bornschier (chapter 3) and Martinelli (chapter 4) trace some of the economic, political and social ramifications of the spread of transnational corporations. Basing his argument on accumulated cross-national economic data, Bornschier finds that economic penetration by transnational corporations appears to generate an increase in economic development of less developed countries, but that this effect is reversed in the longer run. In addition, the level of penetration by transnational corporations appears to be associated by increased income inequality in the less developed countries. The implication of these empirical results is that the spread of transnational corporations to the less developed world do not seem to have any effect of equalizing the current pattern of international economic stratification; if anything, the effect would appear to be the opposite. Alberto Martinelli ventures a complex set of hypotheses relating to the political role of transnational corporations; central to these hypotheses are the ideas that, while the transnational corporations are dependent on nation-states for securing the kind of social and political stability required for the functioning of the economic order, their operations in fact intrude on the states' capacities to pursue economic policies that are necessary to maintain social and political stability. With respect to labor, Martinelli stresses the degree to which transnational corporations, intrinsically international in character, pose novel problems for labor because the corporations deal with an internationally diverse and fragmented labor force, and the fact that the corporations profit from this diversity and fragmentation of labor interests. And with respect to technology, Martinelli explores the impact of technology transfers on the international competitive positions of both home and host countries of the transnational corporations. Martinelli's main underlying preoccupation is with the discontinuities and contradictions stemming from two distinct modes of economic and social integration — transnational-corporate and national-state. The final essay in Part I, by Christopher Chase-Dunn (chapter 5), is more methodological in character, arguing that, despite the hostility of some dependency theorists and world-system theorists to positivistic research methods, systematic and comparative cross-national research can enlighten some of the central hypotheses emerging from these two theoretical perspectives.

The two essays in Part II have the issues of international autonomy and dependency as their focus. Fernando Henrique Cardoso's statement (chapter 6), theoretical in character, traces and criticizes a variety of theoretical perspectives that have worked to undermine the idea that development is an autonomous, internally generated socioeconomic process, and to establish, in its place, the thesis that relations of international economic domination and dependency are more central in determining the 'developmental' fate of nations. The essay by Constantine V. Vaitsos (chapter 7) takes as a starting point the trend, noted in this introduction, whereby various strong economies (Japanese, some Western European, etc.), have come to constitute a challenge to American economic domination in the 1960s and 1970s. Parallel to this shift, he argues, is an increase in Western Europe's role in maintaining the dependency of less developed countries, a role manifested by changing trading patterns between the EEC and the Third World, and by a European concern with limiting Third World development of industrial manufacturing capacity.

International and national finance constitute the themes for the two essays in Part III. Building on theoretical contributions from imperialist and dependency theories, Barbara Stallings (in chapter 8) analyzes the changing patterns of Euromarket financial operations in the 1960s and 1970s. In particular, she argues that funds provided by these private capital markets tend to favor the advanced over the less developed countries, and, within the Third World, to favor some nations over others. The political consequences of these lending patterns, she suggests, are to promote uneven development, divide the Third World politically, and to undermine politically progressive regimes and support politically reactionary ones. Makler's essay (chapter 9) also concerns the effects of the differential allocation of credit, though at the national level. In

a case study of Bahia in north-eastern Brazil, he argues that the
allocation of credit tends to hasten the development of what are
regarded as the more 'dynamic' sectors of the economy — sectors,
moreover, that are considered crucial for the state's developmental
goals. Simultaneously, these policies hinder the economic growth
of more 'traditional' sectors, and place at a relative disadvantage
the groups and classes in society that are associated with those sectors. In particular, agricultural interests have been short-changed in
relation to industrial ones in this system of skewed credit allocation.

Part IV returns to political and social themes once again. In a
case study based on Brazilian material, Luciano Martins (in chapter
10) traces a number of new and complex political arrangements
that are emerging with respect to host governments and transnational corporations — arrangements that appear as bargains struck
by agencies of power that are perpetually in potential conflict with
one another. These bargains serve to limit excesses in the exercise of
power of either party, and to establish quasi-legal conditions which
serve to stabilize the working environment of both parties. Basing
his analysis mainly on the Quebecois or French Canadian nationalist movement, Sales (in chapter 11) interprets this movement
(and, implicitly, others as well) in large part to the diminished local
control, which is in turn attributable to the continued presence of
dominant international (especially American and Anglo-Canadian)
economic forces. Finally, in an Epilogue, Charles E. Lindblom offers some reflections on recent developments in the world
economy, and on the intellectual styles of those who observe and
analyze them.

NOTES

1. Among recent contributions to the understanding of this transition are R.
Bendix, *Kings or People* (Berkeley: University of California Press, 1978); P. Ander-

son, *Lineages of the Absolutist State* (London: New Left Books, 1974); I. Wallerstein, *The Modern World System* (New York: Academic Press, 1974).

2. R. Cooper, *The Economics of Interdependence: Economic Policy in the Atlantic Community* (New York: McGraw-Hill, 1968).

3. K. Polanyi, *The Great Transformation* (New York: Rinehart, 1944).

4. R. Robinson and R. Gallagher, 'The Imperialism of Free Trade,' *Economic History Review*, vol. VI (1953), pp. 1-15.

5. E. J. Hobsbawm, *Industry and Empire* (London: Weidenfeld & Nicolson, 1968).

6. M. De Cecco, *Money and Empire: The International Gold Standard, 1890-1914* (Oxford: Basil Blackwell, 1974).

7. For an analysis of the contributions made by those authors, see A. Martinelli, *La Teoria dell'imperialismo* (Turin: Loescher, 1974).

8. A. Gerschenkron, *Bread and Democracy in Germany* (Berkeley: University of California Press, 1943).

9. D. K. Fieldhouse, *The Theory of Capitalist Imperialism* (London: Longmans, 1967); J. S. Galbraith, 'The "Turbulent Frontier" as a Factor in British Expansion,' *Comparative Studies in Society and History*, vol.10 (1968).

10. A. Martinelli, 'Contradictions between National and Transnational Planning: The Role of Labor Unions' (Nyon: International Foundation for Development Alternatives, 1979), Dossier II.

11. P. Katzenstein, 'International Interdependence: Some Long-term Trends and Recent Changes,' *International Organization*, vol.29 (Fall 1975), pp.1021-34; Alex Inkeles, 'The Emerging Social Structure of the World,' *World Politics*, vol.27, no.4 (July 1975), pp.467-95.

12. F. Bergsten (ed.), *The Future of the International Economic Order: An Agenda for Research* (Lexington, Mass.: Lexington Books, 1973).

13. A. Lindbeck, 'The Changing Role of the National State,' *Kyklos*, vol. 28 (1975), pp. 23-46.

14. E. Mandel, *Spatkapitalismus* (Frankfurt: Suhrkamp, 1972); S. Amin, 'Une Crise structurelle,' in *La Crise de l'imperialismo* (Paris: Minuit, 1975).

15. R. Gilpin, *U.S. Power and the Multinational Corporation* (New York: Basic Books, 1975).

16. See R. Keohane and J. Nye, *Power and Independence* (Boston: Little, Brown, 1977).

17. R. Cameron et al., *Banking in the Early Stages of Industrialization: A Study in Comparative Economic History* (New York: Oxford University Press, 1967); R. Cameron, *Banking and Economic Development: Some Lessons of History* (New York: Oxford University Press, 1972).

18. A. Gerschenkron, *Economic Backwardness in Historical Perspective* (Cambridge, Mass.: Harvard University Press, 1962).

19. H. T. Patrick, 'Financial Development and Economic Growth in Underdeveloped Countries,' *Economic Development and Cultural Change*, vol. 14, no. 2 (January 1966), pp. 174-89.

20. ibid., p.174.

21. R. I. McKinnon, *Money and Capital in Economic Development* (Washington, DC: The Brookings Institution, 1973).

22. G. W. Shaw, *Financial Deepening in Economic Development* (Toronto: Oxford University Press, 1973).

23. *New York Times*, 9 October, 1979.

24. T. Dos Santos, 'The Structure of Dependence,' in Charles K. Wilber (ed.), *The Political Economy of Development and Underdevelopment* (New York: Random House, 1973).

25. Board of Governors of Federal Reserve System, *Annual Report of Assets and Liabilities of Overseas Branches of Member Banks of Federal Reserve System*.

26. Chase Manhattan Bank, *Annual Foreign Earnings Reports* (1967 and 1974).

27. The Group of Ten members were France, Belgium, Germany, Italy, the Netherlands, UK, Sweden, Japan, USA, and Canada. This group disbanded in 1972 in favor of the creation of a Group of Twenty under IMF auspices with some participation of less developed countries.

28. There is some debate over the issue of the origins of the Euromarket. For further discussion, see Geoffrey Bell, *The Eurodollar Market and the International Financial System* (New York: John Wiley, 1973).

29. 'Co-financing' refers to the cooperative efforts between private and public lenders. The public agency, i.e. the IMF, provides the loan guarantee, hence assuming the risk. Having an official agency guarantee the loan reduces the risks of default. A default on the private sector becomes a default on the public agency. For a discussion and illustration of co-financing in Peru, see Barbara Stallings, 'Peru and the U.S. Banks: Privatization of Financial Relations' (1978; unpublished manuscript).

30. 'A Survey of American Financial Institutions,' *The Economist*, 22 January 1977, pp. 5-60.

31. A. Ferrer, 'Latin America and World Economy,' *Journal of InterAmerican Studies and World Affairs*, vol. 20 (1978), p. 333.

32. R. C. Garg, 'Brazilian External Debt: A Study in Capital Flows and Transfer of Resources,' *Journal of InterAmerican Studies and World Affairs*, vol. 20 (1978), p. 346.

33. ibid., p. 341.

34. S. Kuznets, 'The State as a Unit in the Study of Economic Growth,' *Journal of Economic History*, vol. 2 (1951), pp. 25-41; also S. Kuznets, *Qualitative Economic Research: Trends and Problems* (New York: Columbia University Press, 1972).

35. International Labor Office, *Multinational Enterprises and Social Policy* (Geneva: ILO, 1973).

36. N. S. Fatemi, G. W. Williams and T. L. T. de Saint-Phalle, *Multinational Corporations* (Cranbury, NJ: A. S. Barnes, 1975); see also the essay by Luciano Martins in chapter 10 below.

37. This line of argument is not inconsistent with the interpretation by Sales, though he stresses not so much the diminution of the nation-state and nationalism as the presumed bases for this weakening: viz. international economic penetration. See chapter 12 below.

38. Fatemi, Williams and Saint-Phalle, op. cit.

39. Martinelli carries this line of analysis further in chapter 4 below.

I

INTERNATIONALIZATION OF
THE WORLD ECONOMY

2

FROM INTERNATIONAL TRADE TO WORLD ECONOMY: A NEW PARADIGM

Charles-Albert Michalet
CEREM, Université de Paris, X, France

The need for further study of a new paradigm in world economics has been brought about by the growing feeling that the traditional analytical framework is not adequate for explaining the unforeseen changes in the international environment, and the new constraints that result from them. This need reflects two different kinds of preoccupations. On the one hand, it appears increasingly obvious that the theoretical frameworks for the great English classics, rethought and refined by the neoclassicists, have no relevance to a certain number of phenomena, old and new, that urgently require to be dealt with: whether it is a question of North-South relations, of the development of the multinational activities of companies or of the new rules in operation on the international monetary and financial system. Challenged by these changes in the field of international economy, the observer realizes that the toolbox of theory, which relates to this area of political economy, does not contain the necessary analytical tools. Armed with traditional concepts, he is defenceless when faced with phenomena outside the limited scope of traditional paradigms: the appearance of a new international economic order, the internationalization of production, the transnationalization of capital circulation no longer fit into the frameworks of the traditional textbooks. On the other hand, this inadequacy is more strongly felt because it is increasingly expected to provide answers to the questions posed by the new international environment. The concerns of the decision-makers are dominated more and more by how to control 'exterior constraints.' Thus, in an economy of prolonged depression, it is important to know if the industrialization of the Third World constitutes a real threat to industrialized countries;[1] if the definition of an industrial policy[2] or even more so that of national planning[3] can be worked out purely on a national basis; if the multinational expansion of companies should be encouraged without limits or, on the contrary, if it is all-important to have a hand in setting the new rules of the game;[4] if the instruments of monetary policy and also those used in the fight against inflation can still be of use in a world where the majority of European currencies are inflating at an uncontrolled rate, where the movement of capital — directed by banks which have become multinational and through international offshore financial centres — is outside all 'regulation.'

Briefly, recognition of the world's needs,[5] reference to the world economy, to the new world-wide economic order, are part of contemporary economic discussion. But these demands seem to become more urgent because their meaning is misunderstood. It is not our aim to give a solution, it must be noted. Nevertheless, if 'societies only ask themselves the questions they can solve,' the question of world economy has become relevant. In elaborating on an earlier study,[6] we simply wanted to ask the question and show the direction of research. To this end, we will deal with two topics, in the form of questions:

1. Why is the framework of international economy no longer relevant?

2. How should an approach be defined in terms of world economy?

WHY HAS THE PURE THEORY OF INTERNATIONAL TRADE LOST ITS VALIDITY?

To question the validity of the pure theory of international exchange is to undertake a criticism of a paradigm. It is a question of showing the limits at the very heart of its logic and not of comparing it with other theoretical paradigms (e.g. the Marxist critique of neoclassical analysis). Strictly speaking, since Adam Smith, the field of international economics has been defined by the explanation of the flow of imports and exports on the basis of international specialization determined by the distribution of production factors.

The first piece of 'heresy' consisted of enlarging the area of reference to include the movement of capital. This widening of the area can be accepted without further comment inasmuch as it does not fundamentally affect the model: goods and services, like capital, are understood in their movements between the nation-states. In the final analysis, these movements are the touchstone of the whole structure and are the basis of 'internationality.' This is exactly what is called into question by two recent manifestations of the change in the international environment, on which we are going to concentrate: the internationalization of production, and the transnationalization of monetary and financial circulation.

The Internationalization of Production

For 20 years, multinational corporations (MNCs) have been in the forefront of the internationalization of production. Because of their investments abroad, MNCs have greatly changed the basis of the accumulation of capital. Henceforth, this no longer corresponds entirely to the country of origin of the MNC. In actual fact, it has been observed that the value of US international production, that is, of goods manufactured outside the USA but under the control of American companies, was four times higher than the value of exports. In the case of Great Britain, it was twice as high; it was considerably higher in the case of West Germany and France.[7] In many cases — in France and Britain, at least — it is the share of profits coming from abroad that allows companies to present positive results to their shareholders. This situation is not without consequences in decision-making within the companies: they reduce their domestic activities, which are less profitable (rationalization), and 'redeploy' their production abroad. Thus the disparity between the economy of the MNC and that of its home country keeps increasing. The relocation of industrial activities abroad undertaken by MNCs conforms to two main strategies.[8] On one hand, MNCs set up abroad to supply the local market (national or regional). It is primarily the existence of protectionist barriers, and secondly local competition (firms of the host country or MNC subsidiaries), that explain local production. This choice corresponds to a policy of export substitution. It concerns first of all other developed countries where the large, lucrative markets are located. It is concerned only with a small number of developing, semi-industrialized countries, mainly in Latin America (Mexico, Brazil, Argentina), where there are social groups with high purchasing power and whose consumption model is duplicated according to that of the home country. It must be noted that this sort of implantation often takes the form of take-over or of equity participation. It corresponds in the final analysis to a process of industrial concentration on a world-wide scale. The number of companies participating in the stagnant world market has decreased since 1973-74. Up till now, this phenomenon of oligopolization has been accompanied by an increase in the number of MNCs, but apparently also by a decrease in the total number of companies.

On the other hand, companies set up specialized manufacturing units components, spare parts, etc. abroad, corresponding to an international segmentation of the production process. The production of these 'workshop affiliates' is for exportation. Implantation of this type of affiliate is confined to a certain number of countries in the underdeveloped periphery where cheap labor is in plentiful supply (South-East Asia, the Caribbean, Mexico). This tendency will increase in the future because it conforms with the strategy of MNCs and, at the same time, with the development policies of the host countries. From the companies' point of view, the situation is no longer the same for 'workshop affiliates' as for 'relay affiliates,' which aimed at a higher market share. Investment incentive is upstream, at the level of the creation of surplus value. In workshop affiliates, thanks to the high degree of specialization of tasks among both workers and management, productivity is at much the same level as in the country of origin. On the other hand, wages are 10-20 times lower; the hours worked are longer and more intensive; strikes and trade unionism hardly exist. Thus, the conditions of the Industrial Revolution in Europe are revived, but in an international setting; that is to say, with the existence of conditions of trade which are unequal in the strict sense as defined by A. Emmanuel.[9] Except for this difference, these conditions have been created by MNCs within their network. Goods that are transferred from one country to another, from the periphery to the center, are not merchandise but products. However the rules of the international trade game, established by MNCs, should not be confused lightly with those of unequal trade; neither should they be interpreted within the traditional framework of international economy. In fact, certain writers have thought to refute all specific ideas on the internationalization of production: the implantation of industries requiring direct labor force in countries where this is plentiful constitutes an application of the Hecksher-Ohlin theory. The change is crucial however: MNCs relocate production units that require a large labor force relative to the criteria of the home country. Since the transferred technology is not changed, its application in certain developing countries can seem, from the host country's factor endowment, like labor-saving. A good level of specialization would without doubt require other types of production. Also, the quasi-equality of productivity levels coexists with the maintenance of pronounced wage differences. The internationalization of production does not therefore lead to the results postulated by the neoclassical theory of international trade. Optimum resource allocation has hardly any better chance of success through the latter than the former — even less so, because the hypothesis of pure and perfect competition in the theory of trade is obviously untenable when MNCs are taken into account. The oligopolistic character of the market is a factor in encouraging multinationalization of firms, and thus the gap between the operating conditions of the international economy and those of the world economy is becoming wider and wider.

In spite of insufficient information on the forms of implantation, it seems possible to say that the strategy for relay affiliates, although it remains predominant, will increasingly be taken over by that of workshop affiliates. It is especially the case for American MNCs, but also for those in Germany and Japan.[10] Besides, through these reasons based on the economic and social conditions of the country, which are all-important, this new tendency can also be explained by the fact that workshop affiliates are less easy to nationalize than relay affiliates (specialization of product, integration into the network of the MNC, difficulty in reconversion, etc.). What can also encourage this type of implantation is the fact that the nature of workshop affiliates' activities corresponds to the aspirations of a growing number of developing countries. In fact, the model of development based on import substitution is increasingly being abandoned in favor of a policy of development through export. In a certain sense, the objectives for the year 2000 of the New International Division of Labor (25 percent of world industrial production in the developing countries and 25 percent of exports of manufactured goods coming from developing countries) coincides with the logic behind workshop affiliates. Also, compensation agreements are being imposed on foreign companies more and more often in order to counteract the structural deficit of balances of payments.[11] This last cause for concern can only be aggravated by the rise in the price of oil.

From this providential convergence of interests between the nation-states and MNCs, there are certain results that discourage over-hasty optimism. Industrial relocation as operated by MNCs can have quite serious implications for the economy of the country of origin: consequences for employment, first of all, as a result of relocating industrial units abroad. The net result is difficult to see. Roughly speaking, it is a matter of knowing to what extent the new exports to developing countries (equipment, industrial complexes, know-how) can succeed in making up for lay-offs caused by the move. Relocation affects labor-intensive industries first of all, as has already been noted, and other industries are characterized by their strong capital ratio. Setting up workshop affiliates abroad, or more frequent use of local subcontracting (also by application of compensation agreements), will have — in fact, already has — consequences for the industrial structure of developed economies. Foreign suppliers are progressively replacing traditional subcontractors in the countries of origin. The governments of these countries are aware of the dangers. Interminable speeches are made about the necessity for readjustment, restructuring, redeployment; sometimes they even result in the instigation of programs to deal with the situation.

The growing interdependence between the North and South has now become a part of official discussion on economy. It is not that some new fact has been discovered, however. For a long time, industrialized countries have been and have remained dependent on the South for the supply of their raw materials and also as an outlet for some of their products. Conversely, the peripheral countries rely heavily on northern industries as markets for their products and on revenues from exports, as these constitute practically their only financial resources. Henceforth, manufactured goods will also be exported along with traditional products. The major buyers remain the same inasmuch as the exchanges between countries of the periphery remain at a very low level. Thus the new international division has not changed the basic direction of flow. It will only change the composition of this flow for a limited number of countries and products.[12] The control of production in developing countries has not changed in any fundamental way, either. Industrial MNCs in developed countries achieve a similar level to mining or agricultural and food-processing MNCs. Industrial MNCs tend to take over, inasmuch as the share of direct investments in the primary sector declines. In the final analysis, through industrial relocation abroad, the position of the South in the world economic system is largely determined by the strategy of MNCs.

What is new and important, on the other hand, is that the internal structure of the countries of origin and of the host countries is upset by the existence of MNCs. In both cases the nation loses its national unity. Paradoxically, it would be necessary to increase the GNP outside the national territory by following the implantation area of MNCs, while at the same time deducting the activity of those local subsidiaries whose operations must be seen in a wider context. Briefly, ideas of national and international, of domestic and foreign, of exterior and interior, and of frontier limits that used to define the existence of an international economy, are losing their validity. The outline of nation-states is becoming blurred and the power of the state over economic activity is lessened.

Exchanges of merchandise between states are also changing in nature. Although the flow continues to be measured at the moment of crossing the national frontier, a growing part — estimated at approximately one-third — is made up of circulation of products between units composing MNCs. The internationalization of the flow is more intense because the international division of labor within MNCs is further extended, as is the case with the proliferation of workshop affiliates. The integrated and planned area of MNCs is gradually taking over from that of international economy. The prices of products that are internalized are fixed by the MNCs. They escape price-setting by the market. The rules for the fixing of transfer prices are not well known. But there is no reason to think that prices are set on a rational basis, which would turn MNC planning into the 'dual' of a pure competitive market. There is not yet a single planning center, but rather a situation of oligopolistic competition, which shows, after more than half a century, that Lenin was right and Kautsky wrong.

Relocation of production capital abroad has not only introduced a greater interdependence between the states, which could be evaluated in the same way as the interdependence caused by the growing share of foreign exchange in a country's GNP; the change is not quantitative, it is natural. Henceforth, the country of origin and the country receiving direct investments are placed in a relationship of interpenetration. A variable fraction of the industry in both is controlled from abroad, is an integral part of the whole economic and planning area of the same firms. This interweaving of national and multinational economic territory, this resiting of the bases for accumulation by firms, has made definition of national borders largely insignificant. The nations have been changed into simple territories in which capital can be increased outside the restraints imposed by state control. Thus, on a purely economic level, it seems that international relations in the sense of exchanges developing between independent national entities are disappearing. The transnationalization of the main economic actors is the negation of national divisions. Their growth strategy is worked out at a world level in the first instance; they create structures and mechanisms that, by their very nature, go beyond national frontiers. Finally, because of their dynamic nature, MNCs have been (and still are) the primary agents in the emergence of a world economy. But the foundation of such a world economy is not limited to the internationalization of production capital. The circulation of liquid capital organized by multinational banks (MNBs) is also taking on an increasingly marked transnational dimension.

The Transnationalization of Monetary and Financial Circulation

The currency of the country is no longer under the exclusive control of the Prince. This mark of sovereignty is called into question by the transnationalization of monetary and financial circuits. The first basis of this trend is in the multinational dimension taken by the principal agents. MNCs come into the picture again because their liquid assets are made up of very large sums in different (national) currencies. Once again, statistical evaluation is very imprecise. According to an official US Senate Report (the Rybicoff Report),[13] the liquid assets of MNCs had a value representing almost three times the total exchange reserves of central banks. MNC finance departments must aim to protect these liquid assets from depreciation of currencies; they are run in such a way that individual currencies are constantly set off against one another. The size of the sums affected by these movements only serves to accentuate any rise or fall in the exchange rates of the different currencies. The disparity between the liquid resources of MNCs and the reserves of central banks taken individually shows that any action taken by the first with regard to a particular currency cannot be combatted by the second. The Prince no longer has complete control over his currency except by making it inconvertible, which would be tantamount to recognition of his own weakness.

In international financial and monetary matters, MNCs are not the most important actors; the most important role is played by multinational banks (MNBs). There is no official definition of MNBs. For our purposes, they can be defined as banks that have developed a network of implantations abroad and that also carry out international operations that can be labelled in currencies other than that of the country of origin. The multinationalization of banks has increased considerably since the second half of the 1960s. In very approximate terms, the share of total profits made outside the country of origin by the big American, European and Japanese banks can be put at between 30 and 50 percent.

The development of the banking network of MNBs can be analyzed — only at a very sketchy level — by analogy with the development of MNCs. Offices of such banks, especially subsidiaries and branches, fit into the national banking system. The central banks do not always have the same control over foreign banks. These latter are not subject to the same working constraints (obligatory reserves, geographic location, spread of activities). For example, foreign banks set up in the USA have greater freedom of movement than American banks. In the case of branches, local control is non-existent; in the case of offshore banking, the local monetary authorities limit their intervention as much as possible. We cannot go further into an analysis of status of branches of MNBs here. What must be remembered, however, is that the world-wide extension of banking networks has a two-fold result.

On one hand, there is the increasing share of activities outside the country of origin, in the global results of the banks. The MNB and the MNC have common features linked to their multinational dimension, for example the fact that the banks have grown on the international scene along with the companies, and the close relations that exist between these two actors (financial participation, loans, personal contacts). The financial group whose major factors are industry and banking realizes, at the highest level, an integration between the two actors. But this is another story. What is important for us here is to note the increasing widening of industrial and banking systems as a result of the intensification of the activities of banks abroad.

On the other hand, the multinationalization of banks comes from their operations on the international monetary and financial markets. Through their intervention on the markets of Eurodollars, Eurocredits and Eurobonds, the banks create money (multiplication of credit on the basis of Eurodollars) and play the role of financial intermediaries. These operations are carried on mainly from international financial centers in Europe, the Middle-East and Asia. Branches of banks that are set up there are without any national control. The rules of the game are fixed contractually between the banks and their clients (MNCs, states, local collectives, public companies) without direct control by the central banks in the host countries or in the home countries. Besides, almost 50 percent of operations in Eurodollars are effected through the international interbank market. There exists therefore a private monetary and financial system which functions parallel to the official system made up of the central banks grouped together and the International Monetary Fund. This system, truly transnational in the sense that it is not subject to any of the constraints applicable to the domestic activities of banks, is undeniably efficient. In part, it has lessened the new difficulties created by the functioning of the system of floating exchange rates for international operations (MNCs, exporters and importers, portfolio managers, treasurers, etc.).

Without laying too much stress on the technical aspect, we would at least like to underline the significance of the formation of a private monetary and financial system in the perspective of the emergence of a world economy. Flexible exchange rates, while they lessen the effects of the constraints resulting from international management of their currency for the states, are in principle favorable to the realization of internal political aims (economic boost, full employment, etc.) and seem contrary to the increasing opening of the economy. Everything has come about as if, all at once, the private banks had generated new structures and new mechanisms in order to safeguard the tendency to the world economic integration. As a result, there has been an undeniable weakening of the traditional tools of monetary policy of the states. The fixing of the discount rate by central banks cannot be carried out without taking into account the interest rate on the Eurodollar market; restrictive credit measures have been largely circumvented by using the international market, through branch banks situated in the financial centers. The system is efficient but still unstable.

This instability has come to light since 1974 as a result of the prolonged recession of industrial economies. Liquid assets in Eurodollars have continued to be fed by the deficit of the US balance of payments. Also, from 1973 they have been swelled by the petrodollars of oil-producing countries with low industrial capacity. The resources of the Eurobanks have become superabundant. Now they have to face up to the low level of credit demand from the economies of the North. The banks have had to look for new ways to use their resources to get the best return possible. Thus the total amount of loans to developing countries and to socialist countries has increased markedly. MNBs use short-term resources to make medium and long-term loans to states whose level of borrowing is extremely high (Brazil, Mexico, Zaîre, etc.). Several socialist countries give over between 30 and 40 percent of their total export returns just to pay the interest on their borrowing. Since 1973-74, more than half of this borrowing is from private banks. These latter have partly taken over from multinational organizations (IMF, IBRD) and from bilateral channels in the directing of capital to the periphery. This new orientation in the circulation of capital is, it must be repeated, the result of the economic situation in the countries of origin. International borrowing has been taken over by the private banks, which have accepted a higher level of risk, inasmuch as the transnational monetary system that they have created has, as a counterpart to the extreme freedom of action allowed to those who use it, the inconvenience of the denial of lender's rights in the last resort. When a large debt cannot be paid back, they have no other recourse than to call in the help of the states of origin. As long as there is no new system set up to deal with this sort of thing — where, for example, the IMF could play the role of central bank for MNBs — a financial crisis could develop into a general economic crisis if the state sector refused to intervene.

The Inadequacy of the Theory
of International Exchange

The traditional concept of international economy as the field of exchange of currencies between autonomous national entities rests, in the final analysis, on the idea of nation-state. It is this that commands the restricted area within which the stocks of production factors are formed. The nation-state cannot enter into a contract with others like it except by the exchange of goods, defined by the idea of specialization. In the classical and neoclassical framework, international exchange is thus confined to the exchange of monies. K. Marx and R. Luxemburg try to explain that international exchange obeys the laws of capital; but they succeed only partially in changing the M-A-M sequence to A-M-A, for they have confined their analyses to the sphere of circulation.[14]

The analysis of MNBs and MNCs makes necessary an urgent reconsideration of the very definition of the nation-state. The immobility of factors is a myth. Capital circulates as much as goods. Migratory movements of population have always existed. It is tempting to maintain that even the land factor is mobile. In fact, the colonial 'dependences' on natural and mineral resources were considered as co-existent with the national territory, an integral part of the Metropole. The political integration of the colonial type, which clearly shows the relative nature of national frontiers, has been succeeded by other forms of foreign presence, an example of which is the implantation of MNCs.

Here the political sovereignty of the host state is not put in question as in the case of the colonialism or of any imperialist occupation (e.g. the Roman or Napoleonic Empires). Nevertheless, the control of the state over certain branches of industry has been lessened. Sometimes the states themselves even officially accord to foreign actors special status ('free trade zone'; 'offshore banking units'). In the case of the countries of origin of the MNCs and MNBs, the state also experiences a loss of power inasmuch as a growing number of companies carry on a large part of their activities and make a large part of their profits outside its frontiers. Thus, the extension of the multinational network of firms and banks changes the outline of economic frontiers while respecting the political borders. The area of the firms does not completely coincide with that of the states, since the firms no longer simply export goods resulting from a national production activity but also relocate part of this activity abroad.

At the same time, it is becoming more and more difficult to admit that the nation-states are trading among themselves, with flexible borders, when the flow of products in fact moves through the complex networks of the organizational structures of MNCs. The nation-states seem to be drained of their internal coherence as a result of foreign implantation and the multinationalization of national firms, and they also seem robbed of their external economic relations by the internationalization of the circulation of goods. By the same token, the paradigm of international economy has no longer any practical application. A new analytical framework is necessary to redefine the status of the state. World economy should be substituted for international economy.

A NEW APPROACH:
THE SYSTEM OF WORLD
ECONOMY

The classic concept of international economy is built on the basis of the nation-states. International exchange seems to be superimposed on this: its addition corresponds to the passage from a closed to an open economy. Such passage is desirable for better allocation of resources, but protectionism still remains the possible alternative to free trade. And what if it were not possible to change direction in this way, at least in terms of economic rationality — the level at which the classical paradigm puts us — for the political choice of stopping free trade must always be born in mind? More precisely, the present situation, our point of departure, does not in itself lead to the risk of a 'copernican revolution': the nation-states would no longer be the alpha and the omega of the structure of international economic relations; it is the world economic system that would determine the relative positions of the nation-states. Using this approach, the world economy could no longer be defined as the sum of the nation-states. As a whole, it is different from the sum of its component parts. Taking national units as a basis does not allow for understanding the actual structure that is being developed. On the other hand, taking the world economy, which is still a developing system, as a point of departure makes what happens at state level unintelligible. To stress the growing interdependence of the states does not sufficiently qualify the special features of the world economy. International specialization is clearly accompanied by interdependence. The parts of a whole are necessarily interdependent inasmuch as they take on a meaning only in relation to one another. But the laws of 'interdependence' are, in the final analysis, those of the reproduction of the system. The problem area therefore lies in a basic disparity in the analysis of the nation-state with regard to the world economy. It would be possible to draw a parallel with what happened in philosophy when humanism was called into question.[15] This does not mean, however, that nations, like men, can be maneuvered or cast aside by an ideological 'coup de force.' Affirming the greater importance of the world economic system over that of the nation-states should not be interpreted as showing that the latter are eclipsed: they continue to exist, but their structure and their relations are determined by the whole of which they are part.

The Emergence of the Problem Area

The recent outlines of a problem area in world economy can be identified by analyzing the relationships between developed and developing countries. There are several interpretations that aim to show, explicitly or implicitly, the unity between these two groups of countries and not their existence in separate worlds, thus raising specific and incompatible theories. The center-periphery dichotomy, as analyzed by S. Amin, aims to show that the social structures of the periphery are an integral part of a world economy dominated by the capitalist mode of production (CMP).[16] It shows how the economic form of peripheral structures is molded by international specialization imposed by the center as a function of its need for supply of raw materials, transferred on the basis of unequal trade: a radical critique on classical optimism, but it does not completely shatter the paradigm of international economy. In fact, the world market remains the center-point of the system and, thus, the sphere of trade remains predominant. This new approach of simple accumulation does not break away from the nation-state concept. It argues for the realization of the conditions of a real national self-reliant accumulation based on the model of the dominant capitalist economies, i.e. with the establishment of a link between the exporting and the luxury goods sectors. It is undeniable that certain preconditions are indispensable to self-reliant development, and these would get the periphery out of the vicious circle of development and underdevelopment. But is it not too late to consider going through the whole story again in a different way? These forms of integration already realized between semi-industrialized economies — are they not already outside the influence of center-periphery, whose paradigm of international economy remains the point of reference in spite of its criticism?

Using the theory of the product cycle to dynamize the theory of international trade, R. Vernon proposes a much more optimistic view of the world economy.[17] The spread of technology linked to a standardization of products leads to a drift in industrial sectors from the USA to the developing countries, via the other industrialized countries. The loss of the technological advantage according to a very Schumpeterian concept of innovation forces American firms to launch new products on their domestic market and/or to transfer abroad — to Europe first of all, then to the developing countries — the production of goods that have become standard and no longer new. The introduction of the factor of technology permits the breaking of patterns of international specialization which formerly condemned economies to remain tied down to their original production location. But this stimulation of trade theory, fruitful though it is, obviously does not question the bases of the paradigms within which it is developing. The transfer of industrial activities is purely and simply a substitute to international trade. When it is carried out by MNCs whose technological advantage has vanished, it is merely a question of production for the local market (relay affiliates).

The proliferation of workshop affiliates, which are not geared to local demand, cannot be taken into account. In the same way, the investment flow between developed countries and from Europe and Japan among others towards the USA cannot be explained by the product cycle pattern.[18] This, in the final analysis, is an excellent theoretical interpretation of the doctrine of the new international division of labor. We have already noted that this latter still follows the traditional paradigm.

In order to get away from the domination of the traditional paradigm, one must come back to Marx: not to Marx on international trade, but to his attempt to expose the laws of operation of the CMP. C. Palloix made a first break-through by using the theory of the movement of capital as expounded in Book II of *Das Kapital*.[19] The changes in capital, according to the three forms of money capital, goods capital and productive capital, are coming about at the moment on an international scale. The paradigm of international economy corresponds to the internationalization of goods capital. The emergence of the world economy is characterized by the internationalization of productive capital (MNCs) and money capital (MNBs). There we have an excellent analytical framework for understanding the stage that the CMP has reached.

Unfortunately, the cycle of capital taken from Book II is a static analytical tool. The objective of Marx, as is well known, was to provide an abstract model for the ideal function of a CMP. One of the basic hypotheses was that the CMP was world-wide. Book III, on the other hand, was to describe the contradictions inherent in the actual operation of the CMP. Paradoxically, there are presuppositions in Book III that seem to be coming about — the extension of the CMP on a world-wide scale, while dealing with the contradictions that could lead to the breakdown of the system, still remains a problem.

In fact, the two statements are probably linked. The internationalization of capital has thwarted the effective realization of lowering the profit rate. At the same time, the direction of movement in capital circulation is clearly indicated, which would allow for reconciliation of the patterns of Books II and III.

From this point of view, and very briefly, the tendency towards the internationalization of productive capital would be interpreted as a response to the over-accumulation of capital in the developed countries. The two types of strategy defined above correspond to two modalities of the struggle against decreasing profits. The cross-investment between developed countries, the creation of workshop affiliates, the world-wide movement towards industrial concentration allow for sharing the total profit made among a smaller number of firms. Setting up in developing countries where salary levels are low, the creation of workshop affiliates, the technical international division of labor within MNCs — all aim at an increase of the surplus value rate by a relocation of the place where value is created to the countries with higher exploitation rates than those of the center. The acceleration of international capital circulation organized by the MNBs and the private international financial and monetary system allows for excess liquid assets to produce a higher rate of return than they might otherwise achieve in their home countries. In this sense, one can recognize a characteristic of imperialism according to Lenin, the stage of capitalism where the export of capital is more important than exports. Lenin also noted the same timing between the stage of imperialism and that of financial capitalism characterized by the constitution of trusts and cartels. What must be added to his analysis is the relocation of the creation of value outside imperialist countries, i.e. the export of capital (as a social relation of production) and not of capital funds.[20] It is without doubt the major feature of the actual operation of underdeveloped capitalist economies. The point is fundamental concerning the change of the peripheral, non-capitalist social formations which are formally dominated by capital. The setting up of production units by MNCs is the final stage in the establishment of social relationships in capitalist production. Trade is only the preparatory stage, undertaken through an injection of cash, and freeing part of the labor-force. It cannot be the instrument of a radical change in the mode of production of the trading countries. The realization of total internationalization of the capital cycle following its three forms means the extension to a world-wide scale of the influence of MNCs.

The emergence of world-wide capitalism, which must not be confused with the imperialism of Lenin or even less with that of Rosa Luxemburg, really rationalizes an attempt to understand a new situation, the change being obscured by the traditional paradigm. Behind all the talk about world interdependence and about the New International Economic Order, what is really aimed for is extension of the CMP world-wide. The analytical perspective should open the field to a better understanding of the ambiguous status of the nation-states.

Several points of reference can be raised which should have been expanded on earlier. First of all, the traditional concept of the nation-state as the most important factor in the international economy as defined and delineated by a specific combination of production factors is called into question by the increasingly marked discrepancy between the political area (the nation) and the economic area. The internationalization of capital means that the capital can no longer be valued on a national basis corresponding to the exercise of the sovereignty of the state. At present, not only is a growing part of production being carried on abroad but, what is really new, the creation of value has also been relocated. National territories are thus placed in a situation of symbiosis, independent of their level of development and, increasingly, of their political regimes. They are thus an integral part of the world system without their national identity necessarily being threatened, as was the case with colonies or empires.[21] Integration is primarily at the economic level. It can be seen in terms of institutions like the EEC, through informal meeting between high-level managers (summits between heads of state; the existence of the trilateral). It has repercussions at the socio-cultural level with the standardization of consumer models, the identifying of products with mass culture and the development of intercontinental tourism. But it also allows for the maintenance of special national characteristics (languages, currencies, legal systems, political institutions, etc.). It can even bring about the exacerbation of regional claims (Catalonians, Bretons, etc.). Although it is less and less based on the use of force (wars, conquests, occupations), the extension of MNCs is still carried out with the active support of the states.

Multinationals and States

The traditional opposition between the multinationals (MNCs and MNBs) and the states, which has been resited in terms defined above, seems oversimplistic. Rather than sticking to a pattern of conflicts, realism makes us consider the relations between the two actors from the point of view of cooperation. The process of multinationalization and the existence of the states form a contradiction, the very vitality of which produces the formation of a world economy as a dynamic result.

On one hand, it is undeniable that the conditions for the appearance of multinationals are inseparable from the economies of their countries of origin. Factors to explain this abound: saturation of the domestic market, non-competitive rise in production costs, development of a technological advantage, accumulation of financial and human resources, etc. Also, the multinational movement is no longer independent of the conditions existing in the other states: protectionism of trade partners necessitates the substitution of local production for exports; competing foreign multinationals induce effects of impulse and counter-attack; and so on. This was the case originally for the states, but the very development of MNCs and MNBs results in undermining the nation-states by splitting them from inside through foreign penetration and the multinationalization of national firms, and also through taking over their external relations. Put in these terms, the relations between the two actors can only be in terms of conflict. The hard core of opposition stems from the double identity of the constituent parts of MNCs and MNBs. They are both internal in and external to the nation-states. They are internal by virtue of assets invested and activity carried on in the country., At the same time, they are foreign (external) because they are either an affiliate of a centrally coordinated world-wide organization or the parent company of an organization whose activities are carried on largely outside the country of origin. The whole question is therefore one of reconciling the transnational dimension of the companies with the purely national objectives of the economic policy of the host states or the countries of origin: stable currency, full employment, external balance, industrial and regional restructuring.

It should be noted that the instruments for economic intervention available to the states — monetary and fiscal policy, controls, planning — have been weakened considerably by the mobility of MNCs: by their financial power, and by the constraints of their strategy and their organization which have been conceived on a global scale. It is significant that the basic principles expressed by the code of conduct of the OECD and by the code in progress in the UN come back essentially to asking MNCs to respect the laws, institutions and political opinions of their host countries. These recommendations could seem trivial. If they are adhered to, they imply that MNCs behave as all good citizens of their host country should. After all, this is only to be expected, and MNCs have long declared this to be their rule of conduct. The problem that remains difficult to resolve is that they should behave like good citizens in all the countries where they have set up and, at the same time, fulfill their own aims. There is some justification for believing that these private aims should have priority over the public policies of the host country; otherwise the coherence of the MNCs would be destroyed.

Conflicts and tensions therefore seem inherent in state-MNC relations, unless, through an act of providence or as a result of economic calculating, the private interests of the MNCs and MNBs become confused with the collective interests of the states. That is what most of the states seem to believe. In fact, from the point of view of the states, whether developed or not, dictatorial or liberal, socialist or capitalist, models in terms of conflict seem less practicable generally than those in terms of cooperation. Generally, all home countries and most host countries take a favorable view of the development of MNC activities. Countries of origin try to promote their own MNCs for the sake of international competition. All of France's industrial policy since 1969, which has gradually replaced the idea of planning, has sought to reinforce the formation of large industrial groups with international ambitions. The public powers have encouraged groupings of companies through considerable financial incentives (subsidies, loans on special terms, reduction of taxes and so on). There is no doubt that the French government's attitude is no exception.

Also, as for the majority of developing countries, the underdeveloped countries are trying to attract foreign investment. Advertising brochures are distributed, information offices are opened which explain to any interested parties the advantages of the economic, socio-cultural, climatic and political conditions of the country. These 'natural' advantages are reinforced by a panoply of concessions ranging from special taxation arrangements for five to ten years to investment loans, via customs exemptions and the host country taking over costs of the infrastructures. In certain cases, the concessions granted to MNCs are extremely generous compared with the treatment of local firms. From this point of view, it is easy to understand that the states have no great desire to increase constraints on the management conditions of MNCs. The latter can easily play countries off against one another by organizing price wars between them.

As has already been noted, the doctrine of the New International Economic Order, supported by the most progressive of the Third World countries and often seen as a threat by rich countries, corresponds to the relocation abroad of MNCs. The attitude of host countries of the periphery toward direct investment from abroad, which China also seems to share, rests in the final analysis on the belief that such investment gives an indispensable boost to development. The study of MNCs basically aims to reduce the negative aspects and enhance the positive side. This is a Proudhonian attitude based on a black-white analysis. While wishing to attract and/or encourage MNCs, but at the same time control them, one tries to escape from the conflict-cooperation dichotomy. But this would be to ignore the very nature of MNCs, which cannot be closely integrated into the host economy, because they must remain part of a whole, whose structure is global. In our opinion, the originality of multinational financial and manufacturing enterprises stems from the very fact that they have solved for themselves the contradiction with which governments are still trying to come to terms. In fact, by analogy with the position of governments, it could be said of MNCs that they cannot develop their activities totally independently of nation-states, in a sort of transcendental world; but neither can they be constricted by state controls. At the very heart of their dynamism, one must look for a particular vs. general dialectic. On one hand, MNCs capitalize on and breed national differences: differences in wage levels, in interest and inflation rates, in levels of development, in production capabilities, in political regimes, in tax systems, in cultural and geographic situations, etc. On the other hand, they are able to rise above these national differences through their integrated, world-wide organization. The homogeneous nature of the companies allows them to exploit national differences, without themselves being affected by them. The result is that MNCs do not seem to pose a direct threat to the existence of nation-states. The era of multinationalism is very different from the era of colonialism, which destroyed existing economic and political structures and institutions. Taking the theory of Hobson[22] further, one can say that MNCs do not directly threaten the nations. Nor do they pose any greater a threat to the states, as was the case in the days of imperialism, defined as a hierarchical order of states guaranteeing world peace (from 'pax romana' to 'pax napoleonic'). All in all, it seems that the internationalization of production and capital circulation does not threaten the nation-states. Finally, the present development can be seen as a new form of economic liberalism.

Thus, what is emerging conforms to the futurist vision of Adam Smith: 'If every nation were to adhere to the noble system of freedom of imports and exports, the different states of a great continent would become like the different provinces of a great empire.'[23] With the exception of this difference, which is a basic one, the internationalization of production, capital circulation and trade go hand in hand. But fundamentally, the emergence of a world economy depends on the continuation of economic liberalism. The great empire is reaching the final limits of its power. This development has perhaps given a renewed topicality to Marx's views on free exchange.[24]

NOTES

1. Y. Berthelot and G. Tardy, *Le Défi économique du Tiers Monde* (Paris: Docu. française, 1979).

2. C. Stoffaes, *La Grande Menace industrielle* (Paris: Colmann-Lévy, 1978).

3. *Rapports sur les options du VIIIe Plan* (Paris: Docu. française, 1979), pp. 22-4.

4. cf. L'élaboration des codes de conduite par les organismes internationaux: International Chamber of Commerce, OECD, UN.

5. A. Cotta, *L'Impératif mondial* (Paris: PUF, 1978).

6. C.-A. Michalet, *Le Capitalisme mondial* (Paris: PUF, 1976) (to be published shortly in English).

7. *Multinational Companies and World Development* (New York: UN, 1973).

8. On the definition of the two strategies, see M. Delapierre and C.-A. Michalet, *Les Investissements etrangers en France: Stratégies et structures* (Paris: Colmann-Lévy, 1976).

9. A. Emmanuel, *L'Echange inégal* (Paris: Maspéro, 1969).

10. cf., for the case of Germany, F. Fröbel, J. Heinrichs and O. Kreye, *Neue Internationale Arbeitsleitung* (Hamburg: Rowholt, 1977).

11. cf., for example, the case of the automobile industry in Morocco: C.-A. Michalet and B. Madeuf (UN Report, mimeo). See also C.-A. Michalet *La Soustraitance international* (OECD Report, not yet published).

12. cf. Berthelot and Tardy, op. cit.

13. Rybicoff Report for the US Senate Committee on Finance: *Implications of MNCs for World Wide Trade and Investment and for US Trade and Labor* (Washington: US Government Printing Office, 1977).

14. On all these points, cf. Michalet, *Le Capitalisme mondiale*, first part.

15. M. Foucault, *Les Mots et les choses* (Paris: Gallimard, 1966).

16. From *L'Accumulation du capital à l'échelle mondiale* (Paris: Edit de Minuit, 1969) to *Classe et nation* (Paris: Edit de Minuit, 1979).

17. R. Vernon, *Les Entreprises multinationales* (Paris: Colmann-Lévy, 1966).

18. J. P. Thuiller, 'Les Investissements directes Européens aux Etats Univ.' PhD Thesis, 1978.

19. C. Palloix, *L'Internationalisation du capital* (Paris: Maspéro, 1975).

20. cf. Michalet, *Le Capitalisme mondiale*.

21. G. A. Arrighi, *The Geometry of Imperialism* (London: New Left Books, 1978).

22. J. A. Hobson, *Imperialism: A Study* (London: Nisbet, 1938).

23. Adam Smith, *The Wealth of Nations* (E. Cannon, 1904; first published 1776).

24. Karl Marx, *Discours sur le libre échange*.

3

WORLD ECONOMIC INTEGRATION AND POLICY RESPONSES:
Some Developmental Impacts

Volker Bornschier
University of Zurich, Switzerland

INTRODUCTION

This paper addresses questions related to impacts of the world economy on national development. It presents some cross-national evidence and investigates the role of economic policy. Multinational corporations (MNCs) as central institutions of the modern world economy imply, owing to their internal division of labor across countries, an internalization of economic relationships previously regarded as international. This means that one should look at MNCs not only as a new feature of the world economy, but as the emergent new organizational form of that system. The market forces that formerly mediated much of the core-periphery structure within the world economy have become less important owing to the direct organizational links by which essential control functions, i.e. entrepreneurial functions, are articulated (Bornschier, 1976).

The massive spread of industrial MNCs in recent decades adds a new element to the classical core-periphery division of labor in the world economy (with the core specializing in industrial production and financial control and the periphery in raw material production). The new form of the hierarchy, which is superimposed over the still active classical one, implies a core-periphery division within industrial and tertiary activities themselves. The core is specializing in control over technology and the innovation process, in control over capital active throughout the world, and in the most advanced and technologically sophisticated industrial products (embodying much human capital) at the beginning of their product cycle; whereas the periphery is engaged in standardized and routinized production either for the domestic or the world market. This process is called 'dependent industrialization' (Bornschier, 1975).

The hierarchies of the world economy have important theoretical consequences for income possibilities, income inequality and types of structural changes (including structural mobility within the system of occupational division of labor) at various levels. Contrary to the argument of Cardoso (1973), I suggest not only classical economic dependence but also dependent industrialization as a major mechanism of preserving underdevelopment — underdevelopment, defined as a process in which the development potential is not, or is only partially, used and in which development is uneven with regard to regions, sectors, organizations, institutional orders and groups of people.

More specifically, the propositions developed elsewhere in more detail (cf. Bornschier, 1980b) are that the peripheral status in either of the two mentioned hierarchies of the world economy is related to greater personal income inequality and to lower long-term economic growth. This effect of the integration with the world economy via MNCs should hold regardless of level of development within less developed countries. For core countries no effects are expected, since they are at the same time headquarter countries of MNCs. The main arguments, beside structural and political distortions within penetrated countries, that are seen as a consequence of MNC penetration are as follows. The redistributive economy implied by the institution of the MNCs is a major contributor to the decapitalization of peripheral countries. This applies to both mentioned hierarchies. With regard to dependent industrialization, an additional cause is seen in the early monopolization of the small domestic markets of effective demand, intensified owing to unequal income distribution. This leads to premature relative stagnation (Bornschier, 1975, 1980b, 1980c).

In the rest of this chapter some recent cross-national findings are discussed in order to evaluate whether or not they suggest support for these propositions. I conclude by discussing recent findings concerning economic policy responses towards MNCs and their impact on economic growth.[1]

MNC PENETRATION
AND ECONOMIC GROWTH

The variable that represents the intensity of integration of a country in peripheral position with the world economy dominated by MNCs is: MNC penetration. This is measured by the total stock of foreign direct investment related to the total stock of capital and to total population, i.e. to both major factors of production. The measure relates to the year 1967 (see n. 1). Since the theory predicts different short-term and long-term consequences of foreign investment, fresh investment of MNCs, i.e. for the years 1968-73, is controlled for. This fresh investment is referred to as 'MNC investment' and is weighted by total GDP in 1968.

The average annual real growth (in percent) of gross national product per capita between the end of 1965 and the end of 1977 is taken as an overall indicator for long-term economic growth.[2] The level of economic development is controlled. This indicator is income per capita in 1965 (logged), and is performed with a function, i.e. a linear and a squared term of logged income (cf. Bornschier, 1980c).

Several control variables are introduced in order to reach an unbiased estimate of the relationship between the level of MNC penetration and the subsequent long-term economic growth. These are: capital formation (GDI in relation to GDP, averaged for the years 1965, 1970, 1973); exports in relation to total product (averaged for the same years); and an estimate of the absolute size of the modern market segment (logged total energy consumption in 1967) (see n. 1).

For the multiple regression of economic growth a sample of 103 countries was used. This is, with only very few exceptions, a full sample of all market economies with a population above 1 million. The socialist countries are, however, heavily under-represented in the sample — only two are included, owing to lack of data.

The regression of economic growth between 1965 and 1977 on the mentioned variables shows the following estimates (standard error of the estimate in brackets).

Economic
growth =

	-0.0263	MNC penetration	$+0.0076$	MNC
	(0.0065)		(0.0025)	investment
	$+13.81$	level of income	-2.49	level of
	(3.63)		(0.61)	income
				squared
	$+0.0664$	capital formation	$+0.0444$	exports
	(0.0335)		(0.0155)	
	$+0.8856$	size		
	(0.2670)			

The constant is -20.48, and $\bar{R}^2$ is 0.39 ($N = 103$).

The regression shows a significant negative impact of the level of MNC penetration on subsequent growth. The estimate is more than four times the standard error. As expected, the short-term effect of MNCs, i.e. fresh MNC investment occurring within the period, has a positive effect which is significant, too. Since the other variables are included here only as controls, their results will not be commented on. Their effect is significant, and the associations go into the expected directions.

The negative impact of MNC penetration on subsequent long-term growth is more pronounced for the 88 less developed countries within the sample (excluding the 15 richest; they are, at the same time, important headquarter countries of MNCs).[3] For the group of 15 richest countries taken separately, there exists virtually no relationship at all.[4] These results are consistent, then, with the propositions.

So far, only total MNC penetration has been considered. The next step relates more specifically to dependent industrialization. A split of total MNC penetration according to economic sectors in which the stock of foreign direct investment is located produces results for the 88 less developed countries that are consistent with the theoretical expectations.[5] The four sectors for which the breakdown has been made cover more than three-quarters of all the stock of capital controlled by MNCs in less developed countries. The measures of 'partial' penetration in manufacturing, mining and smelting, integrated petroleum and agriculture relate again to 1967 and are constructed by weighting the stocks in these sectors with the total stock of capital and total population. One has to note that the partial measures of penetration in these four major sectors of less developed countries are statistically rather independent (the average intercorrelation is only $r = 0.15$).

The regression results are as follows (standard error of the estimate in brackets):

Economic growth =				
	− 0.0617 (0.0175)	MNC penetration manufacturing	− 0.0510 (0.0139)	MNC penetration mining and smelting
	+ 0.0032 (0.0162)	MNC penetration integr. petroleum	− 0.0193 (0.0156)	MNC penetration agriculture
	+ 0.0103 (0.0027)	MNC investment	+ 11.52 (5.44)	level of income
	− 2.05 (1.01)	level of income squared	+ 0.0622 (0.0359)	capital formation
	+ 0.0297 (0.0161)	exports	+ 1.001 (0.289)	size

The constant is − 17.62 and $\bar{R}^2$ is 0.49 ($N = 88$ less developed countries).

The partial penetration effect in manufacturing is significant and negative; the same is true for the partial effect of penetration in mining and smelting. The one for agriculture is negative but not significant. And for penetration of the petroleum sector no relationship exists. Fresh MNC investment (which is not split according to sectors, owing to lack of data) again shows a significant positive effect on growth.

These findings for the partial penetration in sectors correspond to earlier findings (Bornschier and Ballmer-Cao, 1978). One may conclude, then, that dependent industrialization is clearly related to lower subsequent long-term economic growth, whereas the effect of classical dependence (raw material extraction) obviously seems to depend on the world market situation of specific commodities. For the period under study, only penetration in mining and smelting shows a negative impact of the same strength as dependent industrialization.

The findings with regard to the effects of MNC penetration and investment in the sample of 103 countries are consistent with earlier findings which are reviewed by: Bornschier, Chase-Dunn and Rubinson (1978, 1980). Those findings, and the ones presented here, suggest the following conclusions. MNC investment has the short-term effect of increasing the economic growth rate. The higher the cumulated investment of MNCs, however, in relation to the total stock of capital and population — that is to say, the greater MNC penetration, as a structural feature of host countries — the lower the subsequent growth rate. Although MNC investment has been found to make short-term positive contributions to growth, one must note that such investments increase MNC penetration and therefore contribute in the long run to the negative effect associated therewith.

That the growth-reducing consequences of MNC penetration has to date aroused rather mild scholarly and public concern is especially due to two factors. First, so long as overall MNC investment remains high, the negative effect of penetration is partly neutralized.[6] Second, growth is dependent on the level of development in a curvilinear way. This implies, inter alia, that highly penetrated richer less developed countries still realize on average a growth rate that is higher than the one of the average poor LDC, even if these poor ones are not penetrated at all. The last point shows also that the slowing down of economic growth in the long run, which obviously results from high penetration, implies not economic stagnation, but a markedly lower growth rate than one would expect against the background of the growth potential.

Before considering personal income inequality as the dependent variable, I turn to a short discussion of the conclusions with regard to economic growth.

Discussion

With regard to the growth effect of MNC penetration two questions arise. First, one may ask whether the empirical association found can be interpreted in causal terms; i.e., that MNC penetration lowers the comparative growth rate, as the underlying theory suggests. Second, if there exists a causal relationship, by which mechanisms and through what mediating factors is growth affected?

In the case of the first question, I want to make two points which suggest that a causal relationship works. Since the mentioned relationships between MNCs and economic growth in LDCs hold also after controlling for various factors that may be of importance for economic growth, a spurious relationship is unlikely. Beside the controls employed in the model discussed in this paper, various others have been used in previous research, including the growth rate of population, the level and growth of urbanization, capital intensity, and world market position with regard to valuable commodities (Bornschier, 1980c).

A logically alternative explanation of the finding that MNCs retard economic growth in the long run has been discussed by Stoneman (1975, p. 18). He claims that there is little support for it. Stoneman makes the point that the inverse relationship between economic growth and MNC penetration could be due to the fact that 'there is a tendency for countries with poor growth prospects to devote greater efforts to building up a stock of foreign investment in intended compensation.' This possibility, however, can be ruled out empirically since it implies a positive correlation between poor growth performance and fresh MNC investment. This contradicts the findings: MNC investment is high when income growth is also high. Thus, one may conclude that the causal interpretation suggested by the theory has not to be rejected.

Recent research has produced several findings with regard to intervening variables linking MNC penetration and economic growth. Some of these findings will be mentioned shortly. Bornschier and Ballmer-Cao (1978) find for LDCs that MNCs go together with higher personal income inequality. This can explain part of the growth effect, since income inequality is empirically found to be negatively related both to domestic capital formation and income growth (except for very small LDCs). Such a partial explanation is consistent with the finding of a growth effect only for LDCs, only for these countries MNCs are linked with higher income inequality. Furthermore, unequal labor productivity and unequal capital intensity, both within and between economic sectors (as indicated by higher sectoral income inequality), are more accentuated for LDCs if MNC penetration is high (Chase-Dunn, 1975a; Bornschier, 1975, 1980c). Such disparities imply a lower level of integration and linkage effects and thus are likely to contribute to a lower level of overall productivity, so that a given capital input results in comparative lower economic growth in the long run.

Further evidence for a mediating mechanism is found in a test of the decapitalization thesis (Bornschier, 1980c). The thesis maintains that the funds available for investment are, on balance, reduced owing to the operation of the institution of the MNC. Bornschier (1980c) finds MNC penetration related to a lower subsequent growth rate of total domestic investment. Since investment growth is a major determinant of income growth, this explains another component of the negative effect of MNC penetration on income growth.

Moreover, technological dependence owing to control of MNCs over patents can explain a further part of the influence on growth (Meyer-Fehr, 1979). Meyer-Fehr (1978, 1979) suggests also an explanation via the relationship between MNC penetration and a particular foreign trade structure of LDCs which is unfavorable for economic growth.

Lastly, Ballmer-Cao (1979) finds MNC penetration related to a higher level of internal social conflict and to lower executive stability. This is likely to contribute to lowering the possible economic growth rate. It is also likely to affect negatively the ability of the state to pursue a policy of growth independently of the class interests created by foreign capital.

MNC PENETRATION AND PERSONAL INCOME INEQUALITY

Several studies in recent years have related world economic position to personal income inequality within countries (Chase-Dunn, 1975a; Rubinson, 1976; Bornschier, 1975, 1978; Bornschier and Ballmer-Cao, 1978, 1979). These various findings suggest a significant positive relationship between level of MNC penetration and level of personal income inequality in less developed countries. This conclusion can be substantiated by a new analysis which employs 72 countries, i.e. the maximum number of fairly reliable observations on personal income inequality (data spread around the year 1968).

A regression of the Gini index of personal income inequality shows the following results.[7] MNC penetration as an indication of a peripheral position within the world economy dominated by MNCs is again the main test variable.[8] The level of the logged income per capita, 1965, is controlled (a linear and a squared term). This is done because personal income inequality has been found related to level of income in a curvilinear form.[9]

Furthermore, the system type is controlled. This is done by employing a continuous variable. The continuum ranges from 'private capitalism,' where profits accrue to individuals, to 'non-private capitalism,' where profits go to collectives (normally the

state). The measure is public investment as a share of total investment, averaged for the mid-1960s. The fact that profits do not add
to labor income inequalities under non-private capitalism allows
the prediction that the continuous variable 'system type' is
negatively related to overall personal income inequality.

The regression estimates for 72 countries are as follows (standard
error of estimate in brackets):

Income inequality =	0.0829	MNC penetration	+ 42.97	level of income
	(0.0291)		(20.30)	
	− 8.97	level of income	− 0.1739	system
	(3.49)	squared	(0.0482)	type

The constant is 1.21, $\bar{R}^2$ is 0.50 ($N = 72$).

The regression results show a significant positive association between MNC penetration and income inequality. The control
variables are significant and their associations with inequality go
into the expected directions.

Excluding the richest countries from the sample (one of the 15
previously excluded rich countries has no data for income inequality) shows that the relationship between MNC penetration and income inequality is stronger for less developed countries: the
estimate is 0.1021 (standard error: 0.0344) for 58 LDCs.[10]

Disaggregating again, total penetration according to sectors
shows the following results for 58 less developed countries. The
dependent variable is the Gini index and the same controls have
been applied as in the previous model (standard error of estimate in
brackets):

MNC penetration in manufacturing   0.1998 (0.0971), $\bar{R}^2 = 0.49$
MNC penetration in mining and smelting 0.1339 (0.0821), $\bar{R}^2 = 0.47$
MNC penetration in integrated petroleum 0.2039 (0.0871), $\bar{R}^2 = 0.50$
MNC penetration in agriculture   0.0030 (0.0762), $\bar{R}^2 = 0.45$

Three of the four partial MNC penetration measures according to
sectors show substantial positive relationships with income inequality. This is most significant in the case of dependent industrialization and the penetration for the petroleum sector. The
association for agricultural penetration is very small and insignificant, although positive, too.[11]

Discussion

The relationship between the level of MNC penetration and the level of personal income inequality seems to be a fairly consolidated empirical finding. Since time series are lacking, however, the question of the assumed mutual causation remains open. The theory underlying the research assumes causal effects from inequality to MNC penetration and also into the other direction, MNC penetration causing higher income inequality.[12] The argument for the first causal chain is that existing income inequality in less developed countries (effective demand for MNC products) is a prerequisite for MNCs oriented toward LDC markets. This is different from the situation of MNCs active in mineral extraction. They do not rely from the outset of their activities in LDCs on prior income concentration. One may expect, however, a certain link, since such MNCs are likely to favor, other things being equal, less developed countries with a more unequal distribution of power.

However, once active, MNCs in both manufacturing and extraction are assumed to increase personal income inequality, other things being equal. The argument is that the links with the world economy via MNCs act in favor of an economic power concentration within the penetrated countries (Bornschier, 1978; Bornschier and Ballmer-Cao, 1979). Moreover, such links weaken the structural strength of the state (Rubinson, 1976; Ballmer-Cao, 1979) and thus the intervening steering power of the state (Bornschier and Ballmer-Cao, 1979). Furthermore, disparities between sectors, i.e. uneven development, favor higher personal income inequality (Chase-Dunn, 1975).

The studies mentioned have tested several specific hypotheses within the areas described. They employed indicators like the degree of concentration of traditional power (land tenure inequality), the power distribution within the aggregate organizational system outside agriculture (occupational structure variables), the power distribution in the labor market, government share in income and executive stability, as well as the level of social conflict. Their results are suggestive, but do not meet, however, the requirements of strict causal analysis, since measures for change in income inequality are lacking.

To conclude, we know that personal income distribution is more unequal if the level of MNC penetration is high. No empirical evidence is reported that MNCs reduce inequality in less developed countries in the course of their operation, whereas there are several hypotheses with preliminary empirical support for the contrary. This is, then, a suggested area for future research.

ECONOMIC POLICY RESPONSES AND SOME OF THEIR IMPACTS

Up to now, economic policy responses towards MNCs have received little attention in cross-national research. One exception is the work of Berweger and Hoby (1978, 1980).[13] They have established data on economic policies with a content analysis according to two dimensions: first, an intervention dimension, with the two poles liberalism-interventionism, in order to represent the quantitative extent of state intervention in the economy and in the sphere of corporate property; second, a restriction dimension, with the two poles promotion-restriction, in order to examine the qualitative aspect of the extent to which policies are directed against MNCs or are favorable to them. Out of the most important economic policy variables,[14] Berweger and Hoby constructed eight different types of economic policy which they could scale according to whether a policy type is advantageous or disadvantageous for MNCs.

An analysis of the distribution of 73 countries among the eight different policy types leads to the following findings for the period between 1960 and 1977 (Berweger and Hoby, 1978, 1980). All eight types of policy towards MNCs are empirically relevant for the period considered. In the earlier years, however, basically liberal economic policies prevailed, while more recently interventionist policies have become prevalent. In the period up to 1977 a clear polarization has developed: one large group of countries concentrates on 'promoting liberalism' and another large group on 'stop-and-go interventionism.' Up to 1970 restrictive interventionism played an important role, too. The reason for the shifts over time is that both disadvantageously liberal and interventionist countries (with imposed transfer restrictions) have increasingly incorporated investment incentives for MNCs in their economic policy package. In 1960 only 38 per cent of the countries ranked high on the variable 'investment incentives', but by 1977 this figure is up to 89.

'Stop-and go interventionism' has become markedly more frequent over time: in 1960 no country represented this policy type, but by 1977 30 out of 73 did so. It consists of a contradictory combination of restrictive measures against MNCs (including interventions with regard to corporate property rights) and promotion in the form of incentives for fresh investment by MNCs. Rising 'stop-and-go interventionism' can be interpreted as follows. Owing to high MNC penetration, negative structural effects appear and the economic growth rate is lowered in the long run; both contribute to increasing social and political problems. This is seen as a major source of restrictive legislation against MNCs in many countries, especially LDCs. Such restrictions on foreign capital, especially in the context of a general interventionist economic policy, affect the propensity to invest negatively and thus are likely to contribute — at least in the short run — to further lowering of the economic growth rate. This makes the economic and social crisis more acute. A shift in economic policy, represented by investment incentives for MNCs, can be considered an attempt to maintain the short-term positive growth contribution of MNC investment in order temporarily to mitigate the negative structural and growth effect of MNC penetration. Since the positive growth effect of MNC investment is transitory, and MNC investment adds to their penetration and hence to increased subsequent negative effects, such policies can be considered only as patch-ups.

Determinants and Concomitants of Economic Policies

The level of development (as measured by per capita income) occupies a prominent position among the determinants and concomitants of economic policy. The lower it is, the more interventionist and restrictive vis-à-vis foreign capital the economic policy of a host country is likely to be. A similar finding applies, with increasing importance over time, to another aspect of development, namely the level of secondary school enrolment: the higher it is, the lower the degree of intervention and restriction in economic policy towards MNCs.

Among the concomitants or framework variables for economic policy that are rather independent of the level of development, one can point to the voting behavior within international organizations (East-West and North-South cleavages) and the degree of integration into international organizations. The relationship of such variables with economic policy suggest that, although the policies are structurally rooted within host countries, their implementation may be supported by increased political participation and synchronization within the system of international organizations. This might explain why international organizations have become increasingly important, especially for LDCs.

Furthermore, one can observe that, in general, the higher the level of MNC penetration, the less interventionist and restrictive economic policy has been. This linkage, which would normally be expected, is however substantially weakened over the course of time. Thus, increasingly countries are able to adopt an unfavorable policy toward MNCs, despite high MNC penetration. Contrary to this negative, though a considerably weakened relationship with MNC penetration as measured on the basis of capital invested, the association between patent penetration through MNCs and restrictive economic policy is somewhat positive. Although one can assume that restrictive policies towards MNCs are frequently accompanied by regulations concerning the use and abuse of patents (monopolistic practices), the positive correlation would suggest that such regulations have remained generally ineffective because of absent or insufficient control. This permits MNCs to react with alternative strategies towards a changing political climate in the world: they can penetrate countries either on the basis of capital and organization and/or by technology, i.e. by control over patents.

Consequences of Economic Policies

The long-term consequences of economic policy could not be adequately analyzed by Berweger and Hoby (1978, 1980) since there has been an intensification of measures aimed against MNCs only in the second half of the period that they studied. Their findings mentioned below refer, therefore, only to the period studied, and the lags they employed are in general no longer than five years.[15] Furthermore, the findings refer only to economic growth as one of the dependent variables of interest here. Personal income distribution has not yet been considered, because the observations on this variable are scattered over a rather wide range of years over which economic policy of many countries has changed.

The central policy variable of Berweger and Hoby (1978, 1980), which they scaled according to the degree of disadvantage for

MNCs, i.e. measures to counter the MNCs, acts negatively on investment stocks and flows of MNCs. The association with flows is, as one would expect, more significant, but the impact on stocks is clearly accentuated with longer lags. The individual policy types that they analyze, also act in the expected directions. These findings suggest the following conclusions.

Although one can observe that high MNC penetration has acted somewhat against restrictive policy measures in the 1960s, one must observe that such policies towards MNCs, once implemented, can in fact lessen dependency on foreign capital provided by MNCs. This would reduce the future negative impact of MNCs on structure and growth which can be predicted on the basis of the findings discussed in the first section of this paper. However, one cannot conclude that these restrictive policies have themselves had an immediate positive impact on economic growth: quite the opposite is suggested by the findings of Berweger and Hoby.

The more interventionist and restrictive the economic policy, and hence the more disadvantageous for MNCs, the lower the subsequent economic growth. This has been controlled for the level of MNC penetration, and it cannot be explained by relation to prior growth, since the relation between this and subsequent policy formulation is not significant. The same effect as for the scaled policy variable, which contains several policy dimensions, holds also for single policy variables such as the degree of general intervention in the economy, whereas investment incentives (owing to their positive effect on MNC investment) have positive growth consequences.

The negative impact of policies countering MNCs on economic growth deserves some comment. The lower economic growth following from interventionist and restrictive policies can be explained largely by the fact that the propensity to invest is reduced. Since capital formation, in general, has a strong positive influence on aggregate per capita income growth, while foreign investment has negative impact in the long run, one can conclude that an economic policy for long-term growth should restrict foreign capital formation and compensate, or even over-compensate, by promoting indigenous capital formation. The available empirical evidence suggests that restrictive policy toward MNCs has not succeeded in doing this, at least not in general and in the short run.

It remains, therefore, an open question to what extent policy measures unfavorable for MNCs, increasingly implemented recently, have resulted in or initiated a real reconstruction of under-developed economies toward greater satisfaction of basic needs, including a wide redistribution of income and a reduction of economic and regional disparities, and have actually led to more self-sustaining development. Such a reconstruction would be decisive in order for an approach countering forces in the world economy to result in a more even and equitable growth in the long run, despite the short-term intensification of the social and economic crisis suggested by the findings mentioned above.

Yet our available evidence points to severe difficulties for such reconstruction. That interventionist and restrictive policies have a negative impact on subsequent growth, at least in the short run, is likely to imply limited popularity for such policies and the regimes that implement them. This strengthens the hands of those supporting the status quo. This can be seen as a stabilization mechanism built into dependency on the world economy. It frequently seems to leave no choice other than patch-up policy. The contradictory combination of restrictions upon and incentives for the MNCs that has suddenly arisen in recent times is a case in point. It might be interpreted as one of the results of the stabilization mechanism of the status quo. Therefore, it would be rather misleading to consider the increase in investment incentives for MNCs as a host country policy basically in favor of MNCs, as apologists have frequently asserted in recent discussions.

CONCLUDING REMARKS

Investment by MNCs in less developed countries could contribute to faster economic growth if it did not add to, or actually produce, structural imbalances in the longer run, so that the short-term growth contributions are reversed. The experience of the last decades leaves but little hope that there are self-sustaining mechanisms mitigating, or even overcoming, these structural imbalances of dependent industralization over time. The economic policy of states seems not to have counteracted them either, whether owing to a lack of options or will.

The empirical findings do not lend support to the frequently advocated position that high income inequality in the course of development is a necessary sacrifice for faster economic growth. Such sacrifice would make sense only if the lower social strata would also derive advantages in absolute terms, although they would have to content themselves with smaller relative shares. MNCs result in greater income equality and make not for greater but for less economic growth over the longer run. And income inequality, quite apart from MNC presence, results in slower economic growth for the majority of less developed countries. Therefore, a strategy of industrialization relying heavily on inequality and MNCs is not one designed to satisfy the needs of the majority of the population in less developed countries, in regard to faster absolute gains.

The growing dependency on the integration with the world economy dominated by MNCs, as well as on foreign credits, which numerous less developed states suffer in order to mitigate in the short run the long-term structural imbalances that have appeared as a result of dependent industrialization is likely to prove a major structural hindrance for a development policy directed toward the needs of the masses. This constellation is especially likely to frustrate the redistribution of income in less developed countries, because it would weaken the short-term opportunities of MNCs in the domestic markets.

In a broader perspective, one may conclude that a fundamental contradiction is obviously built into the functioning of the world economy, which threatens the working of the system in the long run. Whereas, in the short run, the maximization of the goals of private enterprises requires a large part of the produced surplus to be withheld from immediate consumption by the majority of the population, an effective mass demand is the precondition for balanced and continuous economic growth. This can be achieved only by redistributing a significant part of the surplus to those from which it is withheld by the normal functioning of the economic system. Since such indispensable redistributions in less developed countries do not occur to any appreciable extent, and since, at the world level, there are no independent redistributing agents, the contradiction is assuming dimensions threatening world society.

NOTES

1. The findings to be discussed stem from a research project directed by the author at the University of Zurich Sociological Institute. The financial support of the 'Deutsche Gesellschaft für Friedens- und Konfliktforschung' (DGFK) is gratefully acknowledged. Thanh-Huyen Ballmer-Cao, Gottfried Berweger, Jean-Pierre Hoby, Alexandros Kyrtsis, Peter C. Meyer-Fehr and Jürg Scheidegger participated in the cross-national research. An overview of the findings can be found in Bornschier (1980a, 1980d). The data and indicators employed are in Ballmer-Cao and Scheidegger (1979). For a summary statement of the theory underlying the research see Bornschier (1980b).

2. These new figures are the only ones not included in Ballmer-Cao and Scheidegger (1979). They are computed from time series on GNP per capita in constant market prices and US dollars of the base period 1975-77; see World Bank (1978).

3. For less developed countries the estimate for MNC penetration is -0.0310 (0.0079) and for MNC investment 0.0082 (0.0027); $\bar{R}^2 = 0.40$, $N = 88$. The estimates for the control variables remain very similar, except that the significance of the level of income is substantially reduced.

4. For the rich countries the estimate for MNC penetration is 0.0012 (0.0205).

5. Less developed countries are used for this test because I do not want to include my own estimations for the breakdown according to sectors in rich countries (see Bornschier and Ballmer-Cao, 1978). For the rich countries also, however, the penetration according to different sectors has no effect on growth, as in the case of overall penetration.

6. One has to note, however, that on the average the level of MNC penetration and subsequent fresh MNC investment are not strongly related for LDCs ($r = 0.40$, $N = 88$). For larger LDCs this correlation even drops to 0.18.

7. For the data see again Ballmer-Cao and Scheidegger (1979).

8. MNC investment has been tested, too, as a predictor. But there is no relationship between income inequality and aggregate fresh MNC investment in recent years, either in the total sample or in the LDC sample.

9. So-called U-shape hypothesis; see Ahluwalia (1976), Bornschier (1978, 1980e).

10. Contrary to the case of economic growth, where no relationship was found for rich countries, MNC penetration tends to be related to inequality in the opposite direction as compared with LDCs; for details, see Bornschier and Ballmer-Cao (1978) and Bornschier (1980e).

11. For a theoretical discussion of the connection between different sectoral location of MNC capital and income inequality, see Bornschier (1980e).

12. Although preliminary findings based on two-stage least squares tend to suggest mutual causation (Bornschier and Ballmer-Cao, 1978), the available evidence is not conclusive.

13. The following summary of some of their results and the comments are in part adapted from a section in Bornschier (1980d).

14. General and sectoral state intervention and nationalizations, capital transfer and import restrictions, and investment incentives for foreign capital.
15. Moreover, I would like to mention that Berweger and Hoby (1978, 1980) did not perform analyses employing statistical interactions concerning economic policies. One can think of investigating the impact of MNC penetration on structure and growth under different conditions. This can be done by analyses of covariance.

REFERENCES

AHLUWALIA, Montek S. (1976). 'Inequality, Poverty and Development,' *Journal of Development Economics*, 3, 307-42.

BALLMER-CAO, Thanh-Huyen (1979). 'Système politique, répartition des revenus et pénétration des entreprises multinationales,' *Annuaire Suisse de science politique*.

BALLMER-CAO, Thanh-Huyen, and Jürg SCHEIDEGGER (1979). 'Compendium of Data for World System Analyses,' in Volker Bornschier and Peter Heintz (eds), Special Issue of the *Bulletin of the Sociological Institute of the University of Zurich*, March 1979.

BERWEGER, Gottfried, and Jean-Pierre HOBY (1978). 'Wirtschaftspolitik gegenüber Auslandskapital,' *Bulletin of the Sociological Institute of the University of Zürich*, no. 35, 1-136.

BERWEGER, Gottfried, and Jean-Pierre HOBY (1980). 'Nationale Wirtschaftspolitik und multinationale Konzerne,' in Bornschier (1980a).

BORNSCHIER, Volker (1975). 'Abhängige Industrialisierung und Einkommensentwicklung,' *Schweizerische Zeitschrift für Soziologie*, 1, 67-105.

BORNSCHIER, Volker (1976). *Wachstum, Konzentration und Multinationalisierung von Industrieunternehmen* (Frauenfeld and Stuttgart: Huber).

BORNSCHIER, Volker (1978). 'Einkommensungleichheit innerhalb von Ländern in komparativer Sicht,' *Schweizerische Zeitschrift für Soziologie*, 4, 3-45.

BORNSCHIER, Volker (1980a) *Multinationale Konzerne, Wirtschaftspolitik und nationale Entwicklung im Weltsystem* Frankfurt and New York (forthcoming): Campus (with contributions by Ballmer-Cao, Berweger, Chase-Dunn, Hoby, Meyer-Fehr and Rubinson).

BORNSCHIER, Volker (1980b). 'Weltsystem und weltwirtschaftliche Arbeitsteilung. Das zugrundeliegende sozialwissenschaftliche Bild von der Welt,' in Bornschier (1980a).

BORNSCHIER, Volker (1980c). 'Multinational Corporations and Economic Growth: a Cross-national Test of the Decapitalization Thesis', *Journal of Development Economics*, June.

BORNSCHIER, Volker (1980d). 'Multinational Corporations, Economic Policy and National Development in the World System,' *International Social Science Journal*, March.

BORNSCHIER, Volker (1980e). 'Weltwirtschaft, Entwicklungsstand und Einkommensungleichheit,' in Bornschier (1980a).

BORNSCHIER, Volker and Thanh-Huyen BALLMER-CAO (1978). 'Multinational Corporations in the World Economy and National Development,' *Bulletin of the Sociological Institute of the University of Zurich*, no. 32, 1-169.

BORNSCHIER, Volker and Thanh-Huyen BALLMER-CAO (1979). 'Income Inequality: a Cross-national Study of the Relationships between MNC-penetration, Dimensions of the Power Structure and Income Distribution,' *American Sociological Review*, 44, 487-506.

BORNSCHIER, Volker, Christopher CHASE-DUNN and Richard RUBINSON (1978). 'Cross-national Evidence of the Effects of Foreign Investment and Aid on Economic Growth and Inequality: a Survey of Findings and a Reanalysis,' *American Journal of Sociology*, 84, 651-83.

BORNSCHIER, Volker, Christopher CHASE-DUNN and Richard RUBINSON (1980). 'Auslandskapital, Wirtschaftswachstum und Ungleichheit: Ueberblick über die Evidenzen und Reanalyse,' in Bornschier (1980a).

CARDOSO, Fernando Henrique (1973). 'Associated-dependent Development: Theoretical and Practical Implications,' in Alfred Stepan (ed.), *Authoritarian Brazil: Origins, Policies, and Future* (New Haven and London: Yale University Press).

CHASE-DUNN, Christopher (1975a). 'International Economic Dependence in the World System,' PhD dissertation, Stanford University.

CHASE-DUNN, Christopher (1975b). 'The Effects of International Economic Dependence on Development and Inequality: a Cross-national Study,' *American Sociological Review*, 40, 720-38.

MEYER-FEHR, Peter (1978). 'Bestimmungsfaktoren des Wirtschaftswachstums von Nationen,' *Bulletin of the Sociological Institute of the University of Zürich*, no. 34, 1-105.

MEYER-FEHR, Peter (1979). 'Technologieabhängigkeit und Wirtschaftswachstum,' *Schweizerische Zeitschrift für Soziologie*, 5, 79-96.

RUBINSON, Richard (1976). 'The World-economy and the Distribution of Income within States: a Cross-national Study,' *American Sociological Review*, 41, 638-59.

STONEMAN, Colin (1975). 'Foreign Capital and Economic Growth,' *World Development*, 3, 11-26.

WORLD BANK (IBRD), Economic Analysis and Projections Department (1978). 'GNP Per Capita Series in Constant Market Prices and US Dollars, Base Period 1975-1977,' Washington, Mimeographed: Data run 12 April 1978.

4

THE POLITICAL AND SOCIAL IMPACT OF TRANSNATIONAL CORPORATIONS

Alberto Martinelli
University of Milan, Italy

In the last decade, transnational corporations have been the object of extended research by numerous scholars in various countries, and of careful political scrutiny by international organizations and national government agencies.[1] The accumulating literature focuses, however, mostly on the managerial and macroeconomic aspect of transnational corporations (TNCs), neglecting their political and social impact. This relative lack of concern can be traced, first, to the fact that studies of TNCs are more often made from the point of view of the corporations than from that of the national governments dealing with them, their workers and their consumers; second, to the fact that political and sociological analyses of international economic relations are still a limited field of study; and, third, to the politically loaded character of many issues concerning TNCs.

Yet the relevance of the social and political dimensions of transnational economic operations is undeniable, and it is highlighted by the recent attempts by international and intergovernmental agencies — first of all the United Nations — to work out codes of conduct for TNCs regarding such issues as national sovereignty, employment and working conditions, technology transfers, consumer protection, and environmental protection.

Author's note: The French version of this paper has been published in Arnaud Sales (ed.), 'Développement national et économie mondialisée', a thematic issue of *Sociologie et Sociétés*, vol. XI, no. 2, October 1979.

The aim of this paper is to provide a general theoretical framework for this kind of research. More specifically, I will identify three major areas where the cost-reducing and market-controlling strategies of TNCs have a relevant political and social impact, and for each of them I will: (1) formulate relevant political issues, (2) define them as research questions, and (3) advance some general hypotheses based on existing theoretical models, in order to construct a series of propositions that can be submitted to empirical validation. The three major areas are as follows.

1. *Political Stability and Social Consensus.* I will examine the extent to which TNCs erode national sovereignty or coordinate with nationally based political structures. I will then consider the contradiction between an increasingly interdependent world economy and an increasingly fragmented world polity. I will argue that TNCs profit from diversity in an interdependent world, whereas states are more constrained by their national character and sometimes cannot control the international ramifications of policies aimed at solving domestic problems. I will also argue that the very operations of TNCs can weaken the nation-states' capability to attain standard economic policy goals, such as full employment and balance of payments equilibrium, which are in turn instrumental in maintaining social consensus and political stability.

2. *Labor Market, Work Organization and Industrial Relations.* I will start with the recognition that TNCs, by shifting investments from one country to another and controlling large numbers of workers in different countries, are a major source of concern for labor unions and governments. Labor concerns in home countries about the export of jobs are matched by labor concerns in host countries about the loss of jobs — owing to TNCs' restructuring of taken-over local firms — and on the down-grading of research and skilled jobs. The main theoretical argument here is that controlling a diversified labor market and organizing the productive process on a world scale are ways in which TNCs maintain great flexibility and high profit rates, even when confronted with more organized and politically aware labor unions in the more developed countries. Contrary to the great trading companies and financial holdings of the past, TNCs are in fact complex productive units with articulated and integrated work processes, which reproduce within themselves the international division of labor, but

do not coincide with the division of the world into nations.

3. *Technology Control and Transfer.* The questions in this area will be discussed with reference to debates going on in the United States — which is the TNCs' most important home country — and in the various kinds of host countries. Control of technology, on the one hand, is a main component of the oligopoly power of TNCs and one of their major ways to pre-empt foreign competition, and on the other, is a basic requirement for national economic growth and social development. To what extent are corporate interests in profit maximization and market control consistent with home countries' national interests and with host countries' attempts to up-grade their technology and/or to industrialize? Strategies and counter-strategies by TNCs and nation states will be discussed.

POLITICAL STABILITY
AND SOCIAL CONSENSUS

Relevant Political Issues
and Research Questions

How, and to what extent, do TNCs compromise or erode national sovereignty? How, and to what extent, do TNCs conflict or coordinate with nationally based political structures, especially states? How and to what extent do TNCs' strategy and operations affect host governments' capability to maintain and implement either democratic, revolutionary, or authoritarian national regimes? How and to what extent do TNCs contribute to either the stabilization or destabilization of societies in which they operate? How and to what extent do TNCs 'muddle through' the domestic policy of host countries in order to pursue goals that differ from the national interest?

The researcher's task is to convert these general, politically significant, and often emotionally loaded issues into questions that can be phrased as testable propositions within a theoretical framework. The four sets of research questions can be phrased as follows:

1. Which are the basic factors accounting for the growing process of internationalization of the economy in the postwar period?

2. What are the basic determinants of the continuing existence of the nation-state as the political institution that alone can perform the functions of legitimation and consensus formation, of social reproduction of capital, and of guaranteeing the conditions for capital accumulation?

3. What are the major implications of the gap between a more internationalized economic system and a persistent nationally based political system? More specifically: what are the implications of this gap for the effective performance of the basic nation-state functions of political stability, consensus formation and social reproduction of capital? What are the implications for TNCs' pursuit of their basic goals of profit maximization and growth? What are the implications for the integration of the capitalist system as a whole?

4. What are the conscious strategies that nation-states develop in order to safeguard their sovereignty and pursue their goals? What are the TNCs' counter-strategies to maintain their freedom of action and continue to profit from diversity in the pursuit of their corporate goals? What is the most likely effect of this dialectical relationship between TNCs and nation-states with regard to the problems of system integration and system change, both at the domestic and at the international level?

Hypotheses and Theories

The major hypothesis concerning the growing process of internationalization of the economy in the postwar period is that the most important driving force behind it is the maximization of corporate profit and growth and the drastic limitation of foreign as well as domestic free competition.[2] It is a testable hypothesis, based on a multitude of data on relative growth rates and comparative prices of firms. This hypothesis, which we may call the 'oligopoly hypothesis,' can be framed into different theoretical interpretations, which have been developed in order to explain the growth of direct foreign investment and the rise of the transnational corporation. The best known among these interpretations are: (1) the theory of the firm and imperfect competition worked out in different forms by Kindleberger, Hymer, Caves and others, which in its turn rests on the Keynesian critique of the neoclassical paradigm in economic theory;[3] (2) the 'product cycle' theory and the technological gap theory, which have been developed by Vernon, Hufbauer, Wells and others,[4] and are to some extent related to Schumpeter's theory of economic development, innovation and entrepreneurship; and (3) the Marxist theory of capital concentration and centralization, which traces back to Marx's analysis of the falling rate of profit and of productive sectors' disproportion and was developed by the theorists of imperialism such as Hilferding, Bucharin, Luxemburg and Lenin, and in a revised version by contemporary Marxist and dependencia theorists — such as Baran, Sweezy, Magdoff, Frank, Dos Santos, Cardoso and others.[5]

There are of course significant differences among those theories, but they stress similar elements such as monopoly advantages (Kindleberger), oligopoly competition (Hymer), the setting of barriers to entry (Vernon), and the global strategy of profit maximization of TNCs (Sweezy-Magdoff); and they contribute to an integrated interpretation of the rise of TNCs in the postwar world economy. Those theories provide a better explanation than other interpretations, which update the neoclassical theory of investments in terms of the marginal efficiency of investments in different economic contexts. The theories based on what can be called the 'oligopoly hypothesis' can rather be superseded by other, more recent, ones, in giving account not so much of the rise of TNC, i.e. the initial decision of foreign investment, as of the degree and pattern of further growth. Relevant in this respect are theories focusing on the importance of TNCs' strategic choices in locating their activities so that they can benefit from national differences in the costs of productive factors and in consumption and income patterns (Dunning and others);[6] and theories that relate TNCs' investment decisions to differences in currency areas, risks of exchange rates variations, tariff areas and the like (Aliber).[7] Those interpretations are complementary with the 'oligopoly' ones insofar as they stress another basic feature of TNCs, which is a central proposition of this essay, namely the fact that TNCs profit from the diversity of an interdependent world economy and a fragmented world polity.

The theories based on the 'oligopoly hypothesis' and other analyses of international economic relations take into account a variety of other processes besides capital concentration and oligopoly competition, which help to explain the general great increase of economic interdependence and capital internationalization and specific institutional development of TNCs in the last 30 years.

The most important of them are the impressive development of communication and transport, the uneven pattern of distribution of economic resources in the world, the complementarity of technology and managerial skills and the efficiency of economies of scale in business activity, and the trade and money liberalization in the postwar period as a result of conscious government policies. We will discuss some of those processes later on.

On the basis of all those studies, one can state that TNCs embody the most important processes that have taken place in the international economy in the last decades (foremost of which is oligopoly competition), and that they are the most relevant expression of economic interdependence and the most dynamic component of contemporary capitalism.

The major hypothesis that concerns the second research question is closely related to the first, in the sense that it has to do with the shortcomings of the free market, this time not in preventing the formation of oligopolies, but to bring about a steady, 'spontaneous' growth of the economy and the continuing integration of the system. These shortcomings account for the continuing existence and actual growth of the nation-state. Abundant evidence is available here too drawn from the analysis of major crises of the world economy (1873-96, the 1930s, the present crisis). It was precisely the inadequacy of the market to guarantee the dynamic equilibrium of the system, after a few decades of 'competitive capitalism' in the nineteenth century, that fostered the need for state intervention, at first in the processes of capital reproduction and social consensus formation, which are needed for capitalist social relations to be maintained, and eventually in sustaining demand for purpose of counteracting crises of oversupply and, in some countries at least, in national economic planning. The traditional division of functions between the firms and the market on the one hand, which had the responsibility for production and exchange decisions, and the state authorities on the other, which were in charge of the reproductive functions (schools, basic research, hospitals, social security, etc.), and of setting the general rules within which market interactions could take place, gave way in more recent times to increasing state responsibility in income distribution and in the control of the economic cycle.

The shortcomings of the market system fostered a more active and enlarged role of the nation-state also in another respect, insofar as uneven development and 'market anarchy' laid the ground for the nation-state to become an institutional agent of growth (as Gershenkron puts it) in late-comer or 'second-developer' countries, such as Germany, Italy and Japan.[8] The uneven development of the world economy in the nineteenth century, with the different timing and sequences, provoked protectionist policies — as a reaction to British free-trade hegemony — and the continuing expansion of the territory controlled by the nation-state. This in turn brought about: first, the increasing rivalry among the different national bourgeoisies, because the process of internationalization of economic life was not identical to the process of internationalization of capitalist interest; then the fragmentation of the world economy into relatively isolated trading blocs centered on the several core economies and their peripheries — with a few notable exceptions — and, finally, the collapse of an internationally integrated economy.

The situation was reversed after the Second World War, when a drastic restoration of liberal economic policy took place by way of removal of import controls, lowering of tariffs and partial return to convertibility, under the new hegemony of the United States. Actually, postwar US policy aimed at rebuilding an international economic order in the West and at recasting a bourgeois Europe and a bourgeois Japan, as allies in the global challenge with the Soviet bloc, thus creating the conditions eventually for renewed competition by the successfully rebuilt economies of Western Europe and Japan. Intervention in external economic relations was progressively reduced in the 1950s and 1960s, while a similar trend was apparent in at least some of the other industrialized countries. With the late 1960s and the early 1970s a new tendency has appeared, however: to return again to rather detailed government interventions in the domestic economy, while in international economic relations too, although to a much more limited extent, neo-mercantilist elements are present within a general open system.

The basic hypothesis of the continuing strength of the nation-state, because of the inadequacy of pure market forces to meet the basic needs of the capitalist economy and to guarantee the dynamic equilibrium of the system, is therefore validated, not only for the periods when rivalry prevails, but also when an open hegemonic system is implemented. In fact, a very strong state was necessary to provide a favorable environment for economic interdependence and corporate expansionism; and the rebuilding of Western European and Japanese economies implied also strengthening the respective nation-states. As Gilpin puts it, 'the MNC has prospered because it has been dependent on the power of, and consistent with the political interests of the United States.'[9] Although this does not imply, as Gilpin argues, that the larger configurations of power among nation-states are the primary determinants of the role played by non-state economic actors, since the inherent dynamic of capital accumulation and trade is in itself a powerful determinant of configurations of power and political regimes, there is no doubt that oligopoly and economic interdependence do need strong nation-states for performing basic functions they cannot perform themselves. Actually, the very growth of transnational economic actors has required expanded and more widely differentiated policy interventions by national governments. For instance, the increased role of MNCs' investment decisions in many industries, with repercussions in the entire economy, has raised demands for greater state coordination and planning, insofar as the intensified flow of trade, technology, labor and capital across national borders can increase inflationary tendencies and balance of payments problems for many countries. And, more indirectly, a growing and more diversified economy has increased the need for state intermediation between conflicting and competitive organized groups.

The hypotheses related to the third set of questions can be summarized as follows: the interrelated trends of the growth of TNCs, and of the continuing centrality of the nation-state in the political process, bring about a basic contradiction between TNCs and nation states. From the standpoint of the TNCs, they cannot renounce the traditional bourgeois state functions, which are necessary to create favorable conditions for the viable functioning of their operations — i.e., defending property rights, warranting the free circulation of factors of production, integrating the subordinated classes, legitimizing the capitalist social relations, etc. — while at the same time, they weaken the power of the host nation-state insofar as they reduce its capacity to carry out economic policies, which are in turn instrumental in maintaining social consensus.[10] In other words, TNCs need strong states and stable societies, but cannot help undermining them to some extent. From the point of view of the nation-state, host countries' governments are caught in the dilemma between the need to foster inward direct investments — in order to maximize the positive effects of international economic interdependence on demand and domestic growth — and the need to defend their autonomous power. This contradiction is particularly acute since, as Lindbeck puts it, 'national governments have raised their ambitions to direct the details of the domestic economy, because of a more complex economic process and rising popular demands, at the very time in which international forces have made both many targets and several policy instruments less susceptible of domestic national manipulation than earlier.'[11] We might also mention the conflict between the TNCs' interest in maximizing the profit component of any given output they generate and the nation states' interest in maximizing the local value-added,[12] and the more general contradiction stemming from the fact that TNCs act according to an overall strategy aiming at the highest long-term profits of the whole business, and not of its single parts located in different countries.[13] But here I will concentrate on the contradiction between TNCs and nation-states as a case for working out testable propositions and methods for research.[14]

The propositions are as follows.

1. Nation-states are still the basic political institutions for the generation of social consensus, the legitimation of existing social relations and the reproduction of society.

2. The successful performance of these functions is required by international and domestic capital in order to operate and continue to grow.

3. The successful performance of these functions depends on the government capability to attain standard economic goals, such as full employment, a sustained rate of growth, balance of payments equilibrium, and the maintenance of a certain level of public expenditure; in fact, a successful management of the economy, although for limited periods, has allowed the bourgeois state to confine class conflict to the distribution of resources and has eased social conflict through the payment of higher wages to the organized workers and the granting of welfare benefits to the unemployed, the underemployed, the marginals.

4. Practically each of the standard goals I have listed and each of the state policies implemented to pursue them, are, however, affected and to some extent threatened by the very operations of TNCs.

The specific impact of TNCs on host countries is related to the increasing vulnerability and sensitivity of most modern economies to conditions in other countries, because of the growing interdependence in economic relations.[15] As an example of this increasing vulnerability and sensitivity, interest rate differentials between nations and expected changes in exchange rates can generate enormous financial flows between countries, so that the traditional maneuvering of the interest rate by central banks in order either to stimulate growth or to curb inflation generally produces unintended, and often negative, consequences.

TNCs move at ease in an interdependent world and profit from diversity, whereas governments are more constrained by their very national character and cannot often control the international consequences of policies aiming at solving domestic problems.

The behavior of TNCs conditions the attainment of states' standard economic policy goals in a variety of ways. First, transnational firms, affect both the level of international demand for investment goods and labor and the level of imports and exports. Assuming the level of total intended investment of a transnational corporation as given, there are many alternative possibilities as to their international distribution, and as to the choice of the markets on which to buy the means of production. The choices of TNCs may often influence the level of investments and the balance of trade — and through them on the level of income — in the countries concerned.

Second, TNCs have a direct control of the terms of trade of different countries in many sectors. This control cannot be reduced to the control that oligopolistic firms have on the prices of their finished products. Insofar as TNCs have vertically integrated productive units located in different countries, the prices at which semi-finished products are transferred from one local unit to the next are only accounting items for the firm, but they represent imports and exports for the countries involved. These prices can be changed without affecting in the slightest way the quantities that are bought and sold. But they do affect both the balance of payments and the level of income of the host countries.

Third, TNCs control important international financial flows, insofar as they realize profits, control sources of money and decide investments over an area including many countries. The proportioning of these variables, i.e. self-financing through undistributed profits, external financing and investment expenditures, need be undertaken only for the firm as a whole and not for each national unit. Corporate global strategy may then be at odds with the states' monetary policies, insofar as the difference between financing — both from domestic and external sources — located in the country and investment expenditure in the local branches and subsidiaries represents import or export of capital.

It is useful to clarify the degree of generalizability of these propositions. We must qualify them with relation both to different types of countries — parent countries/host countries, advanced industrial countries/less developed countries and further differentiations within these broad categories — and to different types of corporations — according to such dimensions as industrial sector (extractive, manufacturing, services), degree of capital intensity, primary drive to go multinational (labor cost-reducing, raw materials-oriented, market-oriented), economic structure of the host country and the like. Actually, the propositions I have outlined apply primarily to host states in advanced industrial economies, where standard state economic policies are actually implemented and contribute to national integration and social consensus, and to manufacturing market-oriented TNCs, which are more concerned with the sustained economic growth, the maintenance of the democratic process and some redistribution of income in the host countries.

The opposite combination, of raw materials-oriented TNCs and less developed host countries, asks for some basic qualifications of the propositions I have outlined. It is true that in this case too TNCs cannot substitute for national states in performing the basic functions of maintaining social peace and guaranteeing societal reproduction, which are required for their operations; but these functions can be performed through authoritarian political regimes, stressing coercion over consensus and law and order over legitimation. From the TNCs' point of view it may be preferable to deal with an authoritarian government, which is more simple and easier to influence; this type of state tends to have a more restricted basis of support, which allows it to curb labor demands and favor foreign investments but not to challenge the dominant position of TNCs, mostly in raw materials-extracting industries, and to defend natural resources. The hypothesis holds here too, however, insofar as authoritarian governments tend to rely on nationalistic values which conflict with TNCs' attitudes and exigencies, and insofar as many less developed countries tend to develop strong states because they are in the process of achieving political integration domestically, a trend that is at odds with their subordination to transnational forces. Although they are less concerned with standard economic policy goals — given the fact that they rely on more coercive mechanisms of social integration and control — less developed countries' governments often challenge international capital in order to prove the strength of the state and their ideological commitment to the 'national interest.' But TNCs' operations tend to make state performance of major functions more difficult in less developed countries as well, because their overreaching influence delegitimizes the government and slows down the process of nation-building and social integration.

We can thus conclude that, although TNCs are a major factor in the integration of the world capitalist system and the most visible feature of its interdependence, as we will see in the next section, they also have inherent de-stabilizing effects on various host countries, insofar as they reduce the autonomous power of the state to implement economic policies.

In order to complete the picture, one has to mention also that, by fostering inter-state competition for acquiring financial flows, which they control and do not care about the national distribution of, TNCs are also the source of potential conflict of interest among nations.[16]

We now come to the final sets of research questions, concerning TNCs' and nation-states' respective strategies and counter-strategies and their implications for system integration and change. The starting hypothesis here is that each of these will try to maximize its major goals, which we have assumed to be the state's autonomous power and the corporation's drive toward profit. However, in the pursuit of these goals, both will take into account the goal of dynamic equilibrium of the existing system of social relations. After all, most of the relationships between international capital and nation-states take place between economic and political actors who have vested interests in maintaining the basic patterns of the present society. Thus, TNCs will likely restrain themselves whenever their profit-maximization strategy threatens to stir widespread nationalistic feelings and to imperil the international open system they need; and the host government will probably restrain itself from too overt discriminatory practices against international capital whenever such practices threaten the inflow of foreign investments which are needed in the pursuit of economic growth. More definite hypotheses on the behavior of TNCs and nation-states must take into account the specific conditions under which their respective goals are pursued and the complex pattern of negotiation over those goals.

If one looks at the record of government policies, one can identify a wide array of defensive devices to limit the discretionary
power of TNCs and restore some of the autonomy of the nation-
state. Selective fees for imports and selective subsidies for exports,
increased protectionism in government spending, the use of foreign
aid to sustain and enlarge export quotas, credit and fiscal incentives, public supply of capital, selective subsidies of production, investment, employment, research and development, product standards for environmental protection — all are instances of policies
that can be justified to some extent on the ground that they aim at
managing the economic crisis and at increasing market efficiency.
They are, rather, neo-protectionist policies, which, however, do
not imply dissociation with the open economic system; in fact they
take advantage both of the difficulties that political authorities of
other countries have in controlling them and of the lack of international regulatory agreements in certain areas.[17] The net result of
conflicting pressures toward liberal and protectionist policies can
be assessed only by studying the relations among organized interest
groups, the institutional forms of political representation and their
relative impact on government policy. Even in countries where a
powerful coalition in favor of protectionism is formed, the cost for
implementing such a policy may be so high, in terms of an international 'capital strike,' i.e. in terms of flight of investments and loss
of jobs, that it can make this solution unworkable. The most likely
outcome then is increasing state intervention in the domestic
economy, without seriously threatening continuing integration in
the world market.

How do TNCs react to this kind of strategy? Basically, by intensifying their existing strategies in coping with host governments.
First, they will likely increase their skills in using a wide range of
financial and organizational procedures, which allow them to in-
sure themselves against risks of nationalization and to profit from
diversity; more state intervention will mean more rules and regulations controlling foreign investments, but foreign investors can
continue to take advantage of the difficult implementation of these
rules and regulations both at the domestic and at the international
level, for example through transfer payments, which are very difficult to control.

Second, a more protectionist policy can imply the formation of a
domestic social coalition of local producers competing with TNCs,
government officials and political leaders who want to safeguard

national sovereignty as a basic requirement for effective policies. And we should then expect that TNCs will try to mobilize support among domestic groups, such as business groups related to their operating — who may prefer the alliance with powerful international groups to the uncertain prospects of an independent firm[18] — consulting professionals and government officials. Efforts to mobilize support can take a variety of forms, from legitimate cooptation into the transnational network to bribery (as the recent US Congress Hearings on ITT and Lockheed have shown). Further research is needed on the different attitudes of different types of TNCs with regard to the development of the host countries.

A third major TNC strategy would be that of exerting their influence in the parent country to get that government to bring pressure on the host governments to favor them. This implies not only the lobbying for legislation to be passed in the parent country (such as the 1962 Hickenlooper Amendment in the USA, which required the President to suspend aid to countries that expropriate US property),[19] but also the resort to more covert operations, as the US Congress Hearings on Chile have shown. Here again, there are serious policy differences, and possible conflict of interests among TNCs. These differences imply a diversified impact on US foreign policy, which is by no means confined to taking strong action against host governments' attempts to gain greater control over their economies. The degree of asymmetry of power between the TNCs and their parent government on the one hand and the host government on the other is the other basic variable to be considered here: where the relationship is very asymmetrical, as in the case of most less developed countries, chances for subversion by TNCs are higher. This strategy is greatly helped by the complementarity of views between TNCs and international financial organizations, like the World Bank and the IMF, which can be used to keep host country governments in line by blocking credit, as in the case of Chile, or by setting guidelines for economic policy as a condition for credit to be granted.

TNCs feel at ease in a unified world economy coupled with a fragmented political system, since they can profit from diversity and exploit their greater flexibility to adapt to different environments. But they envisage the danger of political fragmentation reaching the point where it implies generalized protectionism and interstate rivalry, which would imperil their very existence as global units. The position taken by many TNCs in influencing their parent country foreign policy, both in the USA and in other advanced industrial nations, seems to show the TNCs' awareness of the problem and their concern with world integration in the present hierarchical order.

LABOR MARKET, WORK ORGANIZATION AND INDUSTRIAL RELATIONS

Relevant Political Issues and Research Questions

The second major area in which TNCs have politically important and theoretically relevant consequences is that of employment levels, labor market structure, work organization and industrial relations.

The relevant political issue here is how and to what extent TNCs are exploiting labor in host countries. This basic issue can be broken down into a set of more detailed questions, such as how and to what extent TNCs profit from fragmented labor markets in the world economy; how and to what extent the corporate drive to make foreign direct investment can be traced to wage differentials among countries; how and to what extent TNCs maintain and reinforce the international division of labor among workers of different countries; how and to what extent TNCs do not apply fair labor standards in host countries; how and to what extent labor unions of different countries have developed coordinated strategies to deal with TNCs.

The corresponding set of research questions concern the dynamics of the labor market and the organization of work in the process of capital accumulation. First, in what ways does the internationalization of the production process foster better conditions for capital accumulation? Second, what are the factors accounting for divided labor markets? Third, what are TNCs' strategies for organizing production on a world scale, and how do they compare with the previous focus of capital internationalization? Fourth, how do TNCs' strategy and structure affect industrial relations? Fifth, what are the factors leading unions to develop either an international coordinated counter-strategy, or a nationalistic outlook that would threaten the further growth of world capital, and how do these strategies affect industrial relations?

Hypotheses and Theories

I have previously stated that, according to various theories, the postwar trend toward an international economy and the rise of the transnational corporation were the result of firms' drives to maximize oligopoly profit and growth. A complementary set of hypotheses focuses on the search for cheap labor and on the organizational effort to minimize labor costs: capital export has historically represented for the bourgeoisies of advanced industrial countries a major way to re-establish profit margins eroded by the growing bargaining power and political awarness of their working classes. More specifically, the TNC can strengthen both its position on the labor market — by profiting from the fragmentation of domestic labor markets and from the diversification of nationally oriented working classes — and its command over labor in the corporation — by distributing the production process in a variety of hierarchically integrated units located in different countries. This hypothesis can be framed in the Marxist theory of the growth and the spread of capitalist social relations of production to a world level and in the neo-Marxist and neo-institutional analyses of dual labor markets.[20] Marx's 'general law of capitalist accumulation' provides a fruitful starting point: Marx stressed the twin processes of capital concentration and capital centralization, which are due to the two great levers of competition and credit; the former lever drives firms continuously to reinvest their profits and extend their markets as a means of self-preservation, and the latter helps to bring individual capitals together and provides the means for further growth. Capital concentration and centralization guarantee the conditions for continuing accumulation through low wages insofar as more and more capital-intensive production (which goes together with these processes) continuously fosters the industrial reserve army. 'The industrial reserve army during the periods of stagnation and average prosperity weights down the active labor army; and during the period of over-production and paroxysm, it holds its pretensions in check. Relative surplus population is therefore the pivot upon which the law of demand and supply of labor works.'[21] Potential sources of industrial labor, other than the unemployed generated by the process of capital concentration and centralization (such as farm labor and precarious and marginal labor of various kinds), are also used by capital in order to maintain low wages and high profits.

As the process of industrialization goes on, however, all these mechanisms are threatened by the progressive exhaustion of non-industrial labor, by the establishment of labor unions which are able to unite separate individual workers and by the rise of socialist, labor, or democratic parties pressing for social security and fair employment legislation, which reduces capital's discretionary power to hire and fire workers. Actually, all advanced capitalist countries experienced either the rise of wages of the best organized segments of the labor force (generally centrally located in the labor market) or social policies aimed at reducing labor mobility, or both. In all these countries, large enterprises were driven to penetrate pre-capitalist areas in their search for 'latent surplus population,' i.e. unorganized and low wage workers.[22] The outward drive of capital looking for cheap labor was paralleled by the inward integration into the advanced industrial regions of workers from less developed countries. Migrations tend to stratify the labor force along ethnic, social and cultural lines, thus making the emergence of class consciousness and the setting of a unified labor strategy much more difficult.

The general hypothesis can then be specified into a set of testable propositions. First, through outward direct investment and inwards labor migration, capitalists are capable of keeping the cost of labor low and of maintaining flexibility in the use of labor. This does not necessarily mean that wages are kept at a low level of workers, but rather that a dual labor market emerges, where strata of educated and skilled, well paid and well organized workers are separated from a pool of unemployed, underemployed, unorganized, badly paid workers, who are continuously threatened by technological change and by the competition of surplus labor abroad. Thus, the existence of a surplus labor force, either continuously reproduced by technological change or still available in non-industrial areas, allows capital to maintain a strong bargaining position on the labor market. This process should not be seen, however, strictly in market terms, since it also has significant implications for the process of political awareness and mobilization of workers.

Second, as a by-product of the strategy aiming at keeping flexibility and low labor costs, through outward foreign investment and inward labor migration, capitalists are capable of slowing down or blocking altogether the building of a collective identity and a political organization among workers. The capitalist class profits from a unified and highly interdependent market for goods and money and a fragmented labor market, diversified along race, sex, age, cultural, national lines — just as TNCs profit from, an interdependent economy and a fragmented polity. The development of strategies and structures within the firm can be explained not only as a response to more and more complex technological processes and to more and more diversified markets, but also as a device to maintain the control of the labor force.

Third, the corporation uses two basic ways of maintaining profit margins: a 'divide et impera' strategy in the labor market, and a tight coordination and control of workers in the firm's organizational structure of production. The transnational corporation can be seen as the most efficient institutional device for applying these processes at the international level.[23] Unlike the great trading companies in the transitional stage to capitalism, and the large financial holdings at the beginning of this century, TNCs develop an international division of labor within themselves, which reflects the international division of labor among advanced and less developed countries, but does not correspond to the division of the world polity into separate national entities. In this sense, transnational corporations represent the most advanced 'spontaneous' growth of capitalist development, although their rise has been helped also by conscious government policies.[24] The specific character of this new institutional form has far-reaching implications for labor.

The trading companies and the financial holdings of the past exploited a diversified world basically through the market, by enjoying a comparative advantage in their imports of raw materials and cheap-labor agricultural products into the core economies of the system. Although controlling a variety of interests and productive units, they did not integrate them into a unified structure. TNCs, on the other hand, are complex productive organizations with articulated and closely integrated work processes.[25] This has important implications for the mechanisms of integration of the world capitalist system. The contemporary TNCs integrate directly into the world economy through their own hierarchical division of labor, besides contributing to it through the growing interdependence of markets, whereas in the past the international division of labor was reproduced almost exclusively through the market.[26]

The international organization of the firm allows the exercise of a unified command over separate and diversified segments of the labor force, thus taking advantage of diversity in order to block the formation of class consciousness and of a unified labor strategy. Contrary to many studies, I think that the political strength of the working class depends more on the degree of cohesion among its components than on the material conditions of life and work; and for this reason TNCs have a clear advantage in dealing with labor.

This statement introduces us to the final question, of how TNCs' strategy and structure affect industrial relations and which are labor counter-strategies both at the domestic and at the international level. The testable proposition here is that TNCs profit from diversity, in the sense that they confront separated labor unions, can play one domestic working class against the other, and enjoy much greater flexibility in dealing with labor conflict than domestic firms in developed countries.[27] The 'divide et impera' strategy is rooted in the oligopoly character and international structure of these firms. TNCs tend to have higher profits than their domestic competitors wherever they exist and can therefore pay higher wages and show more elasticity in the bargaining process, wherever they confront strong national unions.[28] This can minimize the financial cost of labor strikes and other slow-down methods by duplicating production and by using excess capacity in their subsidiaries abroad. And they can disinvest. Actual shifting of production quotas may not be necessary; in fact, the existence of alternative sources of supply allows management to threaten production-switching, thus weakening labor actions. But both the threat to switch production and the effective switching of investments are effective TNC strategies.[29]

Finally, TNCs' labor policies tend to vary greatly according to the national context in which they operate. General Motors, for instance, tends to negotiate at company level and to stay outside of industry-wide collective bargaining agreements in Great Britain at Vauxhall, but not at the German Opel. In general terms, one can state that, wherever authoritarian governments are in power and laws against strikes are enforced, TNCs find a congenial ground for their operations. But also where democratic regimes exist, with strong labor unions and complex negotiations procedures, TNCs enjoy a clear advantage in terms of flexibility and level of decision-making.

Labor counter-strategies also tend to vary from one country to another, and specifically from predominantly home to predominantly host countries, from advanced industrial to less developed economies, from democratic to authoritarian political systems, in the presence of strong or weak trade unions, etc. The concerns and criticisms expressed by unions in parent countries are often dissimilar to those expressed by host countries' unions, and seem therefore to imply a conflict of interest among them. US labor leaders and spokesmen, for instance, have attacked TNCs for shutting down American productive facilities and locating abroad new processes and products, for exporting technology by direct transplant, licensing, patent agreement and the like, and for exporting capital to build an industrial base abroad at the expense of American industry. But host countries' labor unions are also concerned with loss of jobs owing to industrial take-overs and restructuring, with transferring of R and D facilities from the taken-over firm to the central headquarters of the corporation, with changing work patterns and wage systems, and with limitations to national governments' planning and balanced growth policies.

The net effect of all these concerns will be, according to Hymer, 'that...labor will tend to become more nationalistic and possibly more socialistic as the continued growth of the world market undermines its traditional strategy.'[30] In fact, the outcome does not seem to be so one-sided, since labor counter-strategy in parent and host countries can take at least two basic forms: the former is the one Hymer predicts, i.e. growing nationalism and the entering of labor into a domestic coalition implementing protectionist policies which would threaten the world market; the latter is a strategy of increased coordination and cooperation among labor unions, in order to work out a more unified strategy to check international capital both at the international and at the national level. The first strategy seems to me more likely to be followed (and at the same time more likely to be defeated) both in predominantly parent countries like the USA and in several host countries where national feelings are strong in the labor movement such as France; but, also, the benefits of interdependence appear to be greater than the costs, and the coalition for a continuing international economy is stronger than a neo-mercantilist one. Where this dissociative strategy would be more at the advantage of domestic labor and of most of the country, as in many raw materials-exporting countries, it is unlikely to succeed, because of the weakness of labor unions and of independent political forces in general.

The second strategy is argued for by unions of some advanced industrial countries that are both parent and host countries of TNCs, like Great Britain, Italy, the Netherlands, etc. The basic point made is that protectionist policies like those advocated by the AFL-CIO are short-sighted and ineffective, insofar as the unions are caught in the TNCs' strategy of playing different labor movements one against the other, whereas a more effective labor strategy is that of asking for state and international controls over TNCs and, at the same time, of working in a coordinated way toward lowering wage differentials among countries and fostering the growth of strong unions and democratic governments in less developed countries. This would strike at the primary advantage of TNCs, i.e. their capacity to profit from the international division of labor, although it may widen the gap between organized workers on the one hand and the unorganized and the unemployed on the other. This more long-sighted strategy is, however, also unlikely to succeed, at least in the short run, because it has to overcome two powerful obstacles; the basically national social identity of workers, and the skillful use of structural cleavages in the labor force made by international capital.

TECHNOLOGY CONTROL
AND TECHNOLOGY TRANSFER

Relevant Political Issues
and Research Questions

As indicated above, a major criticism made by US labor unions to US-based transnational corporations is that they export technology at the expense of American industry; this type of criticism is increasingly expressed by labor unions of other industrialized countries as well, the more the process of transnationalization goes on. On the other hand, host countries' unions charge TNCs with preempting domestic R and D development by either closing down or reducing research centers in taken-over domestic firms. We have maintained that oligopoly is a major feature of TNCs, and oligopoly is often based on the control of sophisticated technological innovations. The struggle for the appropriation of advanced technology is not limited to the competition among large enterprises, but directly involves nation-states, because of national security considerations and because of the growing importance of technology as a key factor of production.

Discussions of TNCs' production and dissemination of technology in the home countries often focus on their potential threat to the maintenance of a technological lead over other nations, whereas discussions in the host countries, mostly in less developed countries, consider the extent to which technologies — and, specifically, appropriate technologies — are transferred, as a major yardstick in making a cost-benefit analysis of foreign direct investment.

On the basis of these different concerns, we can formulate a few research questions. Studies on the technological factor in TNCs require a much more selective approach than those on TNCs' implications for political stability and labor market, since they are more numerous.[31] Our analysis will then focus on US-based TNCs only, given the persistent technological lead of American firms in several industries, and will select the specific political aspect of the problem of technology transfer and control.

A first set of research questions asks what have been the major factors for the US technological edge and whether the US lead is now faltering. A second set of questions asks how and to what extent advanced industrial host countries can take advantage of technology transfers. A third set of questions asks how less developed host countries can take advantage of technology transfers, address themselves to the specific problem of appropriate technologies and products, and examine distortions introduced in the host countries and societies by inappropriate products and processes. And a final question focuses on host countries' strategies to capture a large share of benefits in technology transfers.

Hypotheses and Theories

Most studies on TNCs agree that a major factor accounting for the process of internationalization in recent decades is that TNCs are capable of exploiting barriers to entry of various kinds, first of all their technological edge in production. The question that has been raised in the USA, however, is whether TNCs' behavior in this respect is consistent with the continuing superiority of the American economy in the international division of labor. It has been remarked, in fact, that the rate of increase of productivity in the manufacturing sector has been consistently lower in recent decades in the USA than in most other OECD nations, that the rate of new product introduction by established US firms has waned in recent years, and, furthermore, that the rate of formation of new US enterprises created to manufacture and sell new products has come to a virtual standstill.[32] And it has been suggested that these trends can be traced to a reduced lead by the USA in technological innovation, which can be explained in terms of technology transfers from the USA to other OECD nations, either by TNCs or by other means. Without entering into a detailed discussion of the conflicting evidence on the subject, we discuss, first, a simple set of testable propositions, which argue for the continuing technological lead of TNCs — and specifically of US-based TNCs — but combining the 'service economy perspective' with Vernon's product cycle theory, and for the coincidence of TNCs' interests with US interests; and, second, another set of propositions expressing an alternative view.

The proposition of the former view is that knowledge has become a major factor of production and that the competitive advantage of US firms lies in their capacity continuously to develop technical innovations and new products. The major factor accounting for the US origins of many innovations is the fact confirmed by many empirical studies of various sorts, which point out that 'successful innovations tend to be those that respond to the market conditions surrounding the innovations.'[33] The size and diversification of the US market is still a key factor, because of the sharp increase in the costs and risks of innovation. Other important factors accounting for US-based TNCs' lead in technological innovation are the need for support by headquarters in an involuted and complex decision-making process, the size of large-scale US government programs and the greater US government support for R and D than that provided by European states,[34] and — not mentioned by Vernon but I think very relevant — TNCs' fear of losing control of the product cycle if they decentralize R and D facilities.

The second testable proposition is that technological knowledge diffuses to American competitors at a faster rate. During the last century, 20 to 30 years often elapsed before a new product produced in one country was produced in another country. For example, the typewriter or the rotary printing press were first produced in Great Britain 20 years after their introduction in the USA. Now, the diffusion lag is much shorter — in certain industries like electronics, only a few years. It has been shown, for instance, that the average lag between the time a major semiconductor device was first produced and the time it was first initiated outside was, in the 1950s and 1960s, only about two years. This accounts also for a much faster obsolescence of productive processes.

The third testable proposition is that TNCs go abroad in order either to forestall the rise of foreign competitors (according to a version of this view that stresses the 'defensive' aspect of TNCs' operations, as in Kindleberger and Vernon), or to exploit fully the technological advantage in highly concentrated foreign markets (according to a version that stresses the aggressive element of TNCs' strategy, as in Hymer). If one accepts this view, the assumption will follow that decentralization of production abroad fosters American interests, and that technology transfer does not threaten them.

These propositions have been challenged by the advocates of substituting foreign investments with export and domestic investment.[35] This position can be summarized in the saying, 'a dollar earned from direct trade is worth more than a dollar earned from foreign direct investment,' since 'while the MNC no doubt does maintain America's position in existing markets, the US must pay a real economic price in terms of lost tax revenues, impaired domestic economic development and skewed distribution of income in the US.'[36] This position argues also that, by investing abroad, the USA transfers part of its comparative advantage to foreign economies, provides an avenue to further market concentration, and produces unfortunate political consequences in both home and host countries. A central tenet of this view is that, through the export of technology, as well as of capital and managerial skills, the USA has strengthened its industrial competitors. As Gilpin states, 'although this transfer of resources has been accompanied, except in Japan, by the expansion of American control over important sectors of the foreign economy, this does not alter the fundamental fact that a shift in the locus of industrial power has been facilitated.'[37] And this has happened because 'In the modern economy, technology, productive know-how and managerial skills are the critical factors of production'; and 'it is precisely these factors that the MNCs take abroad.'[38]

This debate shows how difficult it is to test major hypotheses on empirical ground. Both views make reference to scattered supportive evidence, but little systematic test of major hypotheses is made.[39] This is one area where more research is needed, focusing on specific types of products and processes.

At the actual stage of knowledge in the field, it seems possible to make three major points on the impact of technology transfer on the decline of US technological lead. The first is that the decline has taken place only with regard to a few advanced industrial countries, mostly West Germany and Japan, whereas for all other countries US-based TNC operations are a major way of maintaining the privileged position of the USA in the international division of labor. The second is that, with regard to advanced industrial countries, the primary cause of the diminution of the US lead is the fulfillment of the European and Japanese capability to generate technological innovations and to reach industrial maturity, coupled with a loss of dynamic innovative vitality in the domestic US economy. And the third is that, as far as government policy is concerned, increased state funding of R and D, changes in tax law and industrial policies make for much more effective strategies than restrictions of US technology transfers abroad.

When one looks at the problem of technology transfer from the point of view of host countries, even advanced industrial ones, the picture looks different from that portrayed by concerned Americans.

This second set of questions can also be addressed by contrasting two different views. To the first view belongs a number of complementary propositions: the first is that, since US-based TNCs received more R and D grants and subsidies from the US government than European firms received from theirs (in the 1960s the USA spent four times as much on R and D as the countries of Western Europe, three to four times as much per capita and double the percentage of GNP),[40] and since they tended to concentrate their investments in R and D-intensive industries, European consumers benefited from advanced technology without the burden of paying for government-sponsored research. A second proposition is that US direct investments have concentrated in industries based on research, such as electronics, chemicals and the like, and that those investments have actually served to bridge technological gaps. It is further argued that not owning a technology is not a handicap in itself, provided that the importing countries have good levels of technological skills and managerial capacities capable of rapidly assimilating advanced technologies.[41] A third related proposition is that, when host countries have not benefited from the potential advantages offered by foreign direct investments, they have not because of their own institutional weaknesses, such as an ineffective and non-coordinated use of R and D facilities, a fragmentation of markets, a set of obstacles to the reaching of optimal dimensions by the domestic firms and the like. In summary, this view argues that no single country can monopolize all advanced technologies, that the different advanced industrial countries develop their own TNCs which specialize in certain areas of technological innovation, and that the different countries can profit from a kind of 'technological multiplier.'

The alternative view criticizes US direct investments as a challenge to European sovereignty. It argues that the combination of the smaller R and D effort in Europe (both public and private) and the brain drain would lead to a widening technology gap between US and European firms; that a more rapid diffusion of technology does not matter if the US companies in the leading sectors, such as electronics, aircraft and nuclear engineering, and in natural resources, maintain a technological lead; that US companies' new entries into the European markets, according to Vaupel and Curhan, were to a large extent (63 percent between 1958 and 1967) take-overs, which reduced European control over its own industrial base and technological growth.[42] Actually, it can be argued that to some extent US companies, through the Eurodollar market, used European capital to buy up European firms.

One can test these two sets of hypotheses by using a variety of data on the growth rates and quality of US investments and, more specifically, on TNCs' entries into high-technology sectors of the European economy, on percentage of acquisitions versus the establishment of new productive facilities, on growth rates and sales of US-based TNCs and European competitors, and the like. Here I want just to discuss a case study — that of the computer industry — as an instance of how research in this area can be conducted.[43]

The computer industry is a typical high-technology industry, where US-based TNCs have been quite active in setting up manufacturing subsidiaries abroad, even in a closed economy like Japan. It is therefore a good case for testing the effects of technology transfers. On the basis of the evidence available, one can state that until recently the computer industry was dominated by US TNCs (primarily IBM), with European and Japanese firms not comparable even to the second-tier US computer enterprises like Honeywell. In 1973, US firms together with their foreign subsidiaries still accounted for 95 percent of the cumulative value of computers installed in the non-communist world, and the situation has not significantly changed in the last few years. However, Japanese firms accounted for 50 percent of shipments in the Japanese market, and European firms accounted for 20 percent of shipments in the local market. It is also worth noting the steady British decline, in spite of the 'enormously important contributions made by English research group to the development of computing technology,' as Jequier puts it.

These facts suggest two reflections: first, technological lead alone does not explain economic success. In this case, the large size of the US market, the innovativeness and affluence of computers' customers and the substantial procurement and development contracts given by the government, together with IBM entrepreneurial skills in conceiving the idea of marketing the 'layman computer,' account for US superiority more than does sheer technological edge. This redefines the paramount importance given to technology in accounting for the dominant portion of the core economy in the system. The second reflection is that government policies do have an influence on outcomes, even in the presence of relevant structural constraints. In fact, European government policies came too late then (there were no reactions to foreign take-overs and no computer science policy until 1964-65), and when they were implemented they were obsessed with the 'IBM model' and tried to build huge 'national champions' capable of competing with the American giants. There were of course good reasons for government sponsoring of domestic mergers, since the size of the market is an important asset in computer industry, but, mostly in France, the policy had the primary goal of fostering the national prestige, without paying too much attention to economic feasibility and convenience.[44] Procurement policies, in the form of either overt preferences as in Great Britain or de facto preferences through 'advice' and 'suggestions' as in France and Germany, were also used without too much success, whereas more sound policies such as R and D support by government came only lately. The Japanese policy seems to be more effective, as far as it strives: (1) to develop services for leasing computers to the users, thus relieving industries

from the financial burden of serving as a banker to the customers;
(2) to develop a common technology among firms that remained
independent, without forcing them to merge against their will;
(3) to encourage the setting up of small research units in the USA,
which could profit from American technology and skilled personnel;
and (4) to encourage the penetration of the American market by
Japanese firms.

The last strategy seems particularly important in order to
forecast whether present US hegemony will come to an end. There
is an increasing trend by Japanese and German firms to develop
productive facilities in the USA. For example, there is the case of
Amdahl of California. This firm, formed by a former IBM
manager, aimed at becoming a major competitor of IBM and got
into severe financial problems in the carrying out of this ambitious
project; Fujitsu, which is one of three large computer firms in
Japan, was ready to provide the necessary investment funds, thus
getting an access into the US market and into the most advanced
technology in the field.

In spite of these recent trends, however, the computer industry
case shows a continuing hegemony by US-based TNCs, with
limited adverse effects of technology transfers for the US economy,
although the increasing aggressiveness of Japanese and German
transnational firms and the growing government support for R and
D, both in German universities and in French non-academic institutions, may threaten to some extent the dominant position of the
USA. In any case, US-based TNCs are the major instrument for
enhancing the dominant American position, and Japanese and Germany TNCs are the main challengers of that position. TNCs tend
to uphold the home country's interests more than they undermine
them.

It can be argued that computers are a special case, and that in the
related components industry of semiconductors and integrated circuits, foreign competition is more effective, as increasing direct investments in the USA by the other advanced industrial nations
show. But here, too, US-based TNCs, although decentralizing
significant factions of the productive process in low labor costs
countries, maintain a tight control over R and D, and over the
technologically most sophisticated stages of the process.

The question of technology transfer is significantly different, according to the degree of development of the host country considered. As the UN study, *Multinational Corporations in World*

Development,[45] points out, whereas for developed economies technology flows and payments move in both directions between buyers and sellers, for developing countries the flow is in one direction. In the late 1960s, 'payments' by 13 developing countries representing 65 percent of the total population and 56 percent of the total GNP of developing countries for patents, licenses, know-how and trademarks, as well as management and services fees, amounted to approximately $1.5 billion, equal to more than half of the flow of direct private foreign investment in developing countries. 'And these payments are growing steadily at a rate which is estimated by the UNCTAD Secretariat at about 20% per annum on the average and are absorbing an increasing proportion of the export earnings of developing countries.'[46]

Costs in themselves would not be a matter of concern, if returns were a real transfer and an effective upgrading of the technological level of less developed countries. But this does not seem to be the case. Less developed countries have weaker domestic industries and internal bourgeoisies, less developed educational systems and less autonomous states from outside influences; and it is therefore more likely that technology is not transferred and/or that the wrong type of technology is applied in the country.

From the literature on technology transfer and less developed countries, one can draw a set of propositions, which are widely framed in the theory of dependencia. This theory states that, contrary to 'stages of growth' and 'modernization' theories, development and underdevelopment are complementary processes and dialectically related aspects of the same world economic structure. In other words, the underdevelopment of certain countries is linked to the development of other economies to which they are subjected, in the sense that unequal exchange processes take place and that chances for development in the dependent economies are severely limited by an hierarchical division of labor in international relations.

This does not mean that growth in the dependent economies does not take place, but that it is a distorted and eterodirected growth. Control of technology by TNCs based in the advanced, industrial countries plays an important role in this respect. Technological innovations tend to occur in the most advanced economies, which enjoy the largest markets, the best infrastructures and the most complete industrial matrices. And TNCs are driven to spread their activities abroad and profit from their technological superiority through the exploitation of their quasi-monopolistic advantages in Third World markets.

Following 'diffusionist' and 'stages of growth' models, which stated the possibility of imitating the process of industrialization that took place in advanced countries, less developed countries have often followed until recently a policy of indiscriminate acceptance of foreign technology and foreign investment, on the assumption that 'the more the better;' but this meant releasing attempts to control the process of growth. Even when an import-substitution strategy through tariffs and exchange barriers was developed with the aim of fostering a domestic industrial base, no control whatsoever was exercised on the type of technology import — with some notable exceptions — on the implicit notion that technology is just a product that can be bought, sold and applied to very different contexts. Patents and licenses were extensively used, with no systematic attempt by the state to organize and manage knowledge and information. Those policies, together with the inherent drive of international capital to spread its operations, thus reproducing and enhancing the international division of labor, have brought about a set of consequences that were criticized by 'dependencia' theorists and which can be formulated as testable propositions. The first is that, in the presence of indiscriminate foreign investments, the dependent economy does not accomplish the transition from the stage of intensive accumulation to that of economic maturity. Lacking 'autonomous technology' and compelled to utilize imported technology, dependent capitalism is crippled, and must insert itself into the circuit of international capitalism. In other words, when, because of import substitution, the local economy reaches the stage of manufacturing capital goods and intermediate products, a more complex know-how is needed, which cannot be found locally and calls for direct participation of foreign firms, through the setting of TNC subsidiaries and branches.

The penetration of foreign technologies into the local economy, as the second proposition states, preempts attempts to develop domestic alternatives by local entrepreneurs. The linkages between R and D laboratories, engineering, and machine building, which have played an important part in relating science to production in the advanced countries, develop very slowly (or do not develop at all). Local entrepreneurs are not motivated to innovate. Local firms do not have chances of learning by doing, since the technology imported is an aggregated package, which remains largely unknown, as the widespread use of 'turn-key' plants shows. The labor market for scientifically trained personnel is small; and research and development institutions, wherever they exist, remain cut off from the productive process.

We come thus to the third proposition, namely the 'marginalization of science' in less developed countries, and the brain-drain of scientists and engineers, who emigrate to the industrialized countries where they can find the proper institutional setting for developing their skills.

A fourth proposition, which stems from the oligopoly character of TNCs is that the technology transferred is often overpriced, thus diverting resources from more profitable outlets and badly affecting the balance of payments. And finally, the fifth proposition focuses on the inappropriate character of imported technologies, which are developed according to advanced industrial countries' needs and do not adapt to the conditions of the labor markets, natural resources and cultural values of the host countries. Barnett and Müeller argue that 'the one characteristic of global corporate technology with the most devastating consequences for poor countries is that it destroys jobs,' being capital-intensive.[47]

At first glance the allegation that TNCs tend to employ inappropriate, capital-intensive technologies seems contradictory with the idea of a profit-maximizing firm, which should make more use of labor where labor costs are lower. But, as Moran points out, there are several testable hypotheses that can give account for that choice in non-dependence theory.[48] A first hypothesis suggests that foreign firms when deciding on the establishment of a new plant do not in fact compare the marginal cost of the capital-intensive technique with the marginal cost of the labor-intensive technique, but rather compare that cost with the total cost of designing a new process to accommodate local factors' propositions. The research made by the 'Plannungsgruppe Ritter' on the degree of sophistication of plant transferred to developing nations supports the hypothesis discussed by Moran: Ritter's research team found out that 'two-thirds of the firms transferred up-to-date plants, since neither working plans nor the designs of tools had to be altered, and thus a transfer of technology could be conducted with least effort.' Lack of specialists in the home country, preventing a simplification of the transferred production processes, contributes to this choice.[49]

Two other hypotheses are suggested by Chudson and Wells and focus on conditions that exist in the host country. According to them, capital-intensive technologies may be adopted because foreign managers more or less consciously try to economize on scarce supervisory skills or overhead costs, and because co-partners in less developed countries insist on sophisticated technology for reasons of prestige.[50]

The propositions help to explain the preference for relative capital-intensive technologies, inappropriate for the host countries, but they fail to stress the most important character of the technology employed by TNCs: the fact that it is applied within a coherent and integrated productive process. Actually, TNCs in different industries use different technologies, not necessarily capital-intensive, and they can use different technologies at different stages of their production. For instance, there is abundant evidence that in textiles and electronics TNCs have located the labor-intensive stages of their production process in foreign subsidiaries in the Third World, from where they export goods to developed country markets.

What is important is that, whatever technology is used, the production that takes place in the host country is a part of a tightly integrated process, which is controlled from the center. There is contrary evidence, such as the Ford low-cost model Fiesta, which is referred to as the 'modern Model T,' which is designed for full production in low-cost labor — Asian — countries. But it is a very limited evidence, and the main factor against the proliferation of those experiments is the TNCs' determination to maintain full control over the organization of production. A firm that takes over or starts a new plant, either to serve a local market or to reduce labor costs, will soon be driven by its profit-maximizing strategy to integrate the plant into its international network of productive facilities. The choice of technology will respond to this need of integration more than to the country's specific needs; and the type of technology employed might be either labor- or capital-intensive, but it will very likely be subjected to the control of the center, whose goals are not nessarily those of the host economy where the subsidiary is located.

We come now to the last research question: what strategies can host country governments work out in order to capture a larger share of benefits in the use of technologies by local subsidiaries of TNCs? Or, in other words, are there feasible alternatives for achieving technological growth while reducing dependency? Several policies have been suggested. The first is the disaggregation of the package of foreign inputs, by obtaining technological and managerial skills through commercial channels separately from capital and by progressively increasing the activities performed by local producers (public and/or private), including the design of intermediate and end products, and marketing.[51]

The disaggregation of the package allows local firms to identify the components of technical knowledge, thus enabling the enterprise to master imported technology. This 'learning by doing' requires a second type of policy, which can broadly be defined as the implementation of a national science and technology policy. Less developed states should develop R and D programs and facilities, should upgrade and reorganize higher education and the school system in general, should set up agencies for economic forecasting, and should coordinate an institutional network of government agencies, labor unions, business and professional associations in order to guarantee a conscious management of knowledge.

But a national science policy is not feasible and effective if it is not framed into a national economic policy. A third major set of policies is therefore required, aimed at controlling foreign investment, at directing it to specific sectors according to a national development plan, and at regulating such matters as licensing of foreign patents, and regulating the percentage of foreign capital in firms and banks operating the country and the repatriation or reinvestment of profits and the rate of disinvestment of TNCs from local subsidiaries.

Finally, the state can influence national economic development by directly controlling basic industries, like energy sources, raw materials, capital goods and public utilities; by progressively nationalizing these sectors and/or setting up joint-ventures with TNCs.[52] By undertaking large investments in those sectors, and by requiring relevant flows of goods and services, the state can also develop and encourage the development of the required technologies.

The implementation of those policies, runs however, into a series of serious constraints, such as the difficult access to larger amounts of financial resources — which are to a large extent monopolized by TNCs and by TNC-related international banks and international monetary organizations — and requires a set of conditions, first of which is the existence of a powerful domestic social coalition committed to national independence and autonomous development. Whether these basic constraints can be overcome and these conditions met in less developed countries are first of all political issues.

NOTES

1. This essay stems from a larger study made for the United Nations Center on Transnational Corporations of New York. Most of the literature in this field uses the term 'multinational corporations' (MNCs). I prefer the less commonly used term 'transnational corporations' (TNCs), since it conveys better the idea of firms that transcend national boundaries, while having a well identifiable base in a parent country.

2. I mean the limitation of free market competition as it is described in many standard economics textbooks. Competition is by no means absent in the contemporary international economy, but it is primarily 'oligopoly competition.'

3. C. P. Kindleberger, *American Business Abroad* (Yale University Press, 1969); S. H. Hymer, *The International Operations of National Firms: A Study of Direct Investment* (MIT Press, 1976); R. E. Caves, 'International Corporations: The Industrial Economics of Foreign Investment,' *Economica*, vol. 38 (February 1971).

4. R. Vernon, *Sovereignty at Bay* (Basic Books, 1971); G. Haufbauer, 'Theories of International Trade and Technological Progress,' in R. Vernon (ed.), *Technological and International Trade* (National Bureau Committee for Economic Research, 1970).

5. For a discussion of Marx's theories of crises see, among others, P. Sweezy, *The Theory of Capitalist Development* (Monthly Review Press, 1956). For a discussion of the 'classical theory of imperialism' see, among others, A. Martinelli, *La Teoria dell'imperialismo* (Loescher, 1974). For a recent appraisal in English of 'dependencia' theory see the special issue of *International Organization* (Winter 1978) on 'Dependence and Dependency in the Global System,' edited by J. A. Caporaso. Best known works include P. Baran, *The Political Economy of Growth* (Monthly Review Press, 1957); A. G. Frank, *Capitalism and Underdevelopment in Latin America* (Monthly Review Press, 1967); F. H. Cardoso and E. Falletto, *Dependencia y desarrollo en America Latina* (Instituto Latinoamericano de Planificación Economica y Social, 1969); T. Dos Santos, *La neuva dependencia* (CESO, 1968); H. Magdoff and P. M. Sweezy, 'Notes on the Multinational Corporation,' *Monthly Review* (October 1969).

6. J. H. Dunning, 'The Determinants of International Production,' *Oxford Economic Papers* (November 1972).

7. R. Z. Aliber, 'The Multinational Enterprise in a Multiple Currency World,' in J. H. Dunning (ed.), *The Multinational Enterprise* (Praeger, 1971).

8. A. Gerschenkron, *Economic Backwardness in Historical Perspective* (Harvard University Press, 1962).

9. R. Gilpin, *U.S. Power and the Multinational Corporation* (Basic Books, 1975), p. 41.

10. Actually, in some cases, TNCs can either 'extend' the power of a host state, like Aramco in Saudi Arabia, or affect that power in a very marginal way, such as when they confront powerful states, like Japan or West Germany. But, in general, the contradiction I have outlined holds for host countries.

11. A. Lindbeck, 'The Changing Role of the National State,' *Kyklos*, vol. 28 (1975), p. 36.

12. J. H. Dunning, 'The Multinational Enterprise: The Background' in J. H. Dunning (ed.), *The Multinational Enterprise* (Allen & Unwin, 1971).

13. H. Magdoff and P. M. Sweezy, 'Notes on the Multinational Corporation,' *Monthly Review* (October 1969).

14. A. Martinelli and E. Somaini, 'Nation States and Multinational Corporations,' *Kapitalistate*, vol. I (1973).

15. R. N. Cooper, *The Economics of Interdependence* (McGraw-Hill, 1968). R. Keohane and J. Nye, *Power and Interdependence* (Little, Brown and Co., 1977).

16. For a discussion of this issue see Martinelli and Somaini, op. cit.

17. It must be noted also that protectionist policies, while reducing international interdependence, can be compatible with foreign investments by TNCs, as it was in the case of Latin American countries in the 1950s.

18. S. Hymer, 'The Internationalization of Capital,' *Journal of Economic Issues* (March 1972), p. 288.

19. For a discussion of this issue see J. Levinson and J. De Onis, *The Alliance that Lost its Way: A Critical Report on the Alliance for Progress* (Quadrangle Books, 1970).

20. P. Dohringer and M. Piore, *Dual Labor Market* (Harvard University Press, 1977).

21. K. Marx, *Capital* (International Publishers, 1967), vol. 1, p. 630.

22. This was of course not the only reason for moving abroad, other reasons being the search for cheap raw materials and for markets.

23. A. Martinelli, 'Multinational Corporations, National Economic Policies and Labor Unions,' in L. Lindberg, et al. (eds), *Stress and Contradiction in Modern Capitalism* (Lexington Books, 1975).

24. Robert Gilpin takes the contrary view that government policies were the primary and most important factor in determining the rise of multinational corporations: see Gilpin, op. cit.

25. N. Poulantzas, *Classes sociales et capitalisme aujourd'hui* (Maspero, 1975).

26. A. Martinelli, 'International Capital and Social Classes', *Annual Register of Political Economy* (1977); G. Arrighi, *The Geometry of Imperialism* (New Left Books, 1978).

27. Domestic firms in many less developed countries also confront a very fragmented working class, but without having the sophisticated organization of work that TNCs have.

28. J. Gennard, 'The Impact of Foreign-Owned Subsidiaries on Host Country Labor Relations: The Case of the United Kingdom,' in R. J. Flanagan and A. R. Weber (eds), *Bargaining without Boundaries* (University of Chicago Press, 1974).

29. A. Martinelli, 'Multinational Corporations, National Economic Policies and Labor Unions,' in Lindberg et al., op. cit.

30. S. Hymer's essay in Lindberg, et al. op. cit.

31. C. Cooper (ed.), *Science, Technology and Development: The Political Economy of Technical Advance in Underdeveloped Countries* (Frank Press, 1973); B. R. Williams (ed.), *Science and Technology in Economic Growth* (John Wiley, 1973); H. Giersch (ed.), *Science and Technology in Economic Growth* (John Wiley, 1973); H. Giersch (ed.), *The International Division of Labor, Problems and Perspectives* (J. C. B. Mohr, 1974); Gilpin, op. cit.; R. Vernon, *Storm over the Multinationals* (Harvard University Press, 1977); C. F. Bergsten, T. Horst and T. H. Moran, *American Multinationals and American Interests* (Brookings Institution, 1978); The National Research Council, *Technology, Trade and the US Economy* (National Academy of Sciences, 1978).

32. National Research Council, op. cit., pp. 50-1.

33. Vernon, op. cit., p. 61.

34. This greater support was much more sizable in the 1960s than at present.

35. P. Musgrave, *United States Taxation of Foreign Investment Income* (Harvard Law School, 1969); US Congress Senate Committee on Labor and Public Policy, *The Multinational Corporation and the National Interest*, 93rd Congress, 1st session (1973); AFL-CIO testimony in US Congress Senate, *Hearings before the Subcommittee on International Trade of the Committee on Finance*, 93rd Congress, 1st session (1973).

36. Gilpin, op. cit., p. 168.

37. ibid., pp. 188-9.

38. ibid., p. 187.

39. Bergsten, Horst and Moran in their recent book, *American Multinationals and American Interests* (op. cit.) make some progress in this respect.

40. A. Young, *The Research and Development Effort in Western Europe, North America and the Soviet Union* (OECD, 1965).

41. J. G. Maisonrouge, 'How a Multinational Corporation Appears to Its Managers,' in G. W. Ball (ed.), *Global Companies* (Prentice-Hall, 1975).

42. W. Vaupel and L. P. Curhan, *The Making of Multinational Enterprise* (Harvard Business School, 1967).

43. J. Jequier, 'Computers', in R. Vernon (ed.), *Big Business and the State* (Harvard University Press, 1974).

44. For a discussion of French economic policy, see J. Zysman, *Political Strategies for Industrial Order* (University of California Press, 1977).

45. United Nations, *Multinational Corporations in World Development* (UN, 1973).

46. UNCTAD, *Transfer of Technology*, TD 106 (10 November 1971).

47. R. J. Barnett and R. E. Müller, *Global Reach* (Simon & Schuster, 1974).

48. T. H. Moran, 'Multinational Corporations and Dependency: A Dialogue for Dependentistas and Non-Dependentistas,' in *International Organization*, op. cit. (n. 5).

49. J. Ritter, 'The Development of Labor-Intensive Technologies for Developing Countries,' in Giersch, op. cit., pp. 448-9.

50. W. A. Chudson and L. T. Wells, Jr., *The Acquisition of Proprietary Technology by Developing Countries from Multinational Enterprises* (UN Study Group on Multinational Enterprises, 1973).

51. ibid., p. 51.

52. State control is in itself no guarantee of reduced technological dependency (see L. K. Mytelka, 'Technological Dependence in the Andean group,' *International Organization*, op. cit.), but it is likely to reduce it.

5

THE USES OF FORMAL COMPARATIVE RESEARCH ON DEPENDENCY THEORY AND THE WORLD-SYSTEM PERSPECTIVE

Christopher Chase-Dunn
Johns Hopkins University, USA

Dependency theory and its reformulation as the 'world-system perspective' have created a major transformation in the study of social change and economic development.[1] The focus on national societies as the independent unit of analysis, which characterized modernization theories, has been replaced by an elaboration of the transnational, international and world-contextual relations, which affect development (Villamil, 1979). This new focus provides the theoretical space for a reinterpretation of the Marxian vision of capitalist development, in which it is understood that capitalism has always been imperialist and 'international' and the capitalist mode of production is a feature of the world economy as a whole (Wallerstein, 1979; Chase-Dunn and Rubinson, 1977). This new perspective, while in need of further clarification, at least holds the promise of a theory that will enable us to understand the underlying tendencies of capitalist development and the transition to socialism. This paper argues (1) that the task of theoretical formulation can be aided by formal comparative research on the mechanisms of dependency and the processes of world-system development; and (2) that quantitative studies of dependency processes can be useful to policy-makers and political movements in the peripheral countries. This is in response to arguments that have alleged that quantitative research is not appropriate for the study of dependency processes.

THE CRITIQUE OF CROSS-NATIONAL
STUDIES OF DEPENDENCY

It is striking to note that, although dependency theory was created and elaborated primarily by Latin American social scientists, and some of the best historical case studies have been done by Latin Americans, they have done virtually none of the many quantitative cross-national studies of dependency. This is due to two factors: (1) the relative concentration of the means of quantitative research in core countries; and (2) differences in the philosophy of science. The first of these causes must be deplored as one of the consequences of uneven development between the core and the periphery. Just as the creation of new technology for material production is concentrated in core countries by the long-run operation of international power dependence relations, so the resources for expensive social research and the utilization of sophisticated techniques of analysis tend to be so concentrated.[2] If, as I argue below, at least some of these techniques are powerful tools which can be used for the purposes of the oppressed as well as of the oppressors, then we should make every effort to see that social scientists in the periphery gain access to these tools. This is not to demean the power of non-quantitative research and theoretical imagination. This power is demonstrated by the fact that dependency theory itself emerged in the periphery.

The other cause of the concentration of quantitative studies of dependency in core countries is the existence of philosophical and methodological objections to this kind of research among many Latin American social scientists. Many of these objections are raised in a critical article by Fernando Henrique Cardoso (1977). Cardoso contrasts his own dialectical approach[3] to what he sees as the 'structural-mechanistic' assumptions of cross-national analysis. Although some other Latin American dependency theorists, for example Osvaldo Sunkel (1973), seem to be less opposed to formal comparative research, the objections raised by Cardoso are widespread and, in fact, are shared by many North American and European social scientists.

My own position is that the main defects of most contemporary social sciences are theoretical rather than methodological. Much or even most of what passes for sophisticated quantitative research is meaningless 'number-crunching,' but this is primarily due to its lack of theoretical content, its tendency to raw empiricism. Quantitative research that is grounded in theory can be used to test propositions that are derived from competing theories, and to elaborate and refine concepts that are parts of theories.

Rather than addressing general problems in the philosophy of science, this paper will focus on the particular issues raised about the appropriate methods of studying dependency.[4] My response is to Cardoso (1977) and the other authors who have made similar criticisms (Bach, 1977; Irwin, 1977; and Palma, 1978).

I will discuss six issues raised by the critiques of cross-national studies of dependency: (1) concept formation, (2) dialectics and contradiction, (3) singularization, (4) the internal-external problem, (5) historicism, and (6) critical theory, determinism and political practice. In order to not misrepresent the authors I am criticizing, let me quote extensively from the most clear and important of the critiques of cross-national studies, that of Cardoso (1977). Discussing alternative approaches to his own dialectical-structural method of studying dependency, Cardoso laments:

> dependency came to be consumed as a 'theory,' implying a corpus of formal and testable propositions. I was always reluctant to use the expression 'theory of dependency' because I was afraid of formalizing the approach. Nevertheless, Latin Americans and North Americans began to make the effort to create a 'theory'. . . some North American specialists began clamoring for 'internal consistency' in the theory of dependency and established a body of hypotheses deduced from the principle of dependency in order to test them empirically. In this type of reformulation of dependency, the concepts must be one-dimensional and precise and must refer to clearly established variables. With their help it ought to be possible to measure the continuum that goes from 'dependency' to 'independence' and to characterize variable degrees of dependency.
>
> However, this kind of definition of the notion of dependency also modifies the 'theoretical field' of its study: instead of making a dialectical analysis of historical processes, conceiving of them as the result of struggles between classes and groups that define their interests and values in the process of the expansion of a mode of production, history is formalized; the specific contribution that these analyses of dependency might make from a methodological point of view (that is, the idea of contradiction) is withdrawn. The ambiguity, the contradictions, and the more or less abrupt 'breaks' in reality are reduced to 'operational dimensions' which, by definition, are univocal but static. The result is somewhat like a dialogue between two deaf people, in which one group says: give me precise concepts, with clear dimensions, and I will tell you, after testing them, if the relationships among the variables defined within their theoretical framework conform to the hypotheses which you propose.
>
> The other group says: I am not interested in defining univocal concepts; what interests me is pointing out contradictions and formulating relationships in which *the same* thing is transformed into *the other* by means of a process which

takes place in time and which brings certain classes or fragments of classes into relation with others through struggle and opposes them to rival blocs — for example, how one and *the same* 'national' bourgeoisie is internationalized into *something else*, or how 'public servants' are transformed into the 'state bourgeoisie' by redefining the allied and enemy camps. In this analytical perspective, processes involve changes in quality and not merely in degree. [Cardoso, 1977, pp. 15-16.]

Let us now discuss the issues raised by Cardoso and the other critics of cross-national dependency studies.

CONCEPT FORMATION

Cardoso (1977) argues that concepts should not be rigidly defined and/or converted into one-dimensional variables, because the social reality being studied is a dynamic, contradictory reality which is oversimplified by such precision. This objection may be partly based on Marx's notion that theoretical concepts in the social sciences should be reflective of the relational and contradictory character of social processes themselves (Marx, 1958). I think that this is an important methodological idea, but it should not prevent us from making tentative definitions clear in order to see how they may be useful in explaining empirical reality. Operationalizing a concept does not permanently commit us to either the definition or the particular indicator we employ to measure it. Cardoso is right to point out that we should be aware of the assumptions behind converting a concept like dependency into a one-dimensional variable. Indeed, almost all the cross-national studies that have been done assume that dependency is multi-dimensional.

Much of the concern for the implicitly static and mechanistic nature of formal specification of causal models (e.g. Bach, 1977) seems to be the result of a misunderstanding of the logic of causal analysis. All non-experimental research is an attempt to infer underlying causal processes from data. The type of variables used (qualitative, metric, linear or curvilinear, multidimensional or not) and the logic and nature of the causal relations that are built in to the model are up to the theoretical imagination of the researcher. It is true that the most commonly tested models assume one-way causation and linear relations, but these assumptions are by no means necessary to causal modeling.

DIALECTICS AND CONTRADICTION

Cardoso (1977) and Bach (1977) argue that conventional causal imagery should not be applied to dependency processes because these processes are dialectical and contradictory. Presumably, these authors are making a claim about objective reality, and, if we can be clear about what is meant by a dialectical process, there is no inherent reason why a dialectical model cannot be specified and tested.

Many students of social structure prefer to use dialectics as an heuristic aid to thinking about processes of social change. As such, the general notions of contradiction, opposition and qualitative transformation can be quite useful for interpreting complex historical situations, and this heuristic is not at all incompatible with particular causal propositions of a more conventional kind. When we assert that there is a causal relationship between dependence on foreign investment and economic growth, we do not deny the interactive and reactive nature of the relationships between multinational corporations, peripheral states and peripheral workers. What we are asserting is that, on the whole, over many cases, in the long run, ceteris paribus, the more dependent a country is on foreign capital, the slower it will develop economically. The fact that there may be exceptions, or that some countries may be able successfully to combine foreign investment with a certain kind of growth, does not disprove the overall contention. Propositions of this kind can easily be combined with a dialectical heuristic.

More problematic is the attempt to include formal dialectical propositions in a model. If we contend that a particular process or relationship is dialectical it may be possible to specify formally the meaning of this assertion. Although it is unpalatable to many dialecticians, it is possible to translate the notion of contradiction into conventional causal logic. Thus contradiction may be understood as: (1) causal vectors that affect a dependent variable in opposite ways; (2) variables that affect one another (reciprocal causation); or (3) a variable that negatively affects itself over time (negative feedback). It is true that most causal models in social research employ only fairly simple assumptions about feedback, reciprocal causation and interaction, but much more complex forms of causation have been successfully modeled with fairly standard mathematical tools. To say that there is a contradiction between production relations and forms of distribution in a capitalist system is to say that these two constellations of institutions interact in ways that produce changes in both of them. This is merely the use of contradiction as an heuristic that sensitizes us to certain kinds of issues, but we may specify this more exactly as reciprocal interaction between levels of repression and wages, a 'dialectical' proposition which may be easily modeled.

Most serious dialecticians are not satisfied with this simple translation of the central notions of dialects (contradiction, opposition, and qualitative transformation) into conventional causal logic, however. They argue that Aristotelian logic precludes the simultaneous existence of opposites, and so a new logic and mathematics is desired. Work has begun to create a formalized dialectical logic and mathematics (Alker, 1979; Rescher, 1977). This type of work may eventually allow us to construct dialectical models that clearly specify the meaning of opposition, contradiction, synthesis and qualitative transformation in ways that make them disconfirmable and useful in explanation, prediction and social practice. This line of work is suggested by Luca Perrone and Erik Wright (Perrone and Wright, 1973; Wright, 1978). They have elaborated a number of 'modes of determination' which are particularly appropriate to the task of modeling the causal structures of Marxian theory.[5] This logic could certainly be extended to dependency processes. Cardoso's own work is not heavy with Hegelian logic and so he would probably favor the use of dialectics as an heuristic rather than a formalized model.

SINGULARIZATION OF NATIONAL SOCIETIES

The argument is implied by Cardoso (1977) and other critics of cross-national studies (Bach, 1977; Irwin, 1977; Palma, 1978), that one shouldn't combine data on different countries in a single analysis because the countries are 'different.' While Rubinson (1977) has, to my mind, argued persuasively against the methodological singularization of countries, I will reiterate his discussion. Of course, countries, and all other entities in the universe, are different. Of relevance to social theory, however, is the question of differences that are related to the process under analysis.

Przeworski and Teune (1970) argue that comparative research consists only of the identification of system factors that alter the relationships among variables across countries, and thus that only an analysis of covariance design is appropriate for cross-national research. This amounts to elevating a theoretical assertion (that each country is unique with respect to the process of interest) to a universal methodological directive. Many psychologists would undoubtedly make the claim that each individual human being is unique, and so comparisons that aggregate individuals are misleading. It is true that everything is unique, if we want to consider its particularity; but social science is the attempt to formulate those underlying tendencies that reproduce and transform the structures of social systems. Any systematic comparison risks the possibility that incommensurable units have been thrown together, but this depends on the theoretical assertion being studied.

One of the most fundamental assertions of dependency theory and the world-system perspective is that there are systematic differences in the process of development between core and peripheral countries. Cardoso (1977) makes this point in the context of his argument that large samples of countries should not be thrown together in a single analysis. But cross-national analysis does not assume that the development process is everywhere the same. On the contrary, it enables us to study the differences by measuring the power-dependence relations between countries (or their position in the larger world division of labor) to estimate the effects of these relations on the process of development.

It has also been argued that dependency processes themselves differ in different kinds of countries. McGowan and Smith (1978) claimed that dependency processes had different effects in Africa than elsewhere. And Cardoso (1977, p. 23) criticizes cross-national research that does not differentiate between different 'situations' of dependence, 'basic distinctions between class and political structures in an enclave type of economy, a nationally controlled export economy, and an associated-dependent industrialized one.'[6] This type of contention, that there are systematic differences between types of dependency, or dependency processes in different kinds of countries, can be tested by analyzing groups of countries separately, or by using an analysis of covariance design with dummy variables in analysis of all countries (e.g. Bornschier, Chase-Dunn and Rubinson, 1978). The point here is that, while there may well be practical limitations on the availability of data on enough coun-

tries or the accuracy of data presently available, there are not inherent limitations in the strategy of formal comparative research
that preclude its usefulness.

Many of the critics of cross-national research seem to be alleging
that dependency processes are different in every country. If this
substantive claim is true, it makes it difficult to contemplate a
general theory of dependency that is of any use, but even this is not
an insuperable barrier to quantitative research. Indeed, with time-
series data on each country we could construct and test country-
specific models of dependency processes (e.g. Gillespie and
Gillespie, 1979; Hollist and Boydston, 1979; Duvall 1979). But the
substantive idea that dependency processes are completely different
as they affect each country strikes me as a failure to understand the
main insights of dependency theory and the underlying tendencies
of capitalist development on a world scale. This, however, is a
theoretical and empirical question, not a methodological one.

THE INTERNAL-EXTERNAL
PROBLEM

Cardoso (1977) raises a question that is largely substantive but also
has methodological implications: what is the relationship between
'external' aspects of dependency and 'internal' dependent social
structures? He argues that much of the best work on dependency
focuses on structures and processes that are, for the most part, national in scope. One of the most fundamental insights of the world-
system perspective is that national boundaries are only one institutional feature of the capitalist world economy itself. Economic,
political and social processes of a systematic kind may operate
relatively independently within a particular geographical area, but
there is precious little in the way of social change or economic
development that has remained isolated from the world-wide process capital accumulation. Even the changes in (or maintenance of)
kinship structures have been greatly conditioned in both the core
and the periphery by the types of class formation, state formation
and nation-building that the capital accumulation process has
created. The isomorphic processes by which national communities
elaborate their 'unique' national cultures are largely a reactive response to the centralization and concentration of power and productive advantage in the core states. These, of course, are substan-

tive assertions, but the reification of national boundaries tends to preclude research that can prove the veracity of these claims. Thus the internal-external distinction itself tends to limit the kinds of conclusions that can be drawn from research. I propose that we drop the distinction entirely, or that we be much more precise in our usage of it.[7] There are real boundaries between classes, nation-states, the core, the periphery and the semi-periphery — and also, until the late nineteenth century, between the capitalist world-system and the socioeconomic systems external to it (external arenas). But the discussion of 'internal' structures and processes, as if the national society were the real concrete locus of interaction between classes, firms, kinship groups, etc., whereas 'external' relations of power dependency and exchange are conceived as abstract, is the kind of mystification that dependency theory was intended to overcome. There is nothing abstract about colonialism or imperialism or neocolonialism. There is nothing abstract about the world division of labor between the core and the periphery. Methodological presuppositions that focus our attention on local realities serve only to obscure these real relations. It is understandable why the intellectual servants of core power display this tendency, but I fail to comprehend the same mistake when made by social scientists of the periphery.

Cross-national research itself, which uses the nation-state as the unit of analysis, can obscure or confuse our understanding of the real relations between classes, firms, cities, regions and zones of the world-economy. Elsewhere I have discussed ways in which data originally gathered on nation-states can be transformed to test propositions which do not implicitly reify national boundaries (Chase-Dunn, 1979a).

HISTORICISM AND THE LOGICAL
BOUNDARIES OF A SYSTEM

The word 'historical' means different things to different people and thus causes much misunderstanding. It is used to mean 'old,' 'unique,' or 'anti-deterministic.' Cardoso and Faletto's (1979) discussion of their 'historical-structural' method implies mainly this last meaning. They say:

> For us it is necessary to recognize from the beginning that social structures are the product of man's collective behavior. Therefore, although enduring, social structures can be, and in fact are, continuously transformed by social movements. Consequently, our approach is both structural and historical: it emphasizes not just the structural conditioning of social life, but also the historical transformation of structures by conflict, social movements, and class struggles. Thus our methodology is historical-structural. [Cardoso and Faletto, 1979.].

Other authors use the word 'historical' simply to mean old. Anything not contemporary (to themselves) is dismissed as antiquarian. Often this usage corresponds with the assumption that institutions such as the market and the state are universally rooted in 'human nature.' This attitude is often completely naive regarding the origins, reproduction and transformation of basic social institutions.

The most common and difficult meaning of 'historical' is its implication of uniqueness. Both Marx and Weber were heavily influenced by the German historicist school, which emphasized the extreme uniqueness of particular social institutions and periods of history. This attitude, which precludes any attempt to theorize, was also adopted by the Boasians in anthropology, in reaction to the overly simple nineteenth-century theories of social evolution. The question of uniqueness vs. generality is partly an arbitrary decision regarding the intended scope of any theory. Everything is unique, and everything has general characteristics. The task of science is to formulate what is not unique in a way that explains and predicts changes. For Marx the correct theoretical focus was a mode of production defined as a relationship between technology and social relations in which there is a basic underlying logic that causes the main movements and developments. Each mode of production contains contradictions which result in its transformation into a different system with a different underlying logic. For Marx, then, the task of social science was not to discover the laws of development for all types of social systems: these would be so general as to be vacuous in terms of their ability to explain particular 'historical' developments and transformations. The scope of Marx's theorizing was confined to particular, unique, modes of production, which were themselves, however, very general and abstract systems. This decision about theoretical scope brings up more questions than it solves, in our attempt to extend and reformulate Marx's notion of the capitalist mode of production for the world-economy as a whole. In order to establish the boundaries of a system, we need not determine only its spatial and organizational boundaries, but also the boundaries of its logic. This is why it is absolutely essential to formulate clearly the underlying laws of development. Only then will we be able to distinguish between non-essential reorganizations, which allow a system temporarily to adjust to its own contradictions, and fundamental transformations, which result in changes in the underlying logic. These are the most important issues in the controversy about the transition from feudalism to capitalism (Hilton, 1976; Wallerstein, 1979, pp. 138-51) and the attempts to understand the transition to socialism (Bettelheim, 1975; Sweezy and Bettelheim, 1971).

CRITICAL THEORY, DETERMINISM, AND POLITICAL PRACTICE

A number of other philosophical and heuristic issues are raised by the critics of cross-national dependency studies. Cardoso argues that dependency theory is (or should be) a critical theory that attacks the structures of domination. He implies that quantitative research is necessarily uncritical because it must wear the mantle of 'value-free' science.

First, I would observe that there is an important difference between scientific scholarship and political propaganda, but this boundary is not between quantitative and qualitative research. Both data-cooking and the falsification of historical evidence (or any other kind of evidence) have no place in critical social science. Thus the canon of honesty applies to both qualitative and quantitative social research. On the other hand, any claim of total impartiality is also dishonest. I prefer to know at least the intentional political and class standpoint of the social science I read. There has been a flowering of Marxist and critical research in North America in the last 10 years that supports my contention that formal comparative research can be effectively critical of existing power structures.[8]

Cardoso and Bach argue that the construction of formal models of dependency processes implies a deterministic view of development which ignores the voluntary efforts of individuals and classes to resist and alter the structures that are exploiting and underdeveloping them. First, models in social science are always probabilistic to allow for the complexities and indeterminancies of human behavior. Second, knowledge of the likelihood of a social outcome given certain conditions is a potential contributor to human freedom. As Stalin (unfortunately) pointed out (1952), we do not become more determined by understanding the laws of nature: on the contrary, we become freer. This is true also of the laws of social development.[9] For example, models of dependency that show the size and nature of average effects on a national economy caused by an increase (or decrease) in dependence on foreign investment can be useful in helping policy-makers in peripheral countries avoid the negative consequences of exploitation by multinational corporations. This point is elaborated below.

Another charge that has been made by Bach is that cross-national studies of dependency imply a narrowly 'economistic' view of development. Amin (1976) uses this term to refer to the tendency among Soviet planners to overemphasize industrial development at the expense of other socialist goals, and to underemphasize the importance of 'superstructural' elements in the process of development. While many dependency and world-system theorists do emphasize the importance of the organizational forms of material production, they do not usually ignore ideological and political structures. Indeed, there are some versions of these theories that focus heavily on the cultural and psychological aspects of dependency relations and world-system processes (Inkeles, 1975; Chirot, 1977). In any case, as with most of the issues raised by these critics, this is much more a substantively theoretical question than a methodological one. Quantitative methods can be used to distinguish between these different approaches to understanding development.

There is also the question of the uses of causal models and quantitative research for informing political practice. There are many political organizations and movements that might make good use of the results of research on dependency, but, just as policy-makers and planners cannot apply models mechanically to every situation, so in politics (especially in politics) practice is more an art than a science because of the complex nature of the task of political leadership and practice. This means that, as in medicine, the results of research must be used by informed and artful practitioners.

THE ACTUAL AND POTENTIAL
USES OF CROSS-NATIONAL RESEARCH
ON DEPENDENCY

I will now briefly review the main findings of cross-national studies of dependency and discuss the potential uses of these findings. A review of cross-national studies of the effects of investment and aid dependence on economic growth and inequality is presented in Bornschier et al. (1978), and a summary of the results of the most thorough single research project testing dependency propositions is given in the paper Volker Bornschier included in this volume (chapter 3 above).

The main conclusion of the cross-national research that has been done is that dependence on foreign direct investment has a retardant effect on economic growth and is associated with greater income inequality. This finding by itself tends to support dependency theory at the expense of modernization and neoclassical economic theories of development. We may ask what the effect of these findings has been. Perhaps it is yet too early to tell, but the impression I get is that these results have not had much affect on either development theory or practice. Those who have direct or indirect interests in common with multinational corporations have ignored the findings, even though they are based on careful quantitative research. Those who were sympathetic to dependency theory to begin with did not need to be further convinced by evidence and tended to discount the research techniques employed in these studies.

Perhaps these conclusions are too pessimistic, but it would be naive to suppose that paradigm revolution or the other kind would result from a single set of research findings. It may be that these findings have played some small part in increasing the sensitivity that core-based social scientists have toward the issues of international inequality and exploitation. But the greater part of the new awareness of these features of the world economy has been stimulated by challenges to core power and the slowdown in world economic expansion that precipitated the demand for a New International Economic Order.

I will consider the potential, rather than the actual, uses of these research findings in the hope that their further dissemination might result in more theoretical clarity, effective development policy, and political action. I should emphasize here that theoretical development itself is a contribution to social transformation even when it is not directly employed by planners and politicians. The task of creating a vision of the real underlying tendencies of capitalist development on a world scale is far from complete, and for me this is the most important contribution that social scientists can make. This involves challenging the hegemonic orthodox theories that mystify relations of exploitation. The findings of dependency theory research do this in a very direct way. But beyond the arena of general social consciousness is the world of the planners. Let us consider the uses of dependency research for policy-making.

Cross-national research shows that an increase in the stock of foreign capital (owing to an inflow of capital with consequent purchase of land, labor, etc.) has a short-run positive effect on GNP growth. On the other hand, dependence on an accumulated stock of foreign capital has a negative (retardant) affect on GNP growth after a time lag of about five years, and this negative effect gets larger up to at least 20 years. Research that carefully examines this distributed lag has not yet been done. What we do know is that there is a short-term positive effect followed, after about five years, by a negative effect which gets stronger as times passes. Most probably the negative effect peaks in strength between twenty and forty years and then decreases. If this is true, what are the implications for policy-makers in the periphery? Any government policy that regulates or taxes foreign investment runs the risk of decreasing it and therefore suffering short-run decreases in economic growth, but long-run relative increases. On the other hand, any policy that encourages foreign investment takes the opposite risk: short-run gains and long-run injuries. The class coalitions that compose the regimes of most peripheral countries tend to favor foreign investment to the long-run detriment of national economic growth. Any regime that attempts to reverse this situation faces a short-run economic decline and thus political opposition, which often means the demise of the regime. It requires an exceptionally strong regime, based on class interests that are relatively isolated from the economic linkages of the transnational corporations, to be able to weather the economic effects of increased controls or expropriation of foreign-held property. Of course, this general point is nothing new to the economic nationalists of the periphery, but more precise estimates of the size and timing of the economic effects could be of great use in actual political practice. To be useful these estimates should take into account the particular situation of the country of interest, its history, the particular nature of connections with foreign corporations, the type of investment, the balance of class forces, etc. The methodological problem of linking a general theory of dependence processes with the attributes of individual countries has been discussed and elaborated by Duvall and Freeman (1978).

The studies of the effects of investment dependence on income inequality remain somewhat inconclusive, because it has not been possible to obtain enough data on changes in income distribution over time. There is definitely an association between investment dependence and inequality. This may be due either to effects that dependence has on class structures (as dependency theory argues) or to the tendency for multinational corporations to invest in countries that already have relatively great inequalities. There is some evidence that this second possibility can be discounted (Chase-Dunn, 1975). If it is true that dependence on foreign investment maintains or increases inequality, what policy implications does this have? First, it makes it clear that there are class issues involved in policies toward multinational corporations. The so-called 'trickle-down effects' are discredited. International and peripheral policy-makers are sensitized to the issue, and must address it.

Exactly what ought to be done depends on the mechanisms by which dependence affects inequality. Bornschier and Ballmer-Cao (1979) show that the relationship between investment dependence and income inequality is mediated by several dimensions of national power distribution: the occupational structure, the structure of land tenure, the bargaining position of labor, and the economic strength of the government. These findings suggest governmental policies that might be implemented to alter these effects. Unfortunately, states in peripheral countries are not autonomous actors pursuing the most rational course in the interests of the whole citizenry. The possibilities for implementation of programs such as land reform, progressive labor legislation and the like are constrained by national and international class forces. Dependency creates an alliance between indigenous and core-ruling classes (Galtung's (1972) 'bridgehead'), in which the indigenous rulers ('liaison elites,' or compradors) tend to dominate the states, which are thus unlikely effectively to regulate multinational corporations in the interest of balanced national economic development or the more even distribution of returns to growth. Thus these findings are probably of more interest to political movements that are not in power than to extant governments.

Bornschier's study of the relationship between policy toward multinational corporations, investment dependence, and economic growth (chapter 3 above) suggests some important lessons for policy-makers in peripheral countries. His finding that regulatory policies have a negative effect on economic growth through their tendency to slow down domestic as well as foreign investment implies the need for either increased incentives for private capital investment or a directly state-sponsored investment program. Since much private domestic capital is in league with foreign capital, we again have the necessity for more basic institutional and political reorganization. The trend toward ambivalent policies of 'stop-and-go interventionism' that Bornschier finds among the peripheral countries indicates that single countries have a difficult time overcoming the power of the multinational corporations. Some may do so, but often at the expense of others (Wallerstein, 1979, pp. 66-94). Concerted international efforts among peripheral countries may be a better strategy for bargaining with multinational corporations than competition between countries for the favors of the companies. The problem here is that international solidarity over any extended period of time is very difficult to maintain, although there have been some successes (OPEC; Andean Pact). And while it may be a more effective strategy for some countries to change their relative position in the world division of labor, state capitalism is not a real challenge to the logic of the capitalist system itself. The world-system perspective implies that state capitalism (or state 'socialism') does not constitute a real break with the laws of uneven development, but rather is only a recent form of the continuation of competitive accumulation in which whole states act as firms (Chase-Dunn and Rubinson, 1979). Of course, little of this follows directly from the results of existing cross-national studies, but neither do the results of these studies prevent us from considering possible alternatives to the presently existing system.

CONCLUSIONS

I have argued that presently available quantitative techniques have been usefully employed to test propositions implied by dependency theory, and that the results of these studies could be valuable for policy-making and political practice. It can be seen from my discussion of dialectical modeling that I am also proposing that further development of formal comparative methods is desirable for the purpose of theory construction and applied research.[10] Just as linear programming and technological development have the potential to solve the problem of production (under the right political circumstances) and to reduce the function of state planning to the 'administration of things' (freeing the populace for more refined pursuits), so a further development of comparative method can help us understand the laws and tendencies of long-run social change. That these possibilities could redound primarily to the favor of the technocrats is a problem for another time.

NOTES

1. J. Samuel Valenzuela and Arturo Valenzuela (1978) correctly argue that this transformation is not a paradigm revolution because social science has not attained the level of consensus necessary to constitute 'normal' science in the Kuhnian sense.

2. Of course there are exceptions. The Bariloche group (Herrera et al., 1975) has produced a sophisticated example of the world-modeling approach, and other applications of quantitative techniques are contained in Ruggles (1974). But the fact remains that none of the many quantitative cross-national studies of dependency has been done by Latin Americans. Seventeen of these studies are reviewed by Bornschier et al. (1978).

3. This approach is more fully explained in the Preface to the English edition in Cardoso and Faletto (1979).

4. Some of these same issues have been raised regarding methods of studying the world-system as a whole by Hopkins (1978) and Bach (1979).

5. Conventional axiomatic theoretical logic has been used by Nowak (1971) to formalize parts of Marx's accumulation model of capitalist development. In my view this formalization adequately represents Marx's theory.

6. Of relevance to this contention is the new finding (Bornschier and Chase-Dunn, forthcoming) that dependence on foreign investment in manufacturing has *larger* negative effects on GNP growth than on foreign investment in extractive industries. Cardoso's (1973) discussion of associated-dependent development leads us to believe that this type of dependence, in which there is a high degree of foreign investment in manufacturing, will have positive effects on aggregate GNP growth. The new finding lends credence to the idea that the differences between the old and the new dependency are more matters of form than substance.

7. Andre Gunder Frank (1979) has attempted to retain the internal-external distinction by clarifying it to refer to internal class relations and external exchange relations. This seems to me to be a grave error, and to make him guilty of charges of 'circulationism' that have been leveled against him (Laclau, 1971; Brenner, 1977). International and transnational relations are not merely relations of exchange: the world market is an institution that obscures the power relations between world classes.

8. I am referring to the work of Albert Szymanski, Erik O. Wright, Michael Reich, Stephen Hymer, Thomas Weisskopf, Michael Hechter, Maurice Zeitlin and others.

9. It should be made clear that, by endorsing the philosophy of science of the Third International, I do not also endorse its politics. It was not 'economistic' methodology that caused the involution of the Soviet state and the utilization of Marxism as a state religion, but rather the threats and opportunities presented by the larger capitalist world economy interacting with class struggles within the Soviet Union (Chase-Dunn, 1980).

10. The first version of this paper contained a review of five types of research design useful for studying dependency theory and the world-system, in which a new design, that of 'multilevel' analysis, was described. This discussion is now included in Chase-Dunn (forthcoming).

REFERENCES

ALKER, Hayward R. (1979). 'Logic, Dialectics, Politics: Some Recent Controversies,' paper presented at the Moscow Congress of the International Political Science Association, 17 August.

ALSCHULER, Lawrence (forthcoming). *Miracles and Muddlers: The Impact of MNCs on Development in Six Third World Countries.*

AMIN, Samir (1976). *Unequal Development* (New York: Monthly Review Press).

BACH, Robert L. (1977). 'Methods of Analysis in the Study of the World-economy: A Comment on Rubinson,' *American Sociological Review* 42 (5): 811-14.

BACH, Robert L. (1980). 'On the Holism of a World-System Perspective,' pp. 289-310 in Terence K. Hopkins and Immanual Wallerstein (eds), *Processes of the World System* (Beverly Hills, Calif.: Sage).

BERGESEN, Albert J. (ed.) (1980). *Studies of the Modern World-System* (New York: Academic Press).

BETTELHEIM, Charles (1975). *Economic Calculation and Forms of Property* (New York: Monthly Review Press).

BORNSCHIER, Volker (1980). 'Multinational Corporations and Economic Growth: A Cross-national Test of the Decapitalization Thesis,' *Journal of Development Economics.* pp. 191-210.

BORNSCHIER, Volker and Christopher CHASE-DUNN (forthcoming). *Core Corporations and Underdevelopment.*

BORNSCHIER, Volker, Christopher CHASE-DUNN and Richard RUBINSON (1978). 'Cross-national Evidence of the Effects of Foreign Investment and Aid on Economic Growth and Inequality: A Survey of Findings and Reanalysis,' *American Journal of Sociology,* 84 (3), 651-83.

BORNSCHIER, Volker, and Than-Huyen BALLMER-CAO (1979). 'Income Inequality: A Cross-national Study of the Relationships between MNC-penetration, Dimensions of the Power Structure and Income Distribution,' *American Sociological Review,* 44, 487-506.

BRENNER, Robert (1977). 'The Origins of Capitalist Development: A Critique of Neo-Smithian Marxism,' *New Left Review,* 104, 25-92.

CARDOSO, Fernando Henrique (1973). 'Associated-dependent Development: Theoretical and Practical Implications,' in Alfred Stepan (ed.), *Authoritarian Brazil* (New Haven: Yale University Press).

CARDOSO, Fernando Henrique (1977). 'The Consumption of Dependency Theory in the United States,' *Latin American Research Review,* 12 (3), 7-24.

CARDOSO, Fernando Henrique and Enzo FALETTO (1979). *Dependency and Development in Latin America* (Berkeley: University of California Press).

CHASE-DUNN, Christopher (1975). 'The Effects of International Economic Dependence on Development and Inequality,' *American Sociological Review,* 40 (6), 720-38.

CHASE-DUNN, Christopher (1979a). 'Comparative Research on World-system Characteristics,' *International Studies Quarterly,* 23(4),   601-24.

CHASE-DUNN, Christopher (forthcoming). 'Old and New Research Designs for studying the World-System: A Research Note,' *Comparative Political Studies.*

CHASE-DUNN, Christopher and Richard RUBINSON (1977). 'Toward a Structural Perspective on the World-system,' *Politics and Society,* 7(4), 453-76.

CHASE-DUNN, Christopher and Richard RUBINSON (1979). 'Cycles, Trends and New Departures in World-system Development,' in John W. Meyer and Michael T. Hannan (eds), *National Development and the World System* (Chicago: University Press).

CHASE-DUNN, Christopher (1980). 'Socialist States in the Capitalist World-Economy,' *Social Problems* 27(5), 505-25.

CHIROT, Daniel (1977). *Social Change in the 20th Century* (New York: Harcourt, Brace and Jovanovich).

DUVALL, Raymond and John R. FREEMAN (1978). 'The State and Dependent Capitalism,' *International Studies Quarterly,* 25(1), 99-118.

DUVALL, Raymond and John R. FREEMAN (1978). 'A Formal and Empirical Analysis of Governmental Dynamics in Dependent Societies,' proposal submitted to the National Science Foundation.

FRANK, Andre Gunder (1979). *Dependent Accumulation and Underdevelopment* (New York: Monthly Review Press).

GALTUNG, Johan (1971). 'A Structural Theory of Imperialism,' *Journal of Peace Research,* 2, 81-117.

GILLESPIE, Michael W. and Heather GILLESPIE (1979). 'Change in Canadian GNP and US Direct Investment: A Case Study of Dependency,' unpublished manuscript, Department of Sociology, University of Alberta.

HERRERA, Amilcar O. et al. (1975). *Catastrophe or New Society? Latin American World Model* (Buenos Aires: Fundacion Bariloche).

HILTON, Rodney (ed.) (1976). *The Transition from Feudalism to Capitalism* (London: New Left Books).

HOLLIST, W. Ladd and Robert J. BOYDSTON (forthcoming). 'Constancy and Change: The Perpetuation of Dependence Amidst Brazilian "Development",' in W. Ladd Hollist and James Rosenau (eds), *World System Structure* (Beverly Hills, Calif.: Sage).

HOPKINS, Terence K. (1978). 'World-system Analysis: Methodological Issues,' in Barbara H. Kaplan (ed.), *Social Change in the Capitalist World Economy* (Beverly Hills: Sage).

HOPKINS, Terence K. and Immanual WALLERSTEIN (1967). 'The Comparative Study of National Societies,' *Social Science Information*, 6(5), 25-58.

INKELES, Alex (1975). 'The Emerging Social Structure of the World,' *World Politics*, 27, 4.

IRWIN, Patrick H. (1977). 'Cross-sectionalism: Mismatching Theory and Model,' *American Sociological Review*, 42(5), 814-17.

LACLAU, Ernesto (1971). 'Feudalism and Capitalism in Latin America,' *New Left Review*, 67, 19-38.

MARX, Karl (1958). *Grundrisse* (New York: Vintage Books, 1973 edn.).

McGOWAN, Patrick and Dale SMITH (1978). 'Economic Dependency in Black Africa: A Causal Analysis of Competing Theories,' *International Organization*, 32(1), 179-235.

NOWAK, Leszak (1971). 'Problems of Explanation in Marx's *Capital*,' *Quality and Quantity*, 2.

PALMA, Gabriel (1978). 'Dependency: A Formal Theory of Underdevelopment or a Methodology for the Analysis of Concrete Situations of Underdevelopment?' *World Development*, 6(7/8), 881-924.

PERRONE, Luca and Erik O. WRIGHT (1973). 'Lo Stato nella Teoria Funzionalista e Marxista-Strutturalista,' *Studi di Sociologia*, 11.

PRZEWORSKI, Adam and Henry TEUNE (1970). *The Logic of Comparative Social Inquiry* (New York: Wiley).

RESCHER, Nicholas (1977). *Dialectics: A Controversy-Oriented Approach to the Theory of Knowledge* (Albany, NY: SUNY Press).

RUBINSON, Richard (1977). 'Reply to Bach and Irwin,' *American Sociological Review*, 42(5), 817-21.

RUGGLES, Nancy D. (ed.) (1974). *The Role of the Computer in Economic and Social Research in Latin America* (New York: National Bureau of Economic Research).

STALIN, J. V. (1952). *Economic Problems of Socialism in the U.S.S.R.* (Peking: Foreign Languages Press, 1972 edn).

SUNKEL, Osvaldo (1973). 'Transnational Capitalism and National Disintegration in Latin America,' *Social and Economic Studies*, 22 (1), 132-76, University of the West Indies, Jamaica.

SWEEZY, Paul and Charles BETTELHEIM (1971). *On the Transition to Socialism* (New York: Monthly Review Press).

VALENZUELA, J. Samuel and Arturo VALENZUELA (1978). 'Modernization and Dependency: Alternative Perspectives in the Study of Latin American Underdevelopment,' *Comparative Politics* (July), 535-57.

VILLAMIL, Jose J. (ed.) (1979). *Transnational Capitalism and National Development* (Atlantic Highlands, NJ: Humanities Press).

WALLERSTEIN, Immanuel (1979). *The Capitalist World-Economy* (Cambridge: University Press).

WALLERSTEIN, Immanuel and Terence K. HOPKINS (1977). 'Patterns of Development of the Modern World-system,' *Review*, 1(2), 111-45.

WRIGHT, Erik O. (1978). 'Modes of Determination and Models of Determination,' in *Class, Crisis and the State* (London: New Left Books).

II

INTERNATIONAL AUTONOMY AND DEPENDENCY

6

DEVELOPMENT UNDER FIRE

Fernando Henrique Cardoso
CEBRAP, São Paulo, Brazil

Not even the Second World War could convince the gullible inhabitants of this planet that the nineteenth century was over. Regardless of the destruction caused by two world-wide conflicts and the massacres of whole populations by Hitlerite political fanaticism, the belief in progress was not shaken. The reminiscence of the horrors of war on a scale that even Goya's fervent imagination had not foreseen, and that required the syntax of a Picasso to symbolize — in *Guernica*, the very incarnation of the irrational — none of this was enough to undermine the general belief in 'progress.' This is perhaps because, in a contradictory manner, it was science that made the maximum destruction possible. Reason, domesticated by technique, helped to construct the possibility of an absolute unreason. Thus the limits of the possible were reached: the destruction of humanity is an exploit within the reach of Dr Strangelove. Yet for a considerable time belief in the victory of reason persisted.

When all this was past, when formal rationality had become a kind of supreme divine law and scientificity had hidden itself behind the high priest's fetish, using its sacredness to disguise the force of the warrior, the businessman and the politician, the most sceptical questions began, little by little, to gnaw at the heart of that monster, the brain. How far had the Century of Enlightenment been reincarnated in the Century of Progress, and how far would the latter make our own era that of the victory of Reason?

Author's Note: This paper was first issued in Spanish by the Instituto Latinoamericano de Estudios Transnacionales, Mexico, as ILET document no. DEE/D/24/E in May 1979.

In this essay, I shall very briefly synthesize the 'development theory' that was worked out in Latin America; I shall show how the reflexive movement criticizing it 'from within' began, through 'dependency theory'; and I shall try to indicate the changes both in the terms in which the problem of development is put, at a moment when demands for a 'new economic order' are becoming stronger, and in the prevailing ideologies concerning the new 'development styles.' As far as possible, I shall make a counterpoint between the thinking that aims to synthesize the periphery's demands for world reform, and the value orientations that are being formed in the advanced industrial societies.

'LATIN AMERICAN' DEVELOPMENT THEORY

The prestige of some ideas created at ECLA concerning economic development could lead to the impression that there exists a set of analytical propositions relative to a 'Latin American theory of development.' Indeed, in recent years, as we shall see further on, Celso Furtado,[1] as well as Osvaldo Sunkel and Pedro Paz[2] gave to the so-called structuralist tradition of analysis synthetic formulations leading to the consolidation of an analytical paradigm. The original formulations, however, contained fragmentary viewpoints on development. If they aroused special interest, it was because they indicated important problems and, in spite of being theoretically unpretentious, took issue with what orthodox economic theory presented as 'established truth.'

In fact, if we take ECLA's *Estúdio Económico* of 1949, or Prebish's article, 'El desarrollo economico de la America Latina y algunos de sus principales problemas,'[3] we see that the predominant concern was not with a 'theory of development' but with an explanation of the inequalities among national economies, which were becoming more acute through world trade. Hans Singer, a United Nations economist, in a cross-national longitudinal study covering a 70-year period,[4] showed that there was a tendency for the prices of primary products to fall in relation to the prices of industrial products exported by the center. Now the theory of international trade, especially in its neoclassical version, had predicted the opposite: that the specialization of production and exchange, by permitting optimum use of the productive factors according to the availability of resources in the respective countries, would cause a tendency toward relative remuneration equalization of the factors of production. As a result, the mechanism of international trade would tend to equalize international differences rather than accentuate them.[5]

Beginning with the Ricardians, and continuing with Ohlin, Aba Lerner, Heckscher and Samuelson, the 'classical' expectation of the theory of international trade would be that the market principle is a lever of equalization provided that there is 'technical progress.' It matters little whether this progress is initially concentrated in industry, since the market mechanism leads to a relative fall in the prices of industrial products compared with agricultural products. This permits exporters of agricultural products to benefit indirectly from the fruits of technical progress. In industry and in the economy, the era of reason found the justification for its proud belief in the effects of progress.

Let us examine the contrast.

— For John Stuart Mill, it should be inferred that 'the exchange values of manufactured articles, compared with agricultural and mining products, have an absolute and indubitable tendency to fall in proportion to the increase in the population and in industry.'[6]

— For Raul Prebish, incomes grow faster in the center than on the periphery, since rising productivity in industrial production is not transferred to prices because the oligopolies defend their profit rate and the labor unions press to keep up wage levels,[7] and thus there is a tendency toward lower prices of primary products in international trade.

It is not difficult to see why these apparently simple statements cause so much ado. They negate the importance of international trade per se, as the foundation for economic equality among nations, and incorporate the explanation both of institutional and structural factors that were situated beyond the sphere of the market and of the free fluctuation of prices: labor union struggles, the organizational capacity of workers and employers in the center, the effects of monopolies.

However, the need for technique, and the belief in its multiplying effects and its relations to wealth (or, more exactly, to the accumulation of capital), etc., was not denied. On the contrary, the emphasis was placed on the setting up of political measures to make it possible for technical rationality to lead to substantive benefits for dispossessed nations and social strata. This is not the occasion for reviewing syntheses or interpretations of ECLA's ideas.[8] It is sufficient to say that the first steps in the analysis of the problems of underdevelopment, while not derived from a theory or a complete analytical system, had a profound effect on key problems posed by other theories, and did so not only by the deliberate defense of alternative policies, but also by looking on the structural level for the conditions of substantive rationality.

This basic perspective was maintained over the course of time, both in ECLA texts and in those of Latin American writers attempting to work out development theory academically. Celso Furtado, for example, states, in a theoretical book on this theme, *Teoria e Política do Desenvolvimento Econômico:*

> Synthesizing, development takes place through a rise in productivity at the level of the economic whole. This rise in productivity (and in *per capita* income) is determined by growth phenomena which take place in particular sectors. Modifications in the structure are transformations in the internal relations and proportions of the economic system, which are basically caused by modifications in the forms of production but which could not be concretized without modifications in the form of distribution and utilization of income.[9]

Income and productivity are the key concepts in Furtado's characterization. The concept of income, he says, corresponds 'to the remuneration (or cost) of the factors used in the production of goods and services. The income generated in a given period may be conceived of as the cost of the production realized, or as the buying power engendered by the production process.'[10]

Furtado observed and stated the relation between the concept of development and that of progress. But, he added, economists had achieved a decisive advance by making this vague idea more precise. This was done by elaborating the concept of 'income flow,' whose expansion can be quantified. 'A rise in the income flow per unit of labor used has been accepted, since the time of the classics, as the best indicator of an economy's development process.'[11]

If Furtado's analysis had stopped at this point, it would merely have redefined Prebish's theory by means of a formalization of neoclassical flavor spiced with Keynesian reasoning. But Furtado introduced other ideas, which, to a certain extent and paradoxically, base structural modifications on modifications governed by demand. These latter modifications, for Furtado, cannot be considered separately from the system of individual and collective preferences.

Thus, Furtado's analysis continually lays itself open to Marxist criticisms (and we shall see in a moment that dependency theoreticians take a firm stand on this point), both because it starts from the notion of income flow without referring to the social exploitation proposed by capitalism, and because it stresses demand and not production as the dynamic element. At the same time, however, it not only reintroduces the structural question of the social division of labor, but also goes on to build a bridge toward fashionable theories about 'another development.' Indeed, Furtado does not use the autonomy of the technical factor in order to explain development, but includes it as a central component of the explanation of the system of preferences, or the system of values. The text sometimes gives the impression that it is the autonomy of this value system that characterizes an authentic development in opposition to mere growth (this is a topic that Furtado discussed elsewhere).[12] However, at least in his work under consideration here, Furtado does not go quite so far in his partial break with the ECLA style of analysis: he qualifies his statements in such a way that the problem of development becomes at the same time a problem of autonomy of values and of rising physical productivity:

> It is only possible to achieve a rise in physical productivity for the whole labor force of any economic system through the introduction of more efficient forms of utilization of resources, leading to the accumulation of capital, or technological innovations, or, more often, the combined action of these two factors. On the other hand, the reallocation of resources accompanying a rise in income flow is conditioned by the composition of demand, which is the expression of the community's value system.[13]

In other words, the synthesis offered by this writer, starting with the use of the analytical instruments that are current in orthodox economics, through the emphasis on structural elements and rationality in the use of factors and continuing to the concern with the value horizon governing all the options, nonetheless remains faithful to the nineteenth century's most classical legacy to contemporary social science: the idea of the optimization of the use of factors, and the critique, initiated by Marxism, of pure formal rationality. Yet at the same time as he makes his gesture of rebellion against formal rationality, Furtado introduces an indeterminate range of options: the value system. The tension between what is wanted (who wants it?) and possible material progress (not only in

physical terms, but also in the techniques of its utilization) constitutes the unsolved equation of development.[14]

Sunkel and Paz's formulation is closer to the revisions of
ECLA's theory that were made in Santiago during the mid-1960s.
They stressed the relation between the idea of progress and that of
development. They show, however, that the optimism inherent in
the belief in the success of reason — technical progress — to solve
social problems was not accepted by development theoreticians.
The concern with the effects of technical progress by accumulation,
distribution of income and the allocation of resources — which
characterized the debate over development — does not derive from
technical progress alone.[15] Anibal Pinto's essay, 'La concentración
del progreso técnico y sus frutos en el desarrollo latinoamericano,'
had already drawn sufficient attention to this point.[16]

Further still, in Sunkel and Paz's book much less emphasis is
given to the dynamic aspects of 'income flow' and variations in demand than to differences in structure. The dependency debate was,
at that time, already gaining followers among ECLA economists:

> The notions of development and underdevelopment lead to a very different ap-
> preciation, since according to them developed economies have a different struc-
> tural formation from that which is characteristic of underdeveloped ones, given
> that the structure of the latter is, to a significant degree, a result of the relations
> which historically existed and still endure between both groups of countries.[17]

The notion of dependency (which, it is worth repeating, had been
disseminated in Santiago by the sociological critique) is already incorporated in this viewpoint.

> Development and underdevelopment, then, can be understood as partial but in-
> terdependent structures which make up a single system. The principal
> characteristic which differentiates the two structures is that the developed one,
> owing to its endogenous capacity for growth, is dominant, while the
> underdeveloped one, given the induced nature of its dynamics, is dependent; and
> this applies as much between countries as within a single country.[18]

Once the problem of development is thought of as a question
that concerns the 'endogenous capacity for growth,' and when it is
related to the historical determinants that lead to one form of
domination, the politicization of the analysis is only a step away:

this way of seeing development puts the emphasis on action, on the instruments of political power and on the power structures themselves; and, in the last instance, it is these that explain the orientation, efficacy, intensity and nature of the internal and external social manipulation of culture, productive resources, technology and socio-political groups. . . .

In the same way, the aspects related to the capacity for scientific and technological investigation are accentuated as this is the determining element — together with the power structure — for the capacity for action and manipulation, both inside the country and in its links with the outside world.[19]

The idea of 'politics,' in the sense defined above, also includes the idea of 'will' and 'objectives.' In this respect, Sunkel and Paz incorporate what was the prevailing value aspiration among those who criticized the 'perverse effects' (concentration of income and of life opportunities) of the pattern of capitalist development of the periphery:

the concept of development, thought of as a process of social change, refers to a deliberate process whose final aim is the equalization of social, political and economic opportunities, both at the national level and in relation with societies that have the highest standards of social welfare.[20]

In other words, neither Furtado nor Sunkel and Paz — the former in the revised 1975 edition of his book and the latter in 1970 — gave emphasis to the question of 'development styles,' or questioned, as Furtado was to do later on, the possibility and desirability of achieving the same standards of development as the industrialized countries. Greater homogeneity, yes; equality of conditions and opportunities between and within nations, yes; but the presupposition was: with an adequate policy,[21] it is possible and desirable to generalize what has already been achieved in terms of development in the industrially advanced countries.

The legacy of the notion of progress from the nineteenth century, and even earlier, is thus redefined by sifting through politics with egalitarian values. But it remains intact.

THE DEPENDENCY THEORIES[22]

At the same time as the ECLA theories were being developed and practical experience of industrialization policies was revealing the difficulties and conflicts caused by the process of socioeconomic transformation, 'counter-theories' were being produced. The practical consequences of the ECLA viewpoint — and the effective challenges of development — led policy-makers to propose:

1. The necessity of reinforcing the decision-making centers, which could articulate the 'deliberate will' to alter a situation diagnosed as unfavorable; hence, the reinforcement of the state and its modernization through the creation of 'public development agencies,' began to be considered preconditions for improvement in the standard of living of a nation;

2. the necessity of absorbing technical progress, initially through the investment of foreign capital, in order to assure industrialization, which was the means to materialize aspirations toward transformation;

3. the necessity of expanding domestic markets, in order to displace the axis of the main orientation of the economic system from outside to inside the country; to which end some redistributive measures should be supported. First and foremost, there should be an agrarian reform to coincide with the technical development of the rural economy. In this way, there would be a guarantee not only of markets for industrial products but also food supplies for cities, thus correcting the inflationary effects of industrialization policies, without forgetting what, since Prebish, had become fundamental: the incorporation of the cost of a decently remunerated labor force into the prices of export products.

Critiques of these policies came both from left and right. The right's criticisms can easily be understood. They questioned the benefits of industrialization. To support their point of view, they cited the advantages brought by the specialization of production and by free trade. To these critics, the ECLA theses were gross errors or arguments mischievously used by those who were in reality opposed to the capitalist system, but preferred to wage the battle little by little. First, they proposed illusions, like industrialization and Statism, and only later would they show their hand by openly advocating socialism.

The left criticized 'development theories' because they failed to clarify the most important thing: that there can be no 'development' without accumulation of capital, and that the latter is nothing more than the expression of a relation of class exploitation. This critique had in fact appeared before the ECLA theories. In its most primitive form (the version current in the 1930s and 1940s), colonialism and imperialism were denounced as 'brakes on development.' And, of course, for those who believe that there is a difference between 'growth' and 'development,' and that the latter presupposes autonomous decision-making by national systems and a more equitative distribution of the fruits of technical progress, imperialism is by its very definition an obstacle to development. Further still, until the mid-1950s the majority of foreign investments in Latin America were made to control the production and commercialization of agricultural products and raw materials. In general, foreign investors from the central countries preferred to sell finished industrial products to the periphery and to maintain only assembly or repair plants in the underdeveloped countries. From the 1950s on, however, and as a consequence of this same local reaction, foreign companies (conglomerates and multinationals) changed their strategy. The steps taken by the local business community (both public and private) during the Second World War when the flow of imports had been interrupted had shown that there were 'technical' possibilities of industrializing basic consumer goods and substituting imports. The participation of the state in the regulation of the economy and the protection of markets, as well as in beginning the production of basic industrial inputs (steel, petroleum, energy — depending on the country), along with the spreading of ideology favorable to development — all this had created a challenge to the old anti-industrialization policies of foreign capital. From then onwards, the competition for the peripheral countries' domestic markets made the belief in the 'anti-industrialization' role of foreign capital obsolete, at least in countries that represented important potential domestic markets.

It was during the transition from one international conjuncture to another (after the mid-1950s) that ECLA's efforts became repetitive and limited. At the same time, the idea that imperialist relations were founded on an alliance between the 'latifundia' (which, the more simplistic critics added, were 'feudal') and foreign capital became fallacious. The ECLA critique, however, was limited in only one respect: the big investors had begun to act in favor of industrialization. But this would neither fortify the national state (i.e. by amplifying the endogenous content of decisions), nor take for granted the widening market of popular consumers. Agrarian reform, redistributive wage policies, progressive taxation, etc., continued to appear in official rhetoric, especially after the OAS meeting at Punta del Este in 1961, although they did not adjust them to practice. Practice was characterized by the concentration of incomes, the modernization of the state apparatus, and the coupling of the state to multinational big business through policy proposals, joint-ventures, uniting the state productive sector to multinationals and so on.

It was in the mid-1960s when this situation was already taking shape, that the so-called 'dependency approach' gained strength as a 'counter-theory' or 'counter-ideology' that was critical of the formulations of ECLA and those of the traditional left. The left continued to view the alliance of 'latifundium and imperialism' as the major threat to development.

What were the principal theses put forward by the 'dependentistas'?

From the methodological point of view, dependency theories emphasized the historical and structural nature of the situation of underdevelopment and attempted to relate the production of this situation, as well as its reproduction, to the dynamics of capitalism's development on a world scale. The studies of Cardoso and of Frank[23] contained the first more globalizing formulations regarding the historical-structural nature of underdevelopment and critique of those who maintained that the 'obstacles to development' could be eliminated by the modernization of forms of behavior and expectations and by the multiplying and demonstrative effects caused by foreign investment. Emphasis was placed on analyzing the expansion of international capitalism for a better understanding of the nature of underdevelopment, and its structural relation with the external poles of development preceded 'dependency theories.' Some Marxist analyses, especially those of some historians[24] but also those of economists, stressed the connections between the expansion of capitalism and some of its 'distorted' effects on the periphery. It is worth remembering that the idea of 'external dependency' was widely accepted in ECLA's analyses. The coefficient of 'openness' in local economies, for example — repeatedly mentioned in ECLA analyses — measured the relation between imports and the gross national product.

What was specific to the dependency approach, then, was not the stress laid on 'external dependency,' which was thought of as shown above, but rather the analysis of the structural patterns that link central and peripheral economies. Thus, the notion of 'domination' was introduced. There was no attempt to use this concept to show, as Sunkel was to do later, that there should be a component of deliberate will, or of propositions, to characterize 'autonomous development.' On the contrary, the stress was laid on the negative: autonomous development is not probable, ceteris paribus. I do not want to discuss here whether this statement was correct or not. I would like simply to qualify, at the opposite (and discontinuous) pole from dependency theory, what was glimpsed was not autonomous development but: socialism. This, of course, was not made explicit by many writers, but the critique of the possibility of capitalistic 'development,' especially as far as 'national development' was concerned, had been the starting-point for analyses by Dos Santos, Quijano, Marini, Faletto and Cardoso, to mention only a few.

Furthermore, domination was not seen only as between nations: there was some attempt to show how the latter presupposes domination between classes. Not all the authors who would be considered 'dependentistas' put the matter in this way. However, the sociologists in particular (and all those just mentioned are sociologists) were preoccupied wth the specification of patterns of class exploitation and with the constitution of power structures and opportunities for political reaction. These would vary, depending on the extent of the structural link between the local and central economies. This linkage could be 'enclaves,' through national producers or by means of industrial development, which associated local entrepreneurial groups with multinationals. It was this latter form of dependency that, because it was current, attracted most attention: this was the 'new dependency.'

The discrepancies among the viewpoints of the various 'dependentista' authors were fewer, as were those between them and the ECLA thoroughbreds. The break was more in terms of the emphasis placed on the political and on the role of exploitation between classes to explain the characteristics of underdeveloped and dependent economies. This, of course, was not refuted by ECLA, but it was seen as less salient than exploitation among nations.[25]

On the basis of a recent synthesis by authors who were involved not in the elaboration of dependency theories, but rather in the verification of their consistency, I think it is possible to summarize the way in which the 'dependentistas' articulate their arguments in order to describe the situations to which they refer:

1. The situations are those in which there is financial and technological penetration by the developed capitalist centers.

2. This produces an unbalanced economic structure both within peripheral societies and between them and the center.

3. This leads to limitations on self-sustained economic growth on the periphery;

4. and favors the appearance of specific patterns of capitalist class relations.

5. These require modifications in the role of the state to guarantee both the functioning of the economy and the political articulation of a society that contains, within itself points of inarticulation and structural imbalance.[26]

However simplistic the above synthesis may be, it has the virtue of going further than the mere recognition of a relation of 'economic dependence.' It is certainly the basis of the 'dependentistas' analysis. But it is not limited to 'foreign penetration' (financial and technological), nor is this penetration seen as a 'discrete fact.' On the contrary, it is in the movement of expansion of capitalism, and thus through social relations of production that include exploitation and domination, that dependency is registered as a 'specificity.' What is this specificity?

On the one hand, from the economic point of view, there are limitations on self-sustained growth; it is not a question of the absence of locally owned technology in itself, or of the foreign debt alone; both these phenomena are indices of the weakness of capitalist accumulation on the periphery. Thus, it is not merely because one, central, nation-state dominates another peripheral, state that there is dependency. This is the expression (or simply the equivalent) of the international movement of capital, which, although it expands both formally and structurally, on a world scale, is achieved by the union of terms that are different and asymmetrical. The reproduction of capital implies its circulation on the international market, where there is a transfer of surplus value through unequal exchange, and an appropriation of surplus by the central bourgeoisies, owing to the deterioration of exchange terms (superficial aspects of dependency). Yet essentially, it implies the extraction of surplus value through the process of production. And this extraction, in the case of situations of dependency, raises the questions of control ('penetration') of local labor by foreign capitalists (an accidental characteristic, from the point of view of the direct extraction of surplus value, which can also be carried out by national capitalists). To assure the production circuit it also raises the issue of the transfer of the mass of accumulated resources from the periphery to the center. This is why 'deliberations' and 'decisions' made by the periphery encounter real obstacles in the structure of both world trade and the international productive system. It is obvious, moreover, that the analysis of these questions relates both to the dynamics of the relations among classes and to the relations among nation-states, as these are the concrete form of the articulation between local and international bourgeoisies.

On the other hand, from the social point of view, the incomplete and heterogeneous nature of industrialization on the periphery (remembering that an even more scandalous form occurs in agricultural export economies) produces effects that the 'dependentistas' have never tired of pointing out: bourgeoisies that are fulfilled only by associating in production with foreign capital and/or subordinating themselves in world trade; a proletariat that, as industrialization proceeds or as the enclaves and the agrarian and mining export sectors prosper, becomes distant from the rest of the popular mass; 'marginal masses' that are hard to absorb, even when industrialization prospers; a false 'petty bourgeoisie,' which corresponds much more to the formation of large strata of wage-workers (white-collar employees and technicians) generated by the oligopolistic and internationalized form of multinational enterprises than to the concept of 'petty bourgeoisie' that was applicable at the time of European competitive capitalism; a social structure in the countryside which, while subordinating the various classes and strata to big capital, gives rise to a wide spectrum of social relations of production — from peasants ('campesinos') tilling the soil by exploiting family labor-power to wage-earning rural workers, and including a whole range of intermediaries, tenants, semi-compulsory workers, etc.

Finally, on the political level, there emerges a Repressive Producer State. While it presents itself as national, and to this extent achieves consensus, it simultaneously organizes and implements capitalist exploitation. To do this it sometimes enters into conflict with the immediate interests of the local bourgeoisie and the multinationals and turns into a capitalist producer state itself. But at the same time the state becomes a key to the viabilization of private accumulation, to the guaranteeing of the mechanisms of distribution of income, of public spending, of the circulation of goods and the formation of finance capital, which make dependent-associated development viable. The state molds the style of exclusive development, which concentrates incomes and is based on a productive system that is responsive to the demand of high-income strata.

Each of the aspects mentioned here is treated in a different way by each of the authors who worked on the characterization of dependency. The controversies among them are considerable. In spite of this, it is not difficult to show that the dependency approach took on a distinct character in relation to earlier approaches. It is sufficient to re-read the opening pages of this essay, referring to the ECLA theoreticians, in order to confirm the fact that the 'problems' formulated by them are not the same as those formulated by the 'dependentistas' — even though the structuralist methodology is the same.

I shall not make unnecessary comparisons. Before concluding this section, however, I would like to refer to the incorporation by some 'dependentistas' of a theme that, while it was present in the work of some ECLA members, did not take on the dimension it represented on the scale of dependency: the cultural theme. Although 'cultural dependency' has almost always been attributed to the implications derived from the situation of dependency in general, at least one author among the first theoreticians of dependency — Anibal Quijano[27] — posed the question in direct terms. Many others refer, of course, to the question of technological autonomy, and some, such as Sunkel in his well-known article, mention the 'transculturation' caused by the internationalization of the productive system.[28] In any case, the dependency approaches not only stress the historical structural relation between the central and peripheral economies in terms of the expansion of capitalism, depicting it as a relation of exploitation between classes and nations that gives a certain specificity to dependent socio-political structures: they also show, at least in some of their formulations, that there are cultural factors directly linked to the maintenance of dependency.

The writers who formulated 'development theories,' as we have seen, also refer to the importance of a system of beliefs and values. But they do so either by making it a relatively independent variable, capable of generating new demands for the productive system, or by postulating the necessity of cultural autonomy. The 'dependentistas' also propose the ideal of cultural autonomy. However, they concentrate their analysis on the evil effects of cultural dependency. Because they are versed in Marxist theory, they refuse to pose the question of the historical subject of this autonomy without posing the question of the Revolution.

This is, perhaps, the Achilles heel of dependency theories: through what historical agent can dependency be overcome?

Prebish, more modest in his analysis, had answers for the questions he raised. It was not necessary to presuppose a Revolution, nor was there any need for a general critique of bourgeois domination. The modernization of the state apparatus in the peripheral countries would make it possible to unleash policies of industrialization, with control but not rejection of foreign capital, and to force the distribution of the benefits of technical progress in favor of workers and rural laborers. These would be the preliminary measures to ensure equality among nations. The battery of reforming policies would be completed by control of the mechanisms of world trade (UNCTAD was an expression of this later on), a policy of transfer of resources from rich to poor countries and access to technology for the underdeveloped.

Similarly, Furtado, in his early works, insisted that the most important thing is to increase productivity, which presupposes technological innovations and capital investment. The action of the state to discipline demand and to control the transfer of capital and technology without de-nationalizing the economy assures the possibility of development. Even Sunkel presupposes the autonomous power to 'equalize opportunities' and technological creativity in order to achieve 'autonomous development.'

And what about the 'dependentistas'?

Implicitly or explicitly, they either restrict themselves to stating the deformations (or, as ECLA called it, the 'perverse style' of development) generated by the expansion of capitalism on the periphery, or they propose socialism as an alternative. But this alternative does not take shape in the analysis with the same force as the critique of the situation of dependency; or, when it does, it is often anchored in the idea, which I have already criticized so many times,[29] of the inviability of capitalist expansion on the periphery, or of the extreme deformation caused by this process, given the 'growing marginalization' of the population, the existence of a 'lumpen' bourgeoisie, the 'development of underdevelopment' etc.[30]

It is a notable fact that, in spite of the undeniable force of some available characterizations of situations of dependency, subsequent political analysis should have lost hold of the vivacity of the real and taken refuge in a kind of eschatology that reaffirms the validity of the principle of Revolution and at the same time hides the feebleness of its proposals about the ways to arrive at it. This feebleness is hidden by the presentation of a catastrophic picture, which gives the illusion of leading to a radical transformation, given the growing economic impasses, even though it is impossible to obtain any more convincing profile of the class or classes capable of making this leap to negate the existing order.

At this point, it is worth returning to our opening speculations. The 'dependentistas,' like the ECLA group, are the inheritors of the belief in the rationality of history, and they are not afraid even when they discover the ugly face of progress. Was it not Marx who helped us to live with the idea that the positive pole — the accumulation of wealth — has its complement in the opposite pole — the accumulation of misery — and that the development of the opposition between the two comes about in such a way that, mysteriously, we arrive at the supersession of both poles, on condition that the negating force of the exploited destroys those who oppress it? And was not this moment of revolutionary explosion — of violence — even thought of as a precondition for the continuation of progress? Why, then, should the 'dependentistas' doubt and directly threaten the idea of development? Development, yes; capitalism, no. The distribution of the fruits of progress must be different. So must the appropriation of the means by which they are obtained. But the formal components — the model — are given by the very history of the development of capitalism. And the historical agents of this transformation — the exploited masses and, 'primus inter pares,' the proletariat — are also already given in advance by the same theory underlying the explanations of the 'dependentistas.'

The pride with which the 'dependentistas' can treat the ECLA theories at their own origins and say: 'Look, the state that you believe you can reform is the bourgeois state, the expression of all the evils of underdevelopment' is at the same time their Procrustean bed. If the ECLA members are insufficient, the 'dependentistas,' with all their love for a rational and integrated vision based on the experience of the European past, become surprisingly sterile: they proclaim what should not exist, but stop halfway to a concrete critique. They do not manage to make specific, except as a creed, what forces will make the transformation; and they fail to reconstruct totally the notion of the ideal to be achieved: the same development, for the benefit of other classes. As an alternative to ECLA's Reforming State, an image of a Reformed Society is presented; but we did not work out to the bitter end the two key questions that were looming on the horizon: what kind of society, and reformed by whom?

Here it is worth making a detour. At the climax of the reformulation of Latin American development theories, at the very moment when the 'dependentistas' were vigorously expounding on the effects of class exploitation and of international capitalism on the industrialization of the periphery, a challenging political option was being opened up in Latin America: Cuba, and more than that, 'Guevarism.'

The analysis derived from the Cuban revolution, especially Guevara's interpretation of it, placed both the idea of 'development' and the concept of the possibility of a dependent development in check. From 1961, when at the Punta del Este Conference Guevara criticized reformism as the 'revolution of the latrines,' until his Bolivian saga in 1967, when the 'theory of the "foco" ' succumbed heroically together with its founder, the truth is that revolutionary political practice placed the pale academic theories in check (though not checkmate). The political complement of the 'dependentista' theses derived not from the analysis they advanced, but from the graft made into them by Regis Debray's *Revolution in the Revolution*. And when Guevara fell, leaving to history the legacy of his moral integrity and revolutionary courage, and, in addition, the reflections of his *Diary*, Latin American political thought continued to be impotent. It failed to draw from these historical experiences the necessary conclusions. It went no further in reformulating the political questions: Allende was judged from the point of view of the need to destroy the state apparatus, rather than from the usefulness of that apparatus to the revolution. The question of the political theory of the proletariat was not frontally posed even if only in order to reaffirm it. It was simply endorsed in the abstract, and here and there amalgamated with the justification of the Tupamaro guerrilla, the Montoneros and the ERP, without going to the bottom of why Unidad Popular, the Torres' movement, etc., had failed.

The triumph of the nineteenth century in Latin American thought occurred not only in the economic field. In addition to the belief in the rationality of history, this thought also harbored, and still does, the belief in social progress. We have halted on the threshold of the decisive questions in order to maintain the convition that we do not need to ask who are the concrete bearers of the future.

CURRENT CONCERNS

The Fulfillment of Basic Needs

The idea that development aims not to accumulate capital, but to satisfy man's basic needs has become common in the documents produced by meetings of experts and government representatives. It is of course not a new one. However, in the form in which this idea was formulated in the last century by the socialist critique ('to each according to his needs, from each according to his possibilities'), the achievement of this desideratum would require, first, the modification of the structures of political domination and socioeconomic exploitation: equality and the fulfillment of needs would be possible only after the establishment, through the class struggle, of an egalitarian social order. This would lead to drastic political modifications, from social revolution to the establishment of the dictatorship of the proletariat and finally of a society without class domination (with a state reduced to the administration of public affairs). Furthermore, the idea of minimum needs based on a fixed parameter (so many calories, or so many square meters of housing) was repudiated from the point of view that needs were historically created, while their physical limits were seen to be practically non-existent.

What do today's champions of 'need-oriented development' have to say?

In whatever document is chosen, be it the Declaration of Cocoyoc, the Algiers Colloquium or, in the most egalitarian formulation available, the Uppsala Report on 'Alternative Development,' development with such characteristics should be:

> geared to meeting human needs, both material and non-material. It begins with the satisfaction of the basic needs of those, dominated and exploited, who constitute the majority of the world's inhabitants, and ensures at the same time the humanization of all human beings by the satisfaction of their needs for expression, creativity, equality and conviviality and to understand and master their own destiny.[31]

The search for a more 'balanced' style of development did not originate with the strategy that aimed at satisfying basic needs. Well before this kind of formulation gained 'momentum' in international discussion, since 1971, within the system of the United Nations itself there had already existed the so-called 'unified approach' to development. This approach attempted to correct the economistic excesses of the obsession with the growth of per capita GNP, through a kind of planning that could fulfill 'social,' if not 'basic' needs.[32] Through the search for a 'balanced' social and economic development, as Marshal Wolfe, one of the most critical participants of these kinds of studies, recognizes, much of the debate revolved around 'terminological innovations,' and even confusion:

> It cannot be accidental that the interminable discussions of development have left intact the confusion between development conceived as empirically observable processes of change and growth within social systems and development as progress toward the observer's version of the good Society.[33]

However, as is usual with progressive utopias, the generic formulation of the desire to satisfy 'basic needs' — whatever the criteria of the definition may be — led to the creation of a persistent critique of the degree of 'cumulative poverty' produced by the present expansion of the economic system, and made room for the adoption of new critical angles regarding the questions of development.

Limits of Growth and the Question of Non-renewable Resources

For some, 'savage development,' rather than the 'capitalist system' — as in the socialist critique or, less clearly, in that of Latin American 'dependentistas' — was to blame for the world's ills. Thus, the thorny problem of a more coherent and incisive critique of given social situations is avoided in international forums. Instead of capitalism being under fire, the deformations of a 'development style' are crucified. To this argument is added, laterally, the fact that the socialist systems in their actual expression have indeed improved their performance in meeting basic needs, but have not always respected the 'outer limits' that are the other obsession of those who formulated the new development strategy. This has now become more wide-ranging. If its center is still the fulfillment of basic needs, it is complemented by respect for ecological requirements, both in terms of an adequate relation between the local ecosystem and the outer limits that the preservation of present life and of future generations impose, and in terms of the use of adequate technology for rational exploitation of natural and human resources.

Following this line of concern, I believe one positive contribution has added something to the preceding debate about development. At the most general level of analysis, the notion of ecodevelopment, especially in Ignacy Sachs' formulation, synthesizes the new critical attitude toward the awareness that certain natural resources are finite (the theme of 'unrenewable' resources), and draws attention to the existence of outer limits, stressing the predatory and polluting forms of technological advance:

> Ecodevelopment is a style of development which, in each ecoregion, calls for specific solutions to the particular problems of the region in the light of cultural as well as ecological data and long term as well as immediate needs.[34]

In his elaboration, Sachs is not concerned with establishing the utopia of 'community development,' This other line of proposals has been the concern of Asian writers who were influenced by the importance of the peasant economy and by the inability of capitalist development to solve the social problems of the rural population. On the contrary, he stays within the tradition of thought that defends fundamental transformations of both technology and productive systems, but draws attention to the need to take into consideration the fact that, in the political conditions of the present-day world, without self-reliance, without the active participation, of the base of society and without 'appropriate' technology — which respects the outer limits and takes account of local human and natural resources — no reasonable development will be possible. In a sense, Sachs tries to make the notion of formal rationality compatible with that of substantive rationality. Rather than proposing Rational Technology as the motive force of the history of economic growth, he adopts a position according to which the 'reasonable' presupposes mutual adaptation between social and human objectives, available means and technical calculability.

It is perhaps in the tension between a Utopia that is 'communitarian,' and is participated at all levels, on the one hand, and the concern with a 'reasonable' attitude that can take account of the technical base necessary for development and its real limits — with the aim of fulfilling basic social needs — on the other, that there exists the richest contributions brought by this kind of approach to contemporary analysis of development problems.

Self-reliance

In the line of development as a product of community will (from the village level to that of the federation of the interests of underdeveloped and oppressed peoples and states), the key concept is that of self-reliance. In the line of analysis of the new instruments of economic development, there is a predominant stress on appropriate technology and the outer limits. At the core of the problem of meeting basic needs, there remains the question of the political reform needed to achieve this. Central documents for the understanding of these positions (which overlap) are the Dag Hammarskjold Report of 1975[35] and the project on the re-structuring of the international order.[36] In addition, there are the studies of the World Order Model Project.[37]

With the aim of being brief, I shall sum up here the key concepts of self-reliance on the one hand, and of appropriate technology on the other, and I shall lay stress on the proposals for the construction of a new world economic order that is the immediate political result of this strategy.

Self-reliance, as many have already said, does not mean autarchy or self-sufficiency. It implies the 'autonomous definition of development and life styles'[38] to stimulate creativity and to lead to a better use of the factors of production, and to reduce vulnerability and dependency, so that societies can rely more on their own forces of resistance, have confidence in themselves, to be dignified. Self-reliance applies both on a local (community) level and on a national and international level.

There is a clear value component in this definition. Such ideas as 'dignity,' 'self-confidence,' etc. imply choices. And this is no accident: against the 'logic of production' imposed by capital (whose greatest critic but also whose best analyst was Marx), the proponents of other development styles counterpose the 'logic of consumption,' with the aim of eradicating poverty and achieving a better distribution of resources among groups.[39] Together even with the idea of self-reliance is that of better distribution of resources and better organization of consumption styles. With this strategy, such a serious problem in today's world as the 'energy crisis' could more easily be thought through once more. Instead of producing more energy through devastating technical means, it would be possible to balance the use of it: 'we can choose low-energy standards of consumption and in this sense give preference to systems of housing, urban transport and the use of time that consume this low energy.'[40]

It is a logical consequence of this approach that obliges us to re-examine the concepts of technology. Almost tautologically, 'by adequate technology should be understood the invention and utilization of work processes and ways of organizing work that are best adapted to the particular circumstances — both economic and social — of a particular country or sector.'[41] The easy criticism, which says that these notions serve only to reinforce the prevailing mode of domination without changing the production conditions of underdeveloped countries, is energetically refuted by all those who adopt the idea of 'appropriate technology.' This does not signify backward technology, but rather a technological blend that, once again, should be oriented toward the reasonable, without losing sight of the basic aims of development (basic needs), without adopting a purely imitative model of what occurred in the industrialized countries, but also without despising science and the advance of the productive forces.[42] The implementation of technology development policies oriented by these concerns, and by the idea of a self-sustained development aiming to meet basic needs, requires a new model for international relations concerning research and development — one that can transfer technology but at the same time lead to the autonomous creation of technology and the filtering of the kind of technology to be absorbed. All this involves the problem of the training of specialized personnel and of policies that can avoid brain drains.

NOTES

1. Celso Furtado, *Teoria e política do desenvolvimento economico* (5th ed.) (São Paulo: Editora Nacional, 1975).

2. Osvaldo Sunkel and Pedro Paz, *El subdesarrollo latinoamericano y la teoria del desarrollo* (Mexico Siglo XXI Editores, 1970).

3. Raul Prebish, 'El desarrollo economico de la America Latina y algunos de sus principales problemas' (E/CN.12) 89/Rev. 1, 27 April 1950); reprinted in *Boletin Económico de America Latina*, vol. VII (1962), p. 1.

4. Hans Singer, 'The Distribution of Gains Between Investing and Borrowing Countries,' *American Economic Review*, vol. XL (May 1950).

5. Among the twentieth-century writers who reformulated the theory of international trade, it is indispensable to mention: Eli Heckscher, who in 1919 wrote an article on 'The Effect of Foreign Trade on the Distribution of Income,' republished in *Readings in the Theory of International Trade* (American Economic Association, Philadelphia, 1949); Bertil Ohlin, *International Trade* (Harvard University Press, 1933); and Aba Lerner, 'Factor Prices and International Trade,' *Economia* (February 1952). In the present-day neoclassical version, where arguments in favor of the equalizing effects of international trade are taken to an extreme, the most influential writer is perhaps Paul Samuelson, 'International Trade and the Equalization of Factor Prices,' *Economic Journal* (June 1948).

6. J. S. Mill, *Principles of Political Economy* (Ashley edn), p. 703.

7. 'During the cycle of economic expansion, a part of the profits was transferred as wage increases due to the competition between employers and the pressure exerted on them by workers' organizations. In the waning phase, when profits had to be squeezed, the portion transferred to these wage increases lost its fluidity in the center, owing to the well-known resistance to wage reductions. The pressure is thus displaced to the periphery, where it has more strength than would normally be the case, provided that wages and profits are not rigid because of the restrictions on competition. Hence, the less incomes can be squeezed in the Center, the more they have to be compressed on the periphery.' Prebish, op. cit., p. 7.

8. In a recent paper the arguments presented here are developed in greater details: see F. H. Cardoso, 'La originalidad de la copia: la CEPAL y la idea del desarrollo,' *Revista de la CEPAL*, (1977), published in English as 'The Originality of the Copy. ECLA and the Idea of Development,' Centre of Latin American Studies, University of Cambridge, working paper no. 27 (1977).

9. Furtado, op. cit., p. 92.

10. ibid., pp. 89-90.

11. ibid., p. 90.

12. Celso Furtado, *O mito do desenvolvimento económico* (Rio de Janeiro: Paz e Terra, 1974).

13. Furtado, *Teoria e política*, p. 93.

14. Furtado, *Teoria e política* and especially *O mito do desenvolvimento económico*.

15. Sunkel and Paz, op. cit., p. 24.

16. Anibal Pinto, 'La concentración del progreso técnico y sus frustos en el desarrollo latinoamericano,' *Trimestre Económico* (January/March 1965).

17. Sunkel and Paz, op. cit., p. 25.

18. ibid., p. 26. The reference to 'within a single country' appears to be related to 'internal colonialism'; however it remains unclear.

19. ibid., p. 38.

20. ibid., p. 39.

21. Emphasis is the editor's.

22. For reasons I have already explained in other papers (see, for example, F. H. Cardoso, 'Dependency Revisited,' (Institute of Latin American Studies, University of Texas, Austin, 1973); and 'The Consumption of Dependency Theory in the United States,' *Latin American Research Review*, vol. XII, no. 3 (1977), I prefer to avoid the pretentious term of dependency 'theory.' Nevertheless, succumbing to fashion, in this essay I shall also use the expression 'dependency theory.'

23. F. H. Cardoso, *Empresário Industrial no Brasil e Desenvolvimento Económico* (São Paulo: DIFEL, 1964), ch. I; A. G. Frank, 'The Development of Underdevelopment,' *Monthly Review*, vol. 18, no. 4 (1966).

24. See, for instance, Sergio Bagu, *Estructura Social de la Colonia* (Buenos Aires: Editorial El Ateneo, 1952), and Caio Prado, Jr., *Formacâo do Brasil Contemporâneo* (Colonia) (2nd ed.) (São Paulo: Editora Brasiliense, 1945).

25. It should be noted, in passing, that the discussion of the opposition between class and nation gave (and still gives) rise to polemics, misunderstandings, and clarifications. See, especially, F. Weffort, 'Notas sobre "Teoria da Dependência": teoria de classe ou ideologia nacional,' *Estudos CEBRAP no. 1* (São Paulo, 1971), and F. H. Cardoso, 'Teoria de dependência ou análises concretas de situaçoes de dependência?' *Estudos CEBRAP* no. 1 (São Paulo, 1971).

26. R. Duval and B. Russet, 'Some Proposals to Guide Research on Contemporary Imperialism,' unpublished, p. 2.

27. Anibal Quijano, 'Cultura y Dominacion,' *Revista Latinoamericana de Ciencias Sociales*, vol. 12, no. 3 (June-December 1971), pp. 39-56.

28. Osvaldo Sunkel, 'Capitalismo Transnacional y Desintegración Nacional en América Latina', *El Trimestre Econòmico*, no. 38, p. 2.

29. Cardoso, 'Consumption of Dependency Theory in the USA,' and J. Serra and F. H. Cardoso, 'As desventuras de dialética da dependência,' *Estudos CEBRAP no. 23* (São Paulo, 1978).

30. Frank, op. cit.

31. Dag Hammarskjöld Foundation, *Another Development* (Uppsala, Sweden, 1977), p. 10.

32. For an analysis of the various stages of the 'unified approach to development,' as well as an analysis of its successes and limitations, the best document is Marshal Wolfe's essay, 'Elusive Development: The Quest for a Unified Approach to Development Analysis and Planning: History and Prospects,' ECLA, P.V.S.H., 186 (Santiago, 1978).

33. Wolfe, op. cit., p. 80.

34. Ignacy Sachs, 'Environment and Styles of Development,' in William Matthews (ed.), *Outer Limits and Human Needs* (Dag Hammarskjöld Foundation, Uppsala, 1976).

35. 'Que Hacer,' *Development Dialogue*, nos. 1-2 (1975). For complementary documents, see the publication edited by W. F. Chagula, B. T. Feld, and A. Parthasarati: *Pugwash on Self-Reliance* (New Delhi, 1977).

36. Jan Turbergen (coordinator), *Reestructurarión del Orden Internacional (RIO)*, Club of Rome Report (Fondo de Cultura Económica, Mexico, 1977). See also the series of essays published in homage to Turbergen by Anthony J. Dolman and Jan van Ettinger: *Partners in Tomorrow, Strategies for a New International Order* (E. P. Dutton, New York, 1978).

37. See Richard Falk, *A Study of Future Worlds* (The Free Press, New York, 1975). In this paper I shall not consider the ideas of Falk and associates. In a suggestive critical review, Medina Echeverria has said, however, that these studies, owing to their synthetic power, the specific type of projective sociology and the explicit recognition of their utopian nature, present advantages over others of the same kind in a more 'cybernetic' or bureaucratic-institutional version. See Jose Medina Echeverria, 'Las prospuestas de un neuvo órden economico internacional en prospectiva,' *ECLA*, D.S. 1148 (November 1979).

38. Hammarskjöld Report.

39. Celso Furtado was one of the first Latin Americans to review his analytical instruments and reformulate the question of the relative autonomy of Demand: see already quoted books.

40. I. Sachs, 'El ambiente humano,' in Turbergen, op. cit., p. 458.

41. Alexander King and A. Lemma, 'Investigación Cientifica y Desarrollo Tecnológico,' in Turbergen, op. cit., p. 414.

42. See Amilcar Herrera, 'An Approach to the Generation of Appropriate Technology for Rural Development,' Report to UNEP (mimeo). Also see the contributions of Amilcar Herrera and Jorge Sabato to the Campinas Symposium on Technology, São Paulo, 1978.

7

FROM THE UGLY AMERICAN TO THE UGLY EUROPEAN:
The Role of Western Europe in North-South Relations

Constantine V. Vaitsos
Athens University, Greece,
and Sussex University, UK

INTRODUCTION AND MAIN ARGUMENTS

Up to the late 1960s, it was not by building on its colonial heritage, but by reconstructing itself from the war devastations, and by promoting the partial devolution of power back to Western Europe, that the old continent contributed indirectly and positively to various concerns that developing countries confronted in their external sector. Yet, from the present decade, and again as a result of changing European needs and interests, Western Europe might prove to be one of the main stumbling blocks to a number of developmental needs of the LDCs in their relations with the industrialized countries. In several important areas, Europe may even create conditions less attractive for the 'South' than the latter experiences in its relations with the two super-powers. The contours of the North-South conflict find Western Europe in one of their crucial epicentres.

The indirect and positive contribution during the 25 years that

Author's Note: I am grateful to Philippe de la Saussay for his research assistance and hard work in the preparation of this paper. I am also indebted to my colleagues, B. Schaffer, R. Green, R. Jolly and H. Singer, for their incisive comments and suggestions. The responsibility for any remaining shortcomings, obviously, remains with me.

followed the Second World War was largely the outcome of two factors. First, in the process of re-establishing its economic base after the war, Western Europe has been promoting a multi-polar world economic system. The dominance of the USA was partly reduced to the advantage of the rest. A more diversified economic system spreads out the contents of economic power and, thus, it dilutes the latter's political influence. Second, the continent's growing economic needs added to the aggregate demand for resources. This process, in turn, provided additional options and degrees of economic maneuverability for the LDC net exporters of primary goods.

In other ways, though, Western Europe, particularly the larger European countries, was trying to preserve part of the economic character and privileges of its colonial past (for example, in the first and second Yaoundé Conventions). Its economic expansion meant its continuing presence in areas where old colonial ties and present economic interests rendered her an obstacle to necessary change in the Third World.[1] Furthermore, Europe, like the other industrialized countries, was quick to appreciate and exploit a central axiom of international economic relations: the distribution of gains from trade and investment is not independent of the power scenarios of the international market mechanism.

After the late 1960s Europe entered into a new phase of relations. Among the complex — sometimes conflicting and at other times re-enforcing — factors that led to this new position, three stand out. First, in trade relations, Western Europe constitutes the weak side of the OECD triangle: USA-Japan-Western Europe. The latter is the only one that is facing large and growing trade deficits with both the others. The nature of such North-North conflictive positions has a direct bearing on Western Europe's orientation and degree of flexibility towards the growing demands of the South. Second, the same structural resource deficiencies that pushed Europe towards its colonial adventures in the past persist even more acutely today. This creates a structural weakness for Western Europe which, on account of prevailing policies, brings it, as no other industrialized region — including the case of Japan — into direct conflict with the aspirations of a number of resource rich developing countries. Finally, although Western Europe in general and the EEC in particular constitute by far the largest overall trade partners in the LDCs, the old continent is the least integrated area with the growing industrial capabilities of, and aspirations for, manufacturing exports from the developing countries.

For these and related reasons to be analyzed below, and despite the rise of vocal progressive political forces in Western Europe — often effective in alleviating some of the repercussions of repressive regimes in the Third World as far as human rights are concerned — the old continent is likely, in the future, to play a negative role in many key developmental strategies with external sector implications. The rise of progressive political forces in Western Europe, or elsewhere, constitutes a large part of political history, and understanding and evaluating them, a large part of political science. But the extent of international solidarity may prove to be severely limited in those areas (as in our subject matter) where foreign politics constitute a condensed form of key economic interests. Here Western Europe is seen as being in direct opposition to many LDC aspirations, regardless of what political parties dominate Western Europe.[2]

However, an important qualification needs to be made at the outset. The response of Western Europe to the LDCs for a restructuring of the world economy is not only highly complex, but also diverse. Important differences exist, depending on the country one analyzes and its historical ties with the rest of the world. Similarly, important differences exist between distinct class and group interests, as well as within such classes and groups. Furthermore, diverging positions are taken by different Western European economic and social actors, depending on the issues involved. Finally, the differences among various European positions become even more specific, and in a sense more meaningful, if one differentiates between long-term goals — for example, stable resource supplies and competition with other developed countries — and shorter-term objectives, such as adjustment policies to deal with production inefficiencies confronting LDC manufacturing exports.

Thus, there is no single and uniform European position vis-à-vis the LDCs, as there are also, of course, no uniform unique needs on the part of the 'Third World.' Instead, there is a set of complex considerations with conflicting objectives and vested interests depending on the circumstances, time horizon and specific issues involved. In the pages that follow, we will try to point out such important differences between various Western European interests. Nevertheless, and in view of the length of this article, we will also need to limit ourselves and concentrate on the overall position of

Western European countries — as expressed over time by their governments — as well as on common positions of a number of countries, like those taken by the EEC.

THE POSTWAR EVOLUTION OF
EUROPE'S RELATIONS WITH
AND ATTITUDES TOWARDS THE LDCs

The First 25 Years

Right from the initial discussion of the Atlantic Charter between Roosevelt and Churchill in 1941, and as exemplified in the official US circulation of the 'Proposal for Trade and Employment Expansion' in 1945, the Europeans — particularly the main colonial powers — faced the imposition of US terms on their future relations with the LDCs. The US orientation, stemming from that country's own interests — particularly its efforts to contain Soviet expansionism — involved two broad principles: the promotion of formal political — as distinct from economic — independence for the colonies; and the reorganization of the world economy by reducing preference zones and by promoting relatively more open trade relations.[3]

Western Europe attempted to resist this US interference in the former's relations with the Third World, but often failed. On crucial issues, such as in the Suez crisis of 1956, major Western European countries not only did not achieve negotiated settlements for their interests, but had to accept defeat and forced withdrawal. Nevertheless, the Western Europeans continued to maintain an active presence in North-South relations, partly building on their ex-colonial ties, and particularly so in the sphere of foreign direct investments and trade. Thus, by 1967 two-thirds of the number of French and Belgian subsidiaries in the LDCs were located in Africa and especially in French-speaking Africa.[4] An approximately similar proportion of the number of UK subsidiaries in the LDCs were in the English-speaking countries of Africa and Asia.[5] Although a transnationalization process began to take place in the foreign investment patterns of European transnationals — particularly with manufacturing operations moving toward Latin America — the newly independent states in Africa and Asia, from

India to Mali, found themselves heavily controlled by enterprises from the former colonial powers. The latter accounted for more than two-thirds and often above 80 percent of the foreign investments registered in their ex-colonies.[6]

The European country that most fervently attempted to perpetuate economic privileges of the old colonial era was France. In the meeting in Venice at the end of 1956, France included its economic interests over her overseas dependencies as part of the price of her own participation in the EEC. Later, with the signing of the Yaoundé I Convention, France transformed — for the benefit of the French budget — the status of her economic neo-colonies into a similar one for the EEC. The economic disintegration of Africa was conditioned by the separate treatment between English and French-speaking former colonies.[7] France also appears to be the only European country that, up to the present date, has maintained more or less intact her EEC share of trade with her ex-colonies.[8]

Despite such efforts, the dynamics of market expansion and industrial growth and the relative resources availability in the LDCs are proving to be far more potent factors in determining the nature and magnitude of European relations with the LDCs. An anonymous piece of sixteenth-century writing, found in Peru, concluded the following: 'Where there are mines, there are soldiers and consequently generals. And where there are mines one can also find the gospel and hence God. In the places where there are no mines, there are no generals nor God.' The equivalent story applies nowadays with respect to markets and natural resources in the LDCs. Where either or both of them are present, there are business opportunities which will attract the transnational enterprises. Their corporate strategies, and the long-run economic and technological ties they can create between host countries and specific developing countries (DCs), can radically change the composition of economic relations.

The changes that have occurred in the composition of Western Europe's external economic relations involved such differentials in market growth rates, industrial capabilities and resources availabilities in the LDCs. For example, if petroleum is excluded, Africa — with the predominant presence of ex-European colonies — dropped in its share of LDC exports to the EEC from just below half of the total in 1955 to less than one-third in 1975. Instead, Latin America and South-East Asia (the latter specially in the

1970s) took the lead in EEC and European imports. If the case of petroleum is included, then the Middle Eastern share increases dramatically. Equivalent changes have also taken place in the export structure of Western Europe, particularly toward the petroleum producers as well as the newly industrializing LDC countries.

Within the political sphere, the main actors in determining North-South relations were the USA and USSR, or, better, the former as a reaction to the latter. In contrast, Western Europe played — at best — the role of a supporting actor. During those years, political issues related to the Cold War were prevalent. In contrast, the economic significance of the LDCs was, with the exception of being the source for some essential primary inputs, rather limited. Also, the cost of administering a foreign policy on development issues was quite inexpensive. In contrast to the Marshall Plan for Europe, up to 1955 the cost of US development assistance to the Third World had scarcely averaged a few million dollars per year.[9]

In the mid-1950s and early 1960s, two sets of, again, political issues linked to the USA-USSR rivalry significantly increased the industrialized countries' commitment to development matters. The US contribution to aid jumped from a few million dollars, to more than US$3 billion per year by the decade of the 1960s.[10] These political issues referred, first, to the coming independence of several ex-colonies. The first black African country, Ghana, achieved its independence in 1956. Conditioning the political evolution of the newly independent states, in competition with the USSR, was a key concern for the USA. The second political event was the Cuban Revolution, which linked the question of economic development to that of continental security. This, in turn, influenced greatly the US position towards the LDCs. In all of these crucial cases, the effective political role of Western Europe was basically peripheral, if present at all.

The economic realities, on the other hand, presented a completely different picture for Western Europe. The latter, although maintaining a low political profile towards the Third World (except for some aberrations like the Yaoundé I Convention), continued to increase its economic commitment to the LDCs significantly. In so doing, Western European economic actors challenged the hegemony and even surpassed in various cases the activities of US firms. To this we now turn.

The Extent and Composition of
Europe's New Encounter with the LDCs

With the beginning of the 1970s, a new scenario in North-South relations began to evolve, and a novel role for Europe has been undertaken. With this scenario economic conditions and economic, rather than traditional political rivalries, both North-North and North-South, have become much more central.[11] In this context, Europe's evolving interests with respect to its prosperity and economic survival bring it to the forefront of economic rivalry.

Western Europe's Expanding
Presence in the LDCs

The economic and psychological demands of European postwar reconstruction, and the rapid expansion of intra-EEC trade after the Rome Treaty, gave some Europeans an illusion of privacy. Yet, far from demonstrating insularity, European countries experienced a rapid economic expansion into the rest of the world.

Even if trade between EEC members is excluded, Europe appears to be by far the largest customer of the rest of the world, and the largest exporter of goods. By the mid-1970s the EEC accounted for well over one-fifth of the world's exports and/or imports (excluding the volume of intra-EEC trade). With the external trade of non-EEC Western European countries, Western Europe rapidly approaches one-third of overall world trade. In contrast, the equivalent share of US imports dropped to 13.9 percent by 1975, and the Japanese increased to 8.3 percent.

With respect to the LDCs, the EEC represents their main supplier and their main export market. By 1975 the EEC exported to the LDCs 60 percent more than the equivalent value of trade from the USA and imported from them over 73 percent more than the USA. Much larger differences existed between the EEC-LDC trade and that of Japan or the COMECON countries with the LDCs. So, at least as far as trade is concerned, the EEC has a higher orientation, and more at stake in what happens in the Third World than any other country or group of countries in the industrialized world.

For Western European interests, this trade relationship with the Third World takes on particular importance since, excluding intra-EEC trade, the LDCs constitute the main external source of supply for the EEC, accounting for 45 percent of the Community's external imports. Aggregate published statistics on the participation of LDCs in world trade tend to obscure their strategic importance in the prosperity of Western Europe. Among the EEC countries, West Germany registers the highest volume of trade with the LDCs.

In the area of foreign direct investments in the LDCs during the 1970-76 period, although the reported overall flows from the USA accounted for about $22 billion and the EEC's for slightly over $13 billion,[12] the Community's flows of foreign investments in the Third World manufacturing sector matched, if not surpassed, those of the USA. The leader is again West Germany, with about one-third of the EEC total, followed very closely by the UK. France is falling progressively behind in foreign direct investment in the LDCs, while Holland in about to match France in the volume of foreign investment flows to the Third World. Even in areas traditionally dominated by US interest, like Latin America, the sales volume in the manufacturing sector of Western European controlled firms in the mid-1970s was closely rivalling that of US firms.[13]

Thus, in practically every major economic field (including foreign aid, where the EEC contribution exceeded the US equivalent by 1976), the presence of Western Europe is central if not dominant in the LDCs' external sector.

The Separability of Power
Elements

The elements of power become more distinguishable in our times, even if countries try to link such elements in order to improve their overall performance.[14] This separability is felt particularly acutely by Western Europe, with its fundamental and dual vulnerability: its economic survival depends on Middle Eastern oil, and its military survival requires the US arms umbrella. When either is seriously challenged, Europe is ready to compromise.[15]

There is another area of European dependence, that in the medium and longer run will seriously affect relations with the South. This involves Western Europe's relative lack of mineral and commodity resources. Unlike the USA, the USSR, Canada and Australia, who are net overall resource exporters, Europe's prosperity — like that of Japan — depends significantly on its continuous and secure access to these resources from the rest of the world. Both the absolute level and the growth rate of raw material imports (excluding petroleum and petroleum products) by the EEC have been much higher than the US equivalents in the 1970s.

With respect to the composition of Western Europe's imports from the LDCs, petroleum and petroleum products accounted for well over half of the total import bill in the mid-1970s. The second most important group of products was commodities (close to or over one-fifth of all imports from the LDCs), while, interestingly enough, mineral imports were trailing behind manufactured imports from the LDCs. The distinguishing characteristics of the US import structure from the LDCs as compared with the main Western European economies are: its much heavier absolute and relative reliance on manufactured imports (the USA imports 75 percent more from the LDCs than do West Germany, the UK and France put together), and its much lesser dependence on minerals.

On account of this resource dependence, Western Europe is likely to play a significantly negative role in the efforts of those (Third World) countries that will try to organize and control the production, pricing and (especially) the processing of primary inputs.[16] But, it will suit Europe's interests, particularly if aggregate demand picks up again in the West, to help stabilize — even if at slightly higher monetary and un-indexed prices — the export earnings of Third World primary producers in order to avoid the disruptive effects that other alternatives might imply for the European economies. An example of the kind of proposal to originate from Western Europe in this area is the recent suggestion by the West German Chancellor to include the copper of Zaire and Zambia in the European Community export earnings stabilization scheme.[17] This could offer certain short-run concessions to the ailing economies of those two countries, drawing them closer to the area of direct European influence.[18] But, it will also provide the coup de grace for CIPEC (the association of the main developing country copper producers), since a wedge will be driven between the African and the Latin American copper producers.

The governments of Western Europe will certainly be among the strongest supporters for increased exploration and investment in the extraction of primary products in the world; they will take a leading role in pressing for guarantees and inducements for the investments of transnational enterprises, and will foster mechanisms that — in the face of the nationalization of assets in the LDCs — will create alternative means of control over the extraction and marketing of these resources. As will be seen below, one of the

means for achieving this will be the attempt to keep the processing
of primary inputs out of the LDCs.

The Implications of Not Being a
Super-power and of Having Small or
Medium-Sized Domestic Markets

Western Europe is not itself a super-power, nor does it include one.
Consequently, it cannot rely on the international imposition of its
will simply through the exercising of its power. The USA and
USSR, although increasingly conscious of their own limitations,
can — in certain areas — still afford to do so. It will therefore be in
Europe's interest to promote certain stabilizing rules and institutions for international economic relations, which it will seek to
shape so as to suit European interests.

Thus, the countries of Western Europe will be strong supporters
for establishing set rules of behavior for the South in its relations
with the North, especially in trade and in the conduct of the South
vis-à-vis the transnational enterprises (TNEs). In particular, the nationalization of foreign privately held assets, the international settlement of disputes and arbitration, and enhanced opportunities
for European TNEs to participate in new projects of resource exploitation in the developing countries will be high on the European
agenda. In fact, the EEC could become the vehicle for imposing the
first multilateral mandatory code of conduct on host governments
in their relations with the TNEs, through the LDC members of the
pending negotiations for the extension of the Lomé Convention.
This is the complete inverse of what is being discussed in the United
Nations family, namely a code of conduct for the TNEs. Also, the
weight of the EEC institutions might be used collectively to exact
similar concessions from countries that attempt to obtain special
relations or associations with EEC members.[19]

In mineral and commodity trade, the main Western European
countries will, for the reasons presented above, continue to oppose
public intervention in international markets. The meaning of intervention in this context is strictly limited to the public sector,
since a very significant part of this trade is controlled by intra-firm
transactions among affiliates that belong to the same TNEs.[20] In
these cases, the 'market' is superseded by administrative decisions
taken in the corporate headquarters of a relatively small number of
TNEs.

Although the official positions of the European 'hard-liners' coincide, at present, with those of the USA and Japan in this area, their interests might diverge in the future. The USA — excluding petroleum — is a net resource-exporter. Public intervention in the international markets of certain goods might prove to its definite advantage. Already, a proposal has been formally made by US senators and has long been considered by the Department of Agriculture to promote, through a US initiative, the creation of a wheat export cartel.[21] Japan, on the other hand, has already promoted intergovernmental long-run resource supply contracts. The participation of Japanese private firms is often undertaken in consonance with policies set by the Ministry of International Trade and Industry, and after broad agreements have been reached among public authorities. Thus, the European hard-liners might develop into OECD hard-liners in this area in the future.

Further implications arise when one considers jointly the relatively small or medium size of European domestic markets and the presence of large TNEs whose origins and corporate overheads are both concentrated in their home countries. First, since European TNEs obtain a substantial, if not dominant, part of their earnings from their foreign operations, they are likely to intervene more actively to try and influence the foreign policy formulation of their governments in favor of their private interests. Second, the smaller the home market, the stronger will be the tendency to link international expansion and exports to foreign direct investments through a tied structure of inter-affiliate relations. Empirical evidence confirms, in the case of foreign subsidiaries operating in Latin America, that TNEs originating in small European countries (like Switzerland, Sweden and Holland) had a much higher rate of tying inter-affiliate trade transactions to their parents' home economy than either the US firms or those belonging to the larger European countries.[22] Third, the asymmetrical distribution of business activities — consolidated production and sales being spread out internationally while the corporate overhead is concentrated in the home country — implies a much more acute exercising of transfer pricing practices among TNEs that have a small home market. Through such corporate accounting practices, the rest of the world contributes not only to capital earnings in the home country of the TNEs, but also directly — through fiscal losses of the host economies — to the level of income, size of employment and overall level of activities in the home economy of the parent firms.

The Effects of Faltering Economic Growth and Increased Competition Among the DCs and their Economic Actors

For Western Europe, particularly within OECD, the persisting economic slowdown and the combination of structural unemployment and inflation in the 1970s have seriously limited both the willingness and the capacity of governments to negotiate constructively over the proposals presented by the LDCs. This is not simply the effect of a few well-organized groups being able to articulate their cause, given the relatively small margins by which ruling parties have come to power in Europe, and the medium size of each individual economy. There are structural causes, and the following two are central.

First, the economic problems that Western Europe faces vis-à-vis the other industrialized countries will prove to be crucial for its relations with the LDCs. In the triangular relationship between the EEC, North America and Japan, the former, as noted earlier, is the only one that registers significant and increasing commercial deficits with both of the other vertices of the triangle. In fact, the proclaimed commercial 'threat' of the Third World manufactured exports to the EEC turns out, at the aggregate and sectoral levels, clearly to be the residual of Europe's *other* trade relations with the rest of the industrialized countries.[23]

The second crucial issue is the development of certain production conditions which generate structural unemployment in the industrialized countries if inflation is to be held under certain levels. It has been observed for some time that the share of manufacturing output and its employment tend to fall as per capita real income reaches a certain level in a country. In the case of Western Europe, even the absolute level of industrial employment started to decrease by 1970. This took place before either the LDC 'manufactures export boom' or the economic slow-down in the industrialized countries began. Employment in the EEC manufacturing sector stood at about 30,500,000 in 1970, dropped to less than 30,100,000 in 1973 and reached 28,352,000 by 1976. In contrast, manufacturing employment in North America continued to increase up to and including 1974.[24] For countries like the UK, though, the decline in manufacturing employment had started from the 1960s. Furthermore, more disaggregate data at the sectoral level indicate that the percentage decrease in the employment share of the sectors in which the LDC export growth was the highest tended to be (1) more substantial for many European countries than for the USA and Japan, and (2) higher during the 1960s than in the first half of the 1970s — before, that is, the LDC export thrust took place.[25]

Such structural conditions in the Western European economies are likely to afford very limited political elasticity for negotiated concessions to the LDCs. Regardless of the political parties in power, the combined effects of large trade deficits and increased competition from the other countries of the North and secular unemployment problems at home will severely limit the scope for the Third World to obtain better conditions in its negotiations with Western Europe. A taste of what is in store for the LDC relations with Western Europe in this area became evident during the recent round of GATT negotiations.

The Shaping of Future Western European Relations with the LDCs

Western Europe's Position on a New Industrial Division of Labour

In the manufacturing sector there are two product groups that, in quantitative terms, have most potential for substantial relocation of industrial activities to Third World countries. In both, Western European interests are particularly in conflict with the aspirations for a larger LDC participation. These two areas involve the processing of unwrought non-ferrous metals, and the production of primary and secondary petrochemical products.

The first category (which includes metals such as copper, tin, lead, zinc, nickel, bauxite, etc.) ranks second only to petroleum exports from the LDCs. The prior processing of these products in the Third World encounters two fundamental difficulties. First, the industrialized countries have set up a cascading structure of tariff and non-tariff barriers which strongly discriminate against industrial operations in the LDCs. Second, the technology, and in many cases the commercialization, of products from downstream processing of these metals are often controlled by DC-based transnational enterprises. The latter will object strongly, and only reluctantly will transfer their processing skills to the LDCs, since such a relocation of production might threaten the companies' strategic concern in controlling their vertically integrated activities.

According to data prepared by the Secretariat of UNCTAD, the primary candidate for a conflict between the North and the South in this area is the EEC. It accounts for well over half of the LDC exports of unwrought non-ferrous metals to the industrialized world, excluding the centrally planned economies. US and Japanese imports from the LDCs account, individually, for less than one-third of the volume of EEC imports in this area. Furthermore, contrary to what is happening in Japan — where long-run government planning and policy commitments will, in the future, be moving smelting and other processing activities to the LDCs[26] — Western Europe continues to leave the initiative in this area basically to its transnational enterprises. For the reasons mentioned above, the latter will in general strongly object to any serious activity relocation to the LDCs.

In the case of petrochemicals, a major threat to existing DC-based operations appears to be brewing. This is due to the investment plans of the oil-producing countries, including the newcomers, UK and Mexico.[27] Such plans could lead to 'the biggest shifts in the international division of industrial labour ever seen in any industrial branch.'[28] It could also, though, lead to 'a lot of rusting chemical cathedrals in the desert.'[29] More than the availability of technology and investment funds, the key issues involved here are who controls the (import) markets, and how excess capacity will affect prices and the need to 'organize' the markets.[30]

For reasons of geographic proximity — vital in many difficult-to-transport petrochemicals — Europe's position will be central vis-à-vis the Middle Eastern producers. By June 1977 the Arab League representatives had already proposed a tariff arrangement for the EEC market comparable to the GATT multifibre agreement. Except for pollution considerations, the European reaction has been far from welcoming to the prospect of having competitive petrochemical plants on the other side of the Mediterranean.

Manufactured Exports from the LDCs and the 'Commercial Threat' to Western Europe

The dramatic increase in the rate of manufactured exports from some LDCs, which started in 1972, and the repercussions of economic slowdown in the OECD countries from 1974 created major political reactions and affected attitudes towards the LDCs in the industrialized countries. Concern for Third World development is seen as being directly in conflict with the interests of the DCs and their commercial, income and employment levels.[31] Discriminatory trade practices erected against the LDCs, particularly through non-tariff barriers, have proved to be much more common and powerful than the General System of Preferences. Official positions, even among the more progressive European governments, began to harden. Although the LDC export growth (1) was concentrated in a relatively small number of products,[32] (2) originated basically from less than a handful of countries,[33] and (3) had several economic actors from the DCs directly involved and reaping benefits,[34] it was considered a dangerous omen of what the future could hold for a direct North-South conflict.

To put the size and importance of the commercial 'threat' of LDC manufactured exports into perspective, they should be contrasted with the EEC's GDP. Such LDC exports, which, it should be noted, include components and other inputs originating from Europe, accounted for less than one per cent of the GDP of the EEC countries. The same was also true for the US economy. Furthermore, it needs to be understood that, despite increased industrial activity in the Third World, its mid-1970s' share in manufacturing value added (not production) of the world's total had hardly changed from the 1948 figure: in the immediate postwar period, it was 7.3 percent, and in 1973 it was 7.6 percent.[35]

With respect to employment, the presumed export 'threat' from the Third World has attracted particular attention, mainly because such exports are concentrated in a narrow product range, and frequently affect very specific and depressed geographic regions within the industriaized countries. Yet, cyclical and — more importantly, as it was noted above — structural reasons in employment composition and level in the DCs have been shown to outweigh by far any employment effects that LDC exports might have had.[36]

The USA and Japan, on the one hand, and Western Europe on the other, differ greatly in the composition of their imports. Among OECD members, Western Europe is the area least integrated with the manufacturing export activities of the LDCs. Among the major European countries, France is the least integrated. The most comprehensive and up-to-date published information in this area has been collected by the Secretariat of the United Nations Conference on Trade and Development (UNCTAD). It concerns the exports of 422 groups of manufacturing products which accounted for the bulk of such LDC exports during the 1970s. According to these data, the USA and Japan obtained, respectively, 16.7 and 18 percent of their world manufacturing imports from the LDCs in 1976. In contrast, for each one of the EEC countries the corresponding figure was less than 10 percent and for most of them it was in the 5 percent range. The difference between the EEC and the USA-plus-Japan becomes much more pronounced for the 85 faster growing categories of LDC exports. Finally, growth rates in the share of LDC manufacturing exports as compared with world exports destined for the markets of the industrialized countries in the 1970s were spectacular for Japan, high for the USA, West Germany and the Netherlands, and totally insignificant or zero for the UK and France.

The reasons behind this type of European performance can be read from two levels of analysis. First, the structure of Western Europe's aggregate import statistics in manufactures indicates that the nature of its production ties it basically to the industrial activities of its constituting economies (intra-European trade and to the other OECD countries (mainly the USA and Japan) than to the LDCs. Second, the corporate strategies of European-based TNEs demonstrate, in certain specific areas of locational diversification, very marked differences from those followed by their US and Japanese counterparts.

First, we present the case of aggregate trade composition. The major exporter of manufactures to the EEC countries is another EEC member, West Germany. In 1976 she exported to the rest of the EEC about four times the total value of manufactures that the whole of the Third World together exported to the whole EEC area, including Germany. Also, in the 1970-76 period the rate of growth of LDC manufactured exports to the EEC, although very high, was still smaller than that of Japan to the EEC. Furthermore, although the growth rate of LDC manufactured exports to the EEC was higher during the 1970s than that of the USA, the latter still exported nearly twice the total equivalent LDC volume. As a result of the above, and given the performance of European countries in their own export activities, the EEC runs a continuously growing trade deficit of manufactures with Japan and a rapidly decreasing surplus in this sector with North America. Instead, the EEC's trade balance of manufactures with the Third World has been positive and significant. The previous figures strongly support the thesis that the 'commercial threat' from the LDCs' exports of manufactured products to Europe turns out, at the aggregate, to be the residual of the latter's import needs for the other industrialized countries.[37]

As for the activities of the transnationals, the case of Western Europe is, again, largely different from that of Japan and the USA. Foreign direct investments in the LDC manufacturing sector have been basically local market-oriented, regardless of the country of origin of the parent firms. The European-originated transnationals, though, have characteristically had an even lower share of LDC manufacturing exports to the industrialized countries. This is so even in sectors such as electronics and parts of metalworking and other labour-intensive activities, in which a number of US and Japanese TNEs have been active for a decade or more. Recent empirical studies undertaken in various Western European countries confirm this corporate behavior for the UK firms (where manufacturing exports are largely related to resource-processing activities), as well as for the continental European TNEs. In addition to European retailing firms with foreign procurement in clothing, the only recently developing exception in other industrial branches concerns some West German firms and, in certain specific cases, some Dutch enterprises.

Even in those cases in which Western European firms (led by the German enterprises)[38] increased their participation in subcontracting activities in the LDCs, the scope of their activities appeared quite limited in comparison with the US and Japanese firms. For example, more than 50 percent of the EEC imports from the LDCs in electronics in 1975 originated from two far-away-from-Europe city-states: Hong Kong and Singapore.[39] Although some use was made of Tunisia and Morocco, the Europeans scarcely made any serious commitment to their LDC neighbors, preferring 'fly-by-night' investments in the two Asian city-states mentioned. This contrasts with the intensive and studied cultivation of political and economic contacts of Japan in South-East Asia[40] (including, in the future, the People's Republic of China[41]) as well as of the USA in the border industries in Mexico and in Taiwan. The potential labor reservoir for European sub-contracting in the South-Eastern Mediterranean (Egypt) and in the North-Eastern Mediterranean (Turkey) have scarcely been touched. It should be noted, though, that the stronger links established in the manufacturing sector between the USA, Japan and the LDCs might generally involve intra-firm trade among affiliated enterprises. The transfer pricing practices and foreign control implications of such transactions might still leave the LDCs with highly questionable net benefits.

In conclusion, Western Europe's orientation toward industrial integration through sub-contracting with the LDCs presents the following characteristics: (1) it is very small compared with Western Europe's import relations with the other industrialized countries (for example, in 1975 the EEC imports from the LDCs in electronics accounted for only 3.1 percent of their imports from the rest of the world in the same product areas;)[42] and (2) it is only a fraction of similar operations undertaken by the other major OECD countries (for example, in 1972 the then six EEC countries plus the UK imported electronic components from the LDCs that amounted to less than 25 percent of the corresponding US volume).[43]

Instead of expecting that this lower base could, in the future, give the opportunity to Western Europe to increase its imports from the LDCs, a quite different scenario might be expected. The latter might reflect the rather small political and corporate commitment that Western Europe has for industrial cooperation with the LDCs. This is basically the result of the nature of the EEC's production structure and its growing commercial deficit with the other major OECD countries.

The Nature of Western Europe's
'New Economic Deals' with the LDCs

Any significant change in the world industrial division of labor in the North-South context poses the problem of diverging and conflicting interests, as well as perspective among the industrialized countries. For some, the industrial division of labor between the North and the South is a by-product of the competition and division of labor among the already industrialized economies; for others, the reverse is true. In the former case, industrial relocation to the South will take place for two basic reasons and as a direct initiative of the North.

First, some *intra*-sectoral specializations will be sought with the LDCs. Under such a scheme, technology and skill-intensive activities will continue to be concentrated in the DCs, while certain labor-intensive activities will be subcontracted to low-wage countries in the South. Through such concentration of high human capital and value added in the North, the countries involved will be better equipped to face the challenge from other DCs.

Second, certain countries of the North also see their competitive edge and future prosperity in fomenting *inter*-sectoral specializations with the South. Under such a strategy, economic actors in the DCs will move into new and monopolistic or oligopolistic activities which can provide lucrative returns. Such operations might involve activities in electronic microprocessors, space and sea-bed technology, non-traditional forms of energy, armaments production, processing and management of specialized information, etc. More traditional and more competitive sectoral activities could be relocated to the South. The division of labor will not be based on simple relative factor endowments (since several of the relocated activities might be capital-intensive): instead, the industrial division of labor will be based on relatively monopolistic structures and monopolistic returns.

There is, though, a second category of DC interests, which sees the international division of industrial labor as a by-product of the industrial competition and threat from the South and/or the activities of TNEs from other DCs, who have affiliates in the South. In this case, it is thought that any type of serious industrial development in the South should be suppressed, or at least controlled from the North. Otherwise, the LDCs, whatever the springboard of their industrial development, could eventually come to challenge the interests of the North.

Within Europe — indeed, within each industrialized country — there will be some groups that will view the world division of industrial labor as the outcome of North-North competition, and others, that of the North-South. Sectoral policies at the national level will therefore be shaped according to the relative political power of each group . At the regional level involving groups of countries, there exist certain conditions (presently characterizing the Western European economies) under which any common DC policy toward the LDCs will be strongly biased by the lowest common denominator of the former's industrial structure. And this lowest denominator perceives the economic threat as coming from the South. This is patently exemplified in Europe's current industrial policy toward the LDCs through the Lomé Convention. Clearly, this convention is an improvement as compared with its predecessors, the Yaoundé I and II. Reverse preferences were abolished; relatively low negotiating emphasis was placed on aid; more attention was given to marketing promotion and information exchange among the LDCs; the latter participate in deciding how the resources of the European Development Fund are used; a coherent first attempt was made to establish a 'trade union of the poor'; etc. Yet, the Lomé Convention should not be judged by the relics of the colonial period. Instead, attention should be drawn to the asymmetrical interdependences that it creates between the EEC and the South.

In this latter context, two fundamental issues need to be emphasized. First, the LDC membership in the Lomé Convention was not negotiated but was decided unilaterally by the EEC. In doing this, the European countries excluded from the Convention all those ex-British colonies (and the South American countries) that could provide a commercial threat for the most stagnant and inefficient European industries. Economies with an export potential in final consumer products, such as Hong Kong in textiles and clothing, or countries with a growing and diversified local industrial capacity, like India or Brazil, Mexico and Argentina, were excluded.

Second, both the export stabilization scheme (STABEX) and the origin rules for market access to the EEC of the Lomé Convention discriminate in favor of the LDCs' resources and against their labor and industrial development. In the case of STABEX, the LDCs are induced *not* to process their materials, since (except for some cases, such as oils and cocoa derivatives) this would mean that they were not covered by export stabilization mechanisms. (Nor is diversification in the market destination of unprocessed primary materials encouraged.) In the case of origin rules, goods exported by the Asian, Caribbean and Pacific (ACP) countries are handicapped in not having preferential access to the EEC if, given certain limits on ACP/EEC value added, the materials had originated outside of the nations participating in the convention.

This latter provision was partly directed against non-European TNEs, which might use the ACP countries as a base for industrial activity and exports to the EEC.

Europe's interests in the Lomé Convention do not concern the LDCs' industrial development or the establishment of alternative and progressive North-South mechanisms of negotiation and interaction. Western Europe has a merely marginal interest in overall LDC industrial development, except insofar as it provides an export market for its own products. Rather, the EEC's crucial concerns in the Lomé Convention are: the existence of a stable source of supply of primary inputs; and opportunities for directly and indirectly promoting European participation in the important market for infrastructural investments, particularly in Africa.

CONCLUDING REMARKS

Examining in a historical context the relations of Europe with the rest of the world, it has been noted that: 'no other civilization has managed to shape the world in its apparent image, burden or bless others with its technology and thought, exploit, murder, nurture and school other peoples and older civilizations.'[44] In all epochs, the European has tended to have a benevolent image of his contribution to the world: he brought Christianity, regardless of whether this permitted him to exploit better the mines and suppress old civilizations; he organized the civil service and the railroads, regardless of whether this enabled Europe to limit the size of its occupying forces in the colonies and thus reduce the costs of colonising; he educated and improved local productivity, regardless of whether this was to achieve more abundant and cheaper products for European consumption; and so on. Similar benevolent images are being presently projected about the current relations of Western Europe with the LDCs.[45]

In the post-1960 period, and especially during the 1970s, Europe has been rediscovering and intensifying its relations with countries in the South that for decades — indeed, centuries — in the past were subjected to its colonial rule and arrogance. The nature and content of the emerging encounter is undoubtedly taking place within the framework of new multilateral political and economic conditions and within a drastically different world context. This new encounter is not simply consonant with Europe's past history:

it emanates from present European needs and interests and the prospects for its economic and political survival or prosperity.

Within the framework progressive political forces that have
emerged in Western Europe have shown themselves to support
some important internal changes in the LDCs. Yet, in their external
sector the nature of Western Europe's own interests might well
militate in many important areas against any serious contribution
to economic development in the LDCs, regardless of what parties
find themselves in power in Western Europe.

NOTES

1. For a discussion of the European role in South Africa, see K. L. Aldeman,
'The Black Man's Burden,' *Foreign Policy* (Fall 1977), pp. 98 et seq.

2. The limits imposed on international solidarity, when certain crucial domestic
interests are affected, can be seen both in (1) the recent debate on the knowledge of
the British Labour Party's leadership in connection with the sanction-busting activities of UK oil firms in Rhodesia, or even with the UK economic policies towards
Namibia, and (2) the attitude of the French Communist Party to Spain's entrance
into the EEC. Similarly, an acknowledged progressive US senator recently became
one of the main proponents for the creation of an international wheat cartel. The
implications of such a cartel for the food-deficient developing countries was a secondary consideration in view of the senator's electoral base in South Dakota, one of
the main wheat-producing states in the USA.

3. Clair Wilcox, *A Charter for World Trade* (Macmillan, NY, 1949).

4. See United Nations Department of Economic and Social Affairs, *Multinational Corporations in World Development*, E.73.II.A.11 (UN, NY, 1973).

5. See EEC Commission, 'Protecting and Guaranteeing Private Investments in
the Developing Countries: Member States' Policies, Some Ideas for a Community
Approach,' Working Paper (December 1976). See also L. Franko, *The European
Multinationals* (Harper & Row, NY, 1976).

6. See C. V. Vaitsos, 'Foreign Investment Policies and Economic Development
in Latin America,' *Journal of World Trade Law*, vol. 7, no. 6 (November/
December 1973).

7. See R. H. Green, 'The Lomé Convention: Updated Dependence or Departure
Toward Collective Self-Reliance,' *The African Review*, vol. 6, no. 1 (1976), p. 43.

8. France accounted for between 40 and 48% of the EEC share of imports from the African Associate States and Madagascar (AASM) between 1961 and 1976. The equivalent share of French exports to AASM varied between 63 and 71% of the EEC's total.

9. See OECD, Interfutures, 'International Division of Industrial Labour' FUT(77), S.10 (OECD, Paris, 1977), p. 21.

10. There were also some important domestic US interests that contributed to the jump in the foreign aid program, as in the case of the P.L. 480.

11. This conclusion obviously needs to be qualified by taking into account the present situation in sub-Saharan Africa as well as the implications of the changes in Iran.

12. Computed from UN Center on Transnational Corporations, *Transnational Corporations in World Development: A Re-examination*, E/C.10/38 (UN, New York, 1978).

13. See C. V. Vaitsos, *The Role of Transnational Enterprises in Latin American Integration Efforts*, GE.78-63131 (Geneva, UNCTAD, 1978).

14. See W. P. Bundy, 'Elements of Power,' *Foreign Affairs* (October 1977).

15. The threat and partial imposition of an oil embargo during the 1973 Arab/Israeli war forced the US NATO allies in Europe — except for Portugal — to deny transit facilities for the US military assistance to Israel.

16. It should be stressed, though, that in the past US, Canadian and Japanese tariff escalation on imports of processed primary goods was often higher than that of Europe.

17. See *Financial Times* (3 July 1978).

18. In the medium and longer run, though, the nature of this stabilization scheme, unrelated to the prices of manufactured goods, could turn against the interest of the participating LDCs. See A. Emmanuel, 'La "Stabilisation": Alibi de l'Exploitation Internationale,' *Revue de Tiers Monde*, no. 66 (April-June 1976).

19. See EEC Commission, op. cit.

20. See G. K. Helleiner, 'Freedom and Management in Primary Commodity Markets: US Imports from Developing Countries,' *World Development* (January 1978).

21. See *Washington Post* (September 1978).

22. See Vaitsos, op. cit., chapter II.

23. It is only in the clothing sector that imports from the LDCs account for a significant part of EEC world imports. In 1975 the corresponding percentage was 24.3: in textiles it was 11.1%, electronics 3.1%, steel 2.5% and much less in other sectors. See OECD, *Trade by Commodities*, Series-C (OECD, Paris, 1975).

24. See OECD, *Labour Force Statistics* (OECD, Paris, 1977).

25. ibid.

26. *Long Term Vision of Industrial Structure* (Council on Industrial Structure, MITI, Tokyo, 1974).

27. 'Towards the Chemical Glut,' *The Economist* (2 July 1977).

28. See comments and discussion in OECD, Interfutures, op. cit., pp. 47 et seq.

29. *The Economist* (2 June 1977).

30. For a representative petrochemical product, ethylene world consumption for 1985 is expected to be 45 million tons per year. Production capacity — given a conservative estimate of present investment plans — is forecasted to be about 70 million

tons per year, which is double the 1976 level (see *Chemical Insight*, as quoted by OECD, Interfutures, op. cit., p. 50).

31. See *Financial Times* (7 March 1978) and *The Economist* (10 June 1978).

32. Four categories of products (clothing, leather goods, electrical and miscellaneous goods) accounted for well over two-thirds of the LDC manufactures export increase.

33. Three sources (South Korea, Mexico and Hong Kong) accounted for nearly half of the export increase in the 1970-78 period: see UNCTAD, 'Dynamic Products in the Exports of Manufactured Goods from Developing Countries to Developed Market-Economy Countries, 1970 to 1976' (UNCTAD/ST/MD/18, March 1978).

34. On welfare matters, with respect to the international distribution of benefits, the following issues are worth keeping in mind. In addition to the effect on DC consumers, the recent LDC export performance does not simply imply a conflict of interest between the newly industrializing countries and the DCs: rather, it often involves the competitive behavior of different TNEs with subcontracting operation in low-wage areas as well as competition between a few large firms in the DCs (basically retail and trading firms) and smaller producers in the DCs. The very liberal terms offered to foreign industrial firms in export platforms by the LDCs, and the monopoly power of the large retail firms that dominate their trade area, reduce significantly the net benefits accruing to the exporting LDCs.

35. See data of UNCTAD as analyzed by OECD, Interfutures, op. cit., p. 8.

36. See *The Economist* (10 June 1978), p. 85, and *DIW Wochenbezicht* (15 January 1978).

37. See figures in n. 3 above.

38. West Germany accounted for 43% of the EEC's imports of electronic components and related parts from the LDCs in 1975: computed from OECD, *Trade by Commodities*, Series-C (1975).

39. Computed from OECD, *Trade by Commodities*, Series-C (1975).

40. See AMPO, *Free Trade Zones & Industrialisation of Asia* (Pacific-Asia Resources Center, Tokyo, 1977).

41. Any serious cooperation between Japan and China in this field could have extraordinary implications on world trade and competitiveness in certain product areas.

42. Computed from OECD, *Trade by Commodities*, Series-C (1975).

43. Computed from UNCTAD data as cited in OECD, Interfutures, op. cit.

44. See F. Stern, 'The Giant from Afar: Visions of Europe from Algiers to Tokyo,' *Foreign Affairs* (October 1977), p. 113.

45. See for example R. Dahrendorf, 'International Power: A European Perspective,' *Foreign Affairs* (October 1977), p. 76.

III

INTERNATIONAL AND NATIONAL FINANCE

8

EUROMARKETS, THIRD WORLD COUNTRIES AND THE INTERNATIONAL POLITICAL ECONOMY

Barbara Stallings
University of Wisconsin-Madison, USA

The 1970s have witnessed major shifts in the international political-economic context in which Third World countries must operate. Détente has altered the relationship between East and West. The increased economic strength of Europe and Japan, together with the multi-faceted consequences of the Vietnam War, have changed the power relationships within the West. Also in the West, a process of privatization has emerged to challenge the postwar emphasis on governmental activity. And, finally, the rise of the OPEC cartel has created a new international power center, dividing the Third World in the process. The last two items on this list lead to the topic of this

Author's Note: Previous versions of this paper have been presented in various places. I would like to thank participants in the following discussions: Research Committee on Economy and Society of the International Sociological Assocaition, conference on 'Social and Political Challenges to the New International Economic Order,' Bellagio, Italy, April 1979; Latin American Studies Association, panel on 'Nationalist Politics and the New International Economic Order,' Pittsburgh, April 1979; Union of Radical Political Economists, conference on 'The Political Economy of the Third World,' New York, April 1979; and seminar presentations at the Political Science Department, University of Wisconsin, May 1979; Facultad Latinoamericana de Ciencias Sociales (FLACSO), Santiago, Chile, August 1979; Centro de Estudios de Estado y Sociedad (CEDES), Buenos Aires, Argentina, August 1979; and the Instituto de Estudios Peruanos (IEP), Lima, Peru, September 1979. I would also like to thank the Faculty of Economics of the University of Cambridge and the Graduate School at the University of Wisconsin for computer time.

chapter: the increasingly dominant role of private banks as a source of finance for Third World governments. During the 1970s, these private Western financial institutions have taken OPEC's huge petrodollar deposits and, in the process of recycling them, have displaced the public agencies who provided the vast majority of Third World finance in the 1950s and 1960s.[1]

This trend has been widely discussed; both financial publications and less specialized journals have taken up the topic. The resulting literature has ranged widely. It runs from technical concern about interest rates to economic concern about mounting Third World debt and the balance of payments effects to political concern about the stability of individual countries and/or the whole international financial system.[2] Most of it shares one common problem, however, which is the lack of a theoretical framework to explain either the reason the loans are made from the banks' point of view or the consequences of this new form of finance from the recipients' viewpoint. Such a descriptive bias is understandable for a new topic, but it must be remedied. In another work, I am studying the reasons for the loans;[3] here I will attempt to make a contribution toward analyzing the consequences.

The theoretical framework that will be suggested comes from a selective reading of the literature on imperialism, sub-imperialism and dependency. After some comments on this literature, the second section of the paper will deal with the economic consequences of the loans for Third World countries, including the presentation of empirical data on amounts of capital involved, allocation and terms. The third section will concentrate on the political impact of the loans, specifically the undermining of certain progressive trends in the Third World in the past decade. Finally, I will conclude by looking at the effects of the loans on the banks themselves, which will reveal that recent trends have been more contradictory than the previous analysis would suggest. These contradictions will then be used to suggest modification of the propositions derived from the theoretical literature.

A THEORETICAL FRAMEWORK

It has been evident for a long time that unification of the theories of imperialism and dependency is necessary; that we need a framework that can combine the analysis of advanced capitalist and Third World countries to take account of both groups, as independent actors. By this, it is meant that neither should be 'black-boxed' with exclusive attention paid to the other; nor should either be regarded as a passive 'victim' of the other's actions. Recent introduction of the concepts of 'sub-imperialism' and the 'semi-periphery' indicate the need for even further complexity. This paper does not pretend to produce such a total synthesis,[4] but it will draw on certain ideas from all three bodies of literature in order to fashion a framework to deal with the particular subject at hand, namely the consequences of the emerging dominance of private banks in Third World finance.

We begin with some brief comments on theories of imperialism. As will be the case with the other types of theories, it is important to differentiate among the various theories of imperialism. Even limiting ourselves to those writers who consider imperialism to derive from economic factors, classical and modern variants can be distinguished. By classical theorists, the reference is primarily to Hobson, Luxemburg and Lenin,[5] whereas important names associated with the modern theorists are Baran, Magdoff and Sweezy (sometimes collectively known as the 'Monthly Review School'). This latter group has much in common with contemporary European authors such as Amin and Emmanuel.[6]

Both the classical and modern theorists share a primary interest in analyzing the problems of advanced economies, dealing with the Third World mainly as a part of the world affected by the actions of the advanced countries. Little attention is paid to their internal characteristics. The classical theorists are more susceptible to this criticism than the moderns, thus their frequent characterization as 'Eurocentric.'[7]

Although, in line with their focus on advanced countries, the main thrust of theories of imperialism is on the causes of imperialist expansion, we will concentrate here on their analyses of the effects. In this respect, classical and modern theorists differ radically. The classical theorists believed that imperialist expansion would have positive effects for Third World countries. That is, there would be an inflow of capital, which in turn would lead to higher development. Thus, when Lenin spoke of uneven development, he was referring to peripheral countries growing faster than advanced countries:

The export of capital greatly affects and accelerates the development of capitalism in those countries to which it is exported. While, therefore, the export of capital may tend to a certain extent to arrest development in the countries exporting capital, it can only do so by expanding and deepening the further development of capitalism throughout the world.[8]

The modern theorists, on the other hand, say that, far from promoting development, imperialism is the primary cause of underdevelopment. This difference arises basically because the latter group of theorists sees advanced capitalist countries as siphoning capital out of the Third World rather than putting it in. Unequal development here refers to the growing gap between center and peripheral countries.

Profits derived from operations in underdeveloped countries have gone to a large extent to finance investment in highly developed parts of the world. Thus while there have been vast differences among underdeveloped countries with regard to the amounts of profits plowed back in their economies or withdrawn by foreign investors, the underdeveloped world as a whole has continually shipped a large part of its economic surplus to more advanced countries on account of interest and dividends.[9]

To a certain extent, the differences are ones of timing. Thus, in an early stage of investment there is likely to be a net inflow of capital, while at a later stage profits may more than offset the then slower inflows. In the second half of the twentieth century, the modern variant has proved more in line with empirical evidence. It is from this version of theories of imperialism that we will draw.

Turning to theories of dependency, which began to appear in the mid-1960s, we find a very different focus. There is little interest in the reasons for capitalist expansion but rather a concentration on its effects in the Third World. This literature has been heavily criticized in the last few years, and often rightly so. Major criticisms include vagueness, circularity, over-emphasis on international factors, lack of attention to domestic factors (especially class struggle and the state), and failure to analyze the specific nature of the articulation of capitalist and pre-capitalist modes of production.[10]

On the other hand, the critics themselves have often been lax in failing to differentiate among different strands of dependency theory. In part, this is due to a failure to translate much of the dependency literature into English, meaning that many people get their view of dependency theory from the myriad works of Andre

Gunder Frank and a single article by Theotonio dos Santos.[11] Both of these sources do indeed lend credence to the view that dependency theory is an overly simplistic — even mechanistic — analysis whereby Third World underdevelopment is a direct result of external forces. A good indication of this problem is the continual quoting of dos Santos's definition of dependency, which concentrates completely on external factors:

> By dependence we mean a situation in which the economy of certain countries is conditioned by the development of another economy to which the former is subjected. The relation of interdependence between the two or more economies, and between these and world trade, assumes the form of dependence when some countries (the dominant ones) can expand and be self-sustaining, while other countries (the dependent ones) can do this only as a reflection of that expansion, which can have either a positive or negative effect on their immediate development.[12]

More subtle and sophisticated is another strand of dependency analysis that has only recently — after almost 15 years — been published in English. The reference here is to the book written in the mid-1960s by Fernando Henrique Cardoso and Enzo Faletto, which emphasizes the internal aspects of dependency.[13] They concentrate on the domestic class structure and class struggle, with external factors internalized, brought to bear via connections between certain class fractions in the Third World and international forces. As they say,

> In the case of economically dependent countries, the explanation of structures of domination involves establishing the links that may exist between internal and external determinants. These links should not be understood in terms of a mechanical and immediate determination of the internal by the external: it is important to delineate the interconnections between these two levels, suggesting the ways through which external factors are interwoven with internal ones. The concept of dependence tries to give meaning to a series of events and situations that occur together, and to make empirical situations understandable in terms of the way internal and external structural components are linked. In this approach, the external is also expressed as a particular type of relation between social groups and classes within the underdeveloped nations. For this reason, it is worth focusing the analysis of dependence on its internal manifestations.[14]

It is this version of dependency theory that is useful in understanding the highly complex situation in the Third World today whereby certain domestic groups support the attempts by the banks and the International Monetary Fund (IMF) to 'impose order' on 'profligate' governments. External forces are important, but an analysis that only sees them imposing their views oversimplifies to the point of distortion.

A third type of theory that is potentially useful deals with the phenomenon of 'sub-imperialism.' This concept has not been very well developed up to now, but generally it refers to certain regional powers (e.g. Brazil, South Africa, Iran under the Shah) that assume an imperialist-like relationship with respect to their neighbors. Johan Galtung's version of sub-imperialism[15] portrays the United States as a 'super-center' acting through 'favorite countries' in different regions.

> The U.S. is no longer capable, nor willing, to exercise 'policing' activities all around the world. . . .Hence the obvious method is to build on already existing structure, *making use of somebody else's imperialism or aspirations in that direction — in other words sub-imperialism.* The formula is simple: establish a bilateral relation between the U. S. on the one hand and a region on the other, select a 'favorite country' which can support local forces in exercising control so as to maintain a status quo, a law and order pattern compatible with capitalist types of 'development.'[16]

Immanuel Wallerstein's concept of the semi-periphery is very similar to Galtung's sub-imperialism.[17] He portrays the world economy as consisting of 'three *kinds* of states' — 'the upper stratum of core states, the lower stratum of peripheral states. . .and a middle stratum of semi-peripheral ones.'

> The semi-periphery is then assigned as it were a specific economic role, but the reason is less economic than political. That is to say, one might make a good case that the world economy as an economy would function every bit as well without a semi-periphery. But it would be far less *politically* stable, for it would mean a polarized world-system. The existence of the third category means precisely that the upper stratum is not faced with the *unified* opposition of all the others because the *middle* stratum is both exploited and the exploiter.[18]

There are problems with both of the above analyses — the mechanistic nature of Galtung's structural hierarchy and the functional nature of Wallerstein's approach — but there are interesting and useful ideas contained in these emerging theories that deserve to be explored further. As with the domestic class structure, it is clear in the hierarchical structure of nations that a middle group is gaining increasing political and economic importance. Thus it is necessary to study the characteristics of such states; the particular one that will be emphasized in this paper is their openness to cooptation.

To summarize, we can extract the following propositions from the three bodies of literature discussed above. First, from theories of imperialism, we can deduce that center states will benefit at the expense of the periphery as a whole; i.e. there will be unequal development between advanced countries and others. Second, from sub-imperialist theories, we can suggest that some peripheral states will benefit at the expense of other peripheral states; i.e., there will be unequal development within the periphery itself. Third, from dependency theory, we can hypothesize that some social groups or classes will benefit at the expense of other such groups, i.e., there will be unequal development within individual peripheral countries. This third phenomenon, in turn, will provide the key to the process by which the other types of unequal development can take place.

These three propositions will be illustrated in the analysis that follows about the effects of private bank loans in the 1970s. In the concluding section, we will return to the propositions to see if they need modification in light of the empirical evidence presented. The paper does not pretend to be a rigorous test of the propositions; it could not be, since it deals with only one kind of capital flow during a limited period. It is, rather, an attempt to begin formulating a theoretical framework through the presentation and modification of propositions.

ECONOMIC CONSEQUENCES OF PRIVATE BANK LOANS

As is well known, the Euromarkets started on a small scale in the 1950s when the Soviet Union began depositing its surplus dollars in banks outside the United States, mainly in London. This was the origin of the term 'Eurodollar' (a dollar deposited in Europe); the more general definition of a Eurocurrency is simply a deposit made in any given currency outside its country of origin. The markets gained in size and importance during the 1960s, in large part because of a series of US regulations aimed at improving the balance of payments. It was only in the 1970s, however, that these markets finally became large enough to challenge domestic capital markets.[19] Table 1 shows the growth of the markets, dividing them into their main component parts — loans and bonds. The former

TABLE 1
Growth of the Euromarkets, 1970-80 ($ million)

Year	Bonds	Loans	Total
1970	$3,343	$4,730	$8,073
1971	5,153	3,963	9,116
1972	9,696	6,796	16,492
1973	9,779	21,851	31,630
1974	6,832	29,263	36,095
1975	19,913	20,992	40,905
1976	32,518	28,849	61,367
1977	33,976	41,637	75,613
1978	34,279	70,179	104,458
1979	40,982	82,812	123,794
1980*	21,250	31,812	53,062

* January-June

Source: Morgan Guaranty Trust, *World Financial Markets*, various issues.

are medium-term floating-rate instruments, issued directly by commercial banks, while the latter are long-term fixed-rate debt, sold to individuals or institutions via investment banks.[20] Bonds, in turn, can be divided into foreign bonds (denominated in one currency and sold in the respective country) and Eurobonds (denominated in one or more currencies and sold in various countries). Both types of bonds are included in table 1. As the table shows, the relative importance of the two types of finance has varied over the period, with loans gaining increasing dominance in the last few years.

Another crucial change with respect to Euroloans came about in the 1970s as well. Prior to that time, most Euroloans had been issued to US or European multinational corporations and to a few European state corporations and governments. These loans were mainly short-term and essentially risk-free. In the early 1970s, however, for the first time since the Depression, US and European business cycles coincided on the downswing, and banks' traditional customers greatly slowed their borrowing. It was at this point that certain Third World governments began to appear as attractive clients for Euroloans.[21] By the mid-1970s, Third World countries accounted for over half of all Euroloans, although significant participation in the bond market did not come until later.[22] Since Third World governments wanted loans to finance development projects, this meant their maturities had to increase. The banks' risk was also thought to increase with the new borrowers.

Unequal Allocation of Finance

Concentrating on the high-volume period of the 1970s, we first want to ask about the allocation of loans among regions and countries. A first approximation can be made by looking at a geographical breakdown. As table 2 indicates, the North Atlantic area countries of Western Europe, the United States and Canada accounted for over half of all funds (50.6 percent) on the markets. It is also important to note that these countries got 71 percent of the bond finance, which is on more favorable terms than loans (fixed interest rates and longer maturities). Continuing in table 2, we see that the advanced Mediterranean countries received 6.1 percent of Eurofinancing and Eastern Europe 3.3 percent, leaving 40 percent for all other countries.[23] Comparable population figures for these areas are: Atlantic countries, 13 percent; advanced Mediterranean countries, 3 percent; Eastern Europe, 9 percent; and all other countries, 75 percent. Of these remaining areas, Latin America received 18 percent of Eurofinance, Asian Pacific countries 13 percent, the Middle East and North Africa 6 percent, tropical Africa 3 percent, and South Asia almost nothing.

Table 2 gives the strong impression that the richest countries have gotten the lion's share of this money; table 3, which gives a breakdown of loans and bonds by income category for all capitalist countries,[24] confirms this. Here we see the industrial countries receiving 66 percent of total finance; these are the countries with the highest per capita income, $6450 in 1977. OPEC countries, considered to be especially good risks because of their oil wealth, accounted for 10 percent of finance; these countries have a per capita income of $2630. Upper and upper middle income Third World countries (per capita income of $2160) represented 9 percent of total finance; intermediate income countries ($905) received 11 percent; lower middle income countries ($460) accounted for 3 percent; and the poorest group ($200) represented less than one percent.[25]

TABLE 2
Euroloans and International Bonds by Geographical Area, 1972-78

Region	Bonds	Loans	Total	Population
	%	%	%	%
North America	30.4	9.0	16.8	5.8
Western Europe	40.9	29.7	33.8	7.1
Advanced Mediterranean	3.8	7.5	6.1	3.0
Eastern Europe	0.5	4.9	3.3	8.9
Latin America	6.3	25.1	18.2	8.1
Asian Pacific	15.0	11.2	12.6	10.8
Middle East and				
North Africa	1.7	8.8	6.2	3.9
Tropical Africa	1.3	3.6	2.8	8.3
South Asia	—	0.2	0.1	44.2

Sources: B. Stallings, *Latin America and U.S. Capital Markets* (loan and bond percentages); *World Bank Atlas*, 1979 (population).

TABLE 3
Euroloans and International Bonds by Income Category, 1972-78

Category*	Bonds	Loans	Total	Per capita income**
	%	%	%	%
Group of 10	60.3	34.0	43.9	$7995
Other industrialized				
countries	29.6	18.0	22.4	4480
OPEC countries	2.5	14.2	9.8	2630
Higher and upper				
middle-income LDCs	3.2	12.2	8.8	2160
Intermediate-income LDCs	3.3	16.3	11.4	905
Lower middle-income				
LDCs	1.0	4.6	3.3	460
Low-income LDCs	0.1	0.8	0.6	200

* World Bank categories
** Median 1977 GNP per capita

Sources: see table 2.

TABLE 4
Third World Euroloans by Borrowing Country, 1970-78

Country	Amount	Percent
	($ million)	%
Mexico	17,243	17.8
Brazil	16,329	16.9
Venezuela	5,623	5.8
Iran	5,466	5.7
Algeria	5,180	5.4
Philippines	4,589	4.7
Indonesia	4,528	4.7
South Korea	4,359	4.5
Argentina	4,307	4.5
Taiwan	2,245	2.3
Peru	2,074	2.1
Malaysia	2,072	2.1
Others	22,709	23.5
Total	96,724	100.0

Source: Stallings, op. cit.

If we make a final cut — down to the individual country level — to see who the leading borrowers were, we find countries considered to be good risks because of strong capacity to earn foreign exchange through exports. Most are exporters of primary commodities, while the remainder come from the small group of Third World countries that has managed to break into the world market for industrial exports. As can be seen in table 4, Mexico and Brazil alone accounted for one-third of all loans to Third World countries (half of all non-OPEC Third World loans). Four OPEC countries (Venezuela, Iran, Algeria and Indonesia) represented another 22 percent, and six non-oil countries (the Philippines, South Korea, Argentina, Taiwan, Peru and Malaysia) got approximately the same amount. Thus, 12 countries represent the vast bulk (three-fourths) of all Third World loans. The bond market is even more concentrated: there, Mexico and Brazil alone accounted for 44 percent, and five countries received over three-fourths of the Third World total.[26]

It is important to note that lenders are as concentrated as borrowers in the Euromarkets. Only a small number of banks have the capital to operate internationally. As late as 1964, for example, only 11 US banks had branches abroad. This number increased to 125 a decade later, as many regional banks opened branches in London or some of the other offshore centers in order to participate in the Euromarkets.[27] Nevertheless, the market is still dominated by a few large banks. In the medium-term credit market, these banks have tended to be from the United States. Through 1978, the top five loan managers were Citicorp, Chase Manhattan, Morgan Guaranty Trust, Manufacturers Hanover, and Bank of America; this ordering held for loans both to the Third World and to the industrial countries. The bond market is more complex. The German giant, Deutsche Bank, is clearly the top bank in all categories, but there are important regional variations for other issuing houses. Three large US investment banks (First Boston, Morgan Stanley, and Salomon Brothers) dominate the New York market, whose principal foreign borrowers are Canada and the international organizations. The European markets are more diversified for both borrowers and lenders. Looking specifically at Third World bonds, the top banks in the 1970-78 period included three German institutions (Deutsche, Dresdner and Westdeutsche Landesbank), one Japanese (Nomura Securities) and one from the Middle East (Kuwait Investment Co.).[28] In relative terms, US banks have been especially important in Latin America, the Asian Pacific area, and Africa (in spite of the European colonial heritage in this last region).[29]

Unequal Terms of Finance

Having some idea about who has gotten loans from the Euromarkets, we now want to look at the terms on which these loans have been made. Specifically, we want to examine interest rates and maturity structures for various categories of borrowers. A first kind of comparison is between interest rates and maturities across the same income categories we were just looking at in the allocation section. We will do this for a subgroup consisting of loans to public sector entities. The reason for selecting this subgroup is that it is the category in which the Third World is most

TABLE 5
Average Spreads on Public Sector Euroloans
by Income Category, 1972-78

Category	Ave. spread	Ave. maturity
	(%)	(years)
Group of 10	0.89	7.62
Other industrialized countries	1.22	7.01
OPEC countries	1.35	6.92
High and upper middle-income LDCs	1.57*	7.66**
Intermediate-income LDCs	1.45	6.92
Lower middle-income LDCs	1.63	6.72
Low-income LDCs	1.71	6.97
Average***	1.37	7.16

 * 1.42% without Brazil
 ** 6.86 years without Brazil
*** Weighted according to number of loans

Source: Stallings, op. cit.

important; 63 percent of public sector loans went to Third World countries, compared with 41 percent for total loans and bonds.[30]

Table 5 shows the interest rate in terms of the average spread above what is called the London Inter-Bank Offered Rate, or LIBOR. The LIBOR is the rate at which banks can purchase deposits; under normal circumstances, it tends to move in close tandem with the US prime rate. The rate actually charged to borrowers is the LIBOR plus a spread, the size of which depends on the amount of liquidity in the markets and the level of risk a country is thought to represent. Since the LIBOR itself fluctuates, the banks protect themselves by readjusting the rate they charge customers every six months to take account movements in the LIBOR (thus the term 'floating' rates). By taking the spreads at any given point in time, or across a period of time, we should then be able to see the differences between the prices charged to different categories of borrowers.[31]

Returning now to table 5, we see that during the 1972-78 period average spreads ranged from 0.89 percent for the strongest industrial countries (the so-called Group of Ten) to 1.71 percent for the low-income less developed countries. While the difference may not appear large, it would represent, for example, an additional $820,000 on $100,000,000 (a typical size loan). In between the highest and lowest spreads there is a monotonic increase, with one exception. That is, Group of Ten countries pay an average spread of 0.89 percent, other industrial countries 1.22 percent, and OPEC 1.35 percent. The exception to this monotonic progression is the especially high spread for upper and upper middle-income LDCs. This exception is explained by the case of Brazil. Brazil, which accounts for about two-thirds of loans in this category, has traditionally had a policy of offering to pay higher spreads in exchange for longer maturities. Leaving Brazil out, the average spread for upper and upper middle-income countries falls to 1.42 percent. Intermediate income LDCs have an average spread of 1.45 percent, lower middle-income countries 1.63 percent, and lower-income countries 1.71 percent. The average is 1.37 percent.

The maturity structure, also shown in table 5, follows basically the same pattern found with interest rates but less consistently. That is, the Group of Ten countries again have the most favorable terms, with average maturities during the 1972-78 period of 7.62 years. The shortest maturities, however, are for the lower middle-income countries, at 6.72 years, while the low-income countries average 6.97 years. The main exception to the trend is again the high income and upper middle-income category, with exceptionally long maturities of 7.66 years. Again, this is due to the Brazilian policy mentioned above; eliminating Brazil, this time reduces the upper middle-income category maturity to only 6.86 years. The average is 7.16 years.

In general, then, with respect to both interest rates and maturities, the richest countries have received the most favorable terms for their loans, while the poorest countries have had to pay more and have gotten the money for less time. An analysis taking bonds as well as loans into account would greatly reinforce this conclusion.[32] It should be quickly pointed out that this is not a surprising conclusion in any way. In fact, it is exactly what would be expected according to the rules by which bankers play; those borrowers seen to represent the highest risks (and, rightly or wrongly, poorer countries are seen as bigger risks) will be charged more when they are allowed to borrow at all.[33] The more interesting — and relevant — question is what role profit-oriented institutions should play in financing Third World countries.[34]

Public vs. Private Finance

This last point then leads to a discussion of public vs. private finance. Private finance for economic development, although the traditional pattern before the Second World War, is quite controversial. Not only do private banks provide huge amounts of money (over $165 billion since 1970),[35] but they provide money with very few strings attached. Whereas the regional development banks, and especially the World Bank, provide loans for specific projects and closely supervise the spending of their monies, the private sector has been much looser with its funds. In part, this is because the banks lack the capacity to evaluate projects as the World Bank does, but many bankers now argue that the purpose for which money is given makes little difference. 'Money is fungible,' they say; that is, if foreign capital is provided for a priority project, this merely frees local capital that would otherwise have gone for that project, so it can go elsewhere. International agency officials, in paternalistic tones, warn Third World governments against seeing quick easy money as an advantage. For example, Antonio Ortiz Mena, President of the Inter-American Development Bank, said:

> The Eurocurrency market has provided a large volume of financing for the region in the last two years, but...this financing is being obtained on conditions that, without careful planning, can frustrate orderly management of the external debt and even weaken the internal savings efforts of our countries.[36]

Likewise William Gaud, former head of the International Finance Corporation (one branch of the World Bank), warns:

> There are those who have welcomed this growing recourse to the private capital market by the developing countries as a desirable trend. It is said to represent a return to the traditional method of financing economic expansion, leaving the borrowing country free to make its own decisions on how the funds should be spent.... .Nevertheless, I see very real risks for the developing countries in borrowing so heavily in a market with no established lending standards and no overall surveillance to prevent unsound practices.[37]

TABLE 6
Maturities on World Bank and Euroloans
to the Third World, 1970-78

Year	World Bank** maturities	Euroloan maturities
	(years)	(years)
1970	30.4	4.5
1971	27.7	6.2
1972	30.3	7.0
1973	32.9	9.9
1974	27.6	8.7
1975	29.7	5.6
1976	26.1	5.5
1977	25.0	6.1
1978	27.9	7.8
Average*	26.4	7.1

* Weighted according to volume of loans
** Both IBRD and IDA

Source: Stallings, op. cit. (Euroloan maturities); World Bank, *Annual Report*, various issues (World Bank maturities).

In order to compare terms on public and private loans, we have calculated maturities and interest rates for World Bank loans and Euroloans to Third World countries for the period 1970-78. The greatest differences are in terms of maturities, as shown in table 6. The average maturity for World Bank loans was almost four times that of private loans — 26.4 years compared with 7.1 years. Shorter maturities, of course, mean that the borrower has less time to get a project underway before having to begin repayments. (The maturity refers to the time before all principal must be repaid; initial payments begin after a grace period which would usually be longer on a longer loan.) Maturities on public loans vary little by year, while those on private loans are more changeable, depending on market conditions.

Interest rates also are less favorable in the private capital markets, although the differences are less dramatic. In addition, however, the fact that interest rates are readjusted every six months according to the level of the LIBOR provides greater uncertainty

TABLE 7
Interest Rates on World Bank and
Euroloans to the Third World, 1970-78

Year	World Bank** interest rates	Euroloan interest rates
	%	%
1970	5.08	9.52
1971	5.68	8.02
1972	5.11	6.82
1973	4.64	10.38
1974	5.96	12.24
1975	6.16	8.74
1976	6.49	7.38
1977	6.40	7.64
1978	5.49	10.03
Average*	6.20	9.16

* Weighted according to volume of loans
** Both IBRD and IDA

Source: See table 6.

for the borrower. The case of the 1980 interest rate jump is the most dramatic example: many countries' interest payments almost doubled in the course of a few months. The interest rates given for Euroloans in table 7 are the total interest rates that the countries actually paid, i.e. the average LIBOR for the year plus the average spread over LIBOR. As can be seen, interest rates on the private loans average about three points (or 50 percent) higher than those on public (World Bank) loans.[38]

It might appear that an international financial structure that concentrates private loans in the richest Third World countries and public loans in the poorer countries would have equalizing effects, given that public loans are provided on more favorable terms. The problem, however, arises from the rate of expansion of the two types of credits. Euroloans to the Third World have increased 82-fold over the 1970-78 period, while bilateral aid has increased only 181 percent and multilateral aid 374 percent.[39] Thus private capital markets now provide about half of all loans available to the Third World.[40] The obvious consequence is that the small group of countries with access to the private markets has much more capital at its disposal; this has certainly been at least partially responsible for the rapid growth rates of these same countries. During the 1970-77 period, the 12 countries at the top of the list of Third World Euroloan recipients had an average annual GNP growth rate of 7.7 percent, while the rest of the Third World grew at 6.1 percent. The gap is much greater if we eliminate the exceptional case of Saudi Arabia; then other Third World countries grew at only 4.9 percent.[41]

In conclusion, then, an examination of who gets funds from the private capital markets and at what terms provides evidence for two of the three propositions discussed on p. 199. These loans have tended to favor the advanced industrial countries over the Third World, thus leading to unequal development between these two parts of the world economy; and they have tended to favor certain Third World countries over others, leading to unequal development within the periphery.

POLITICAL CONSEQUENCES OF PRIVATE BANK LOANS

The new role of private banks in financing Third World governments has had a variety of political consequences. Here we will focus on three interrelated ones: creating divisions within the Third World in economic/political terms, and thereby limiting Third World demands; directly undermining progressive regimes; and supporting reactionary ones. This is not to say, of course, that the change from the progressive atmosphere in the early 1970s to the more authoritarian one at the end of the decade was due solely to the activities of the international banks. Many factors — domestic and foreign — have been at work, but the banks have been a major force.

Dividing the Third World

As the previous section showed, private loans have been heavily concentrated in a handful of Third World countries, while the others have been left to rely on public sector loans (bilateral and multilateral). The much faster growth rate of private loans (even though their terms are less favorable) has increased the share of capital going to the countries with access to the private markets. It should be added that the skewed distribution of private loans within the Third World is reinforced by a similar pattern of direct foreign investment. A recent United Nations study shows that half of multinational corporations' investment in the Third World is located in ten countries: Brazil, Mexico, Venezuela, Indonesia, Nigeria, India, Malaysia, Argentina, Singapore and Peru. Of the ten, only India is not one of the top borrowers in the Euromarkets.[42]

The focus of this section of the paper is on the political consequences of the unequal distribution of capital and hence the uneven development of Third World economies. The economic differentiation has led to political differentiation and the elevation of countries such as Brazil, Mexico, Saudi Arabia and others to the status of 'semi-peripheral' countries. In a situation quite similar to that of the so-called 'middle class' or 'middle sectors,' these semi-peripheral countries in various regions of the Third World become buffers between the advanced capitalist countries on the one hand and the poorer Third World countries on the other. Furthermore, the semi-periphery is then open to cooptation by the advanced capitalist world, which tries to convince it that its interests are much closer to those of the United States, Europe and Japan than to those of Chad, Bolivia and Bangladesh. This is exactly the phenomenon that Galtung, Wallerstein and others are referring to.

If we look at the history of the Group of 77 (G-77) and the New International Economic Order (NIEO) demands, it is clear that the cooptation of the semi-periphery has been an important force in the G-77's declining militancy.[43] A prime example is the NIEO demand most closely related to international finance — the demand for a debt moratorium and rescheduling. The failure to make any progress on this demand in the course of the North-South negotiations cannot be separated from Mexico's and Brazil's decision to shun the demand for fear of losing their credit rating on the international markets. UNCTAD Secretary-General Gamani Corea made this point clear in explaining why cancelling commercial debt is no longer part of the G-77 demands.[44]

Likewise, the inclusion of Third World representation (usually meaning semi-periphery representation) on the powerful IMF Interim Committee, and their increased voting power, has tended to defuse demands for reorganization of the international lending agencies. Further, proposals exist for

> bringing selected newcomers into the inner circles of international decision-making.... The most apt historical precedent is the inclusion of Japan in the OECD in 1972. It would now seem desirable to invite such major new powers as Iran, Brazil, and Mexico to join the same organization. Saudi Arabia, which now has the second largest monetary reserves in the world, might be invited to meetings of the Group of Ten, which will undoubtedly continue to act as an informal steering group on some international monetary issues.[45]

The importance of these developments is obvious. It was always recognized that the only way a bloc of countries as diverse as the Group of 77 could come together to confront the advanced capitalist world would be to present a package of proposals. This package would combine their various interests, and all would back the entire package, giving support to each others' demands in return for the others' support for their own. As the semi-peripheral countries break ranks on certain issues, this means that the whole concept of a 'united front' must fail. A debt moratorium, for example, is not a very credible threat, as the countries representing the vast majority of that debt refuse in advance to have anything to do with it.

The economic differentiation of the semi-periphery can probably best be viewed as a logical consequence of the uneven nature of capitalist growth patterns. The political differentiation, however, has been increased (though not caused) by the conscious attempts of governments, corporations and banks in the advanced countries to divide the Third World. State Department officials admit, in not-for-attribution interviews, that cooptation of certain middle-level Third World countries was a definite part of US strategy in the North-South negotiations. The decreased militancy of G-77 demands is partially attributed by such officials to this strategy.[46]

Undermining Progressive Governments

Another cause for the decline in G-77 militancy, according to State Department views, came from the disappearance of certain particularly militant leaders such as Velasco of Peru, Echeverría of Mexico and Boumediene of Algeria. This assessment is probably valid, but it must be extended to include the decline of the regimes these leaders represented. Here again the banks played an important role. Many of the most obvious cases are found in Latin America (e.g., Chile under Allende and Peru under Velasco; Jamaica under Manley), but other regions have not been immune. Turkey under Ecevit is another, more complex, example.

In the Chilean case, the private banks played an important though not decisive role in the coalition of foreign governments, multinational corporations and multilateral agencies that helped dump Allende. They were not as important as they were to be several years later in Peru, because they had never been the chief source of funds for Chile. The Allende government came to office when private loans to Third World governments were only beginning; thus Chilean financial dependence was on public sector funds (mainly the US government and multilateral agencies). This financial dependence was very heavy because the United States had tried to build up the Frei government as an attractive capitalist alternative to socialist Cuba. As a consequence, Chile during most of the 1960s had the highest per capita aid flows in the world also the highest per capita debt (except for Israel).[47]

The Allende government was strongly nationalistic; one of its first important steps was to take over the foreign-owned copper mines that accounted for about 80 percent of the country's foreign exchange earnings. In addition, however, Allende also had the announced goal of expropriating large factories and farms, and radically redistributing income, as part of the move from a capitalist mode of production toward socialism. This guaranteed the strong opposition of local propertied classes as well as the US government and most of the major industrial multinationals with investments in Chile; together they effectively blocked Chile's traditional sources of international finance. The banks were brought in mainly through their short-term credits. During the Frei years, Chile had around $220 million in short-term credit lines from US banks. By 1972 only $35 million was still available. The five major New York banks — First National City Bank, Chase Manhattan, Manufacturers Hanover, Morgan Guaranty Trust and Chemical Bank — cut credits completely. Three other banks — Bank of America, Irving Trust and Bankers Trust — left a few lines open.[48] The blockade made imports very difficult and achieved its aim of increasing political opposition for the Allende government through creating economic problems.

In order to understand the actions of domestic groups that joined forces with the outside coalition, it is important to review the Cardoso-Faletto version of dependency theory. Domestic opposition groups were linked in many different ways to international capitalism (including the banks). Some members of the local capitalist class engaged in joint ventures with foreign capital or got loans from the international capital markets. Workers who had jobs in foreign-owned industries were afraid of losing the wage differentials they enjoyed over workers in domestic firms. 'Middle-sector' groups who took consumption cues from the United States were afraid of losing this international life style. And, of course, the military, which was ultimately responsible for the coup, was closely tied to the US military through training and equipment. On the other hand, analyses that indicate that the United States caused Allende's overthrow are simply incorrect. The fall of the Allende regime was brought about by local forces, tied to and aided by international capitalism. Understanding the linkage is crucial.

In the case of Peru, the banks were much more directly involved in the demise of a progressive government.[49] Initially, the banks had been very eager to lend to the military government. On the basis of favorable projections for Peruvian exports (copper, fishmeal and especially oil), the government was able to obtain over $2 billion from the private capital markets and, in the process, avoid the effects of the US credit blockage. Between 1968 and 1975 the Velasco government undertook a series of reforms under an ideology of a 'third way' between capitalism and communism. The most important of the reforms were (1) an extensive agrarian reform centering on the creation of cooperatives; (2) an industrial and mining reform introducing worker participation and profit-sharing; and (3) the nationalization of some key foreign firms, including branches of Standard Oil, ITT, W. R. Grace, Cerro and Chase Manhattan. Government leaders also became major participants in the Group of 77 and principal spokespeople for the demands of the Third World vis-à-vis the advanced capitalist countries. Unlike the Allende government, the Peruvian military did not want to remove themselves from the international capitalist system; they made no pretext of being Marxian socialists. They did, however, want to improve the standard of living of the population and to increase domestic control over economic and political decision-making.

By 1975, serious economic problems provided the excuse for Velasco's replacement by a president much more positively oriented toward international capitalism. When a debt crunch came in early 1976, Peru took an unusual step. Rather than going to the IMF for a balance of payments loan, the government approached the private banks to ask for one. For a series of reasons, six major US banks agreed, and took on the role of setting stabilization terms and monitoring the Peruvian economy. They also demanded and received concessions for private capital in general and foreign capital in particular.

The Peruvian economy took a nosedive as a result of the stabilization measures imposed, but balance of payments problems did not disappear. Wide opposition to the banks' role arose within the international banking community itself (principally because of fears of being made scapegoats and of lacking the necessary clout, experience and expertise to assume the traditional IMF role). The next year the banks sent Peru to the Fund, conditioning their own future loans on Peru's signing a letter of intent with the IMF.[50] The resulting negotiations ended all pretense of Peru being either nationalistic or progressive in either economic or political terms.

It should not be surmised, however, that this outcome was simply the result of the banks (and/or the IMF) imposing their will on a resisting Peruvian government. Well before Peru's negotiations with the banks began in 1976, Velasco had already been replaced, and the government had moved in a more conservative direction. This is another case that can be understood only by looking at the way local elites have become allies of international capitalism through ideological as well as economic channels.

In 1980 another case of bank involvement in undermining a progressive government seemed to be underway in Jamaica. Michael Manley, Jamaican prime minister since 1972, tried a milder version of policies that were found in Chile and Peru. At home, he made serious attempts to redistribute income and some attempts to redistribute property. Internationally, he became an important figure in the nonaligned movement and tried to gain increased revenue for Jamaica by imposing a levy on exports of the foreign-owned bauxite industry. A balance of payments crisis resulted as foreign investment dried up, capital flight occurred, and tourism fell off at the same time that oil prices rose.

Reversing the Peruvian strategy, Jamaica first went to the IMF and signed several stabilization agreements. The measures involved drove the economy into a sharp recession but did not resolve the balance of payments difficulties. When the IMF demanded yet more deflation in the spring of 1980, the government broke off relations with the Fund and tried to deal directly with the banks. The banks, which account for $450 million of Jamaica's $1.3 billion foreign debt, refused to reschedule the loans into longer-term debt or to provide new money. Their only concession, in order to avoid an open default that would cause them trouble with stockholders and bank supervisors, was an agreement to roll over principal payments on 87½ percent of the debt subject to a month-to-month review. Interest payments and payments on the remaining principal would continue.[51] The economic result of the balance of payments crisis was shortages of consumer goods and raw materials; the latter increased Jamaica's already high unemployment rate.

The political fallout of the economic crisis drove Manley out of office in the autumn 1980 election. Economic issues became top political issues, and the leader of the right-wing opposition party charged that Manley's leftist policies were ruining the country. The propertied classes in Jamaica and foreign groups (the banks, industrial multinational and perhaps the US government) hoped for an opposition victory and did what they could to promote one. A basic part of the strategy was to keep pressure on the government by trying to convince potential donors to avoid providing loans until after the election. The banks were an important participant but again worked in close cooperation with local interests.[52]

Supporting Reactionary Regimes

All over the Third World, the governments that have been the favored clients of the international banks have also been among the most repressive in their domestic activities. Iran under the Shah, South Korea, Taiwan, the Philippines, Indonesia, Brazil, Argentina, Chile — all stand high on the list of countries with poor human rights records. The relationship is not coincidental, of course, for the banks (like other multinational corporations) see 'strong' govenments as necessary to assure the stability and predictability that, in turn, will make their investments safe and profitable.[53] When necessary, strong governments are also useful for implementing stabilization programs that will produce sufficient foreign exchange to maintain payments to the banks.

Brazil is an archtypical case. The banks have poured almost $30 billion into Brazil in the past decade, relying heavily on their confidence in the military government. As one banker put it several years ago, 'As long as Mario Simonsen is finance minister, Brazil will put paying its foreign debts before anything else, including social welfare.'[54] Presumably the same could be said of Simonsen's successor, Delfim Netto. Up to now, that confidence has been justified. Although the strategy seems to be changing, the military has carried out policies that eliminated almost all opposition, whether from political parties, labor unions or individual citizens. Tactics ranged from dissolving opposition organizations to jailings, torture and murder. The economic strategy guaranteed that capital was squeezed out of the workers and peasants in order that rapid accumulation could take place. Domestic capital, however, was deemed insufficient, and a 'resource gap' (current account deficit) was specifically planned. The main way of filling this gap was to be loans from the private banks.[55] In addition, of course, Brazil became one of the major havens for foreign industrial investment.

When the Carter administration came to power in Washington, with its professed concern for human rights, some thought that the banks might be enlisted in the campaign. Jimmy Carter himself put an end to such hopes/fears. In a press conference in Brazil in 1978, the following exchange took place:

Q. Mr. President, the American commercial banks are the main Brazilian source of external credit. It seems to some people in Washington that sooner or later, a Congressman may try to establish a link between commercial banking loans and the human rights policy. I'd like your opinion about this subject.

A: Brazil is a major trading partner of the United States in commercial goods and also in loans and, I might say, timely repayments.... It would be inconceivable to me that any act of Congress would try to restrict the lending of money by American private banks to Brazil under any circumstances. This would violate the principles of our own free enterprise system. And if such an act was passed by Congress, I would not approve it.

Q: Which one would be the first place for you — the private enterprise and the private system or the human rights policy?

A: Well, they're both important to us and I don't see any incompatibility...between human right on the one hand and the free enterprise system on the other.[56]

Zaire is another prominent case where private bankers have been heavily involved in maintaining a reactionary regime in power in order to protect their investments. President Mobutu Sese Seko came to power in 1965 with full Western backing and, despite passing flirtations with the socialist countries internationally and nationalizations at home, he remains a Western bulwark in a non-aligned or socialist-leaning continent. His strong anti-communism, together with Zaire's mineral wealth, proved a strong attraction to the private banks. In spite of the fact that Zaire is one of the world's poorest countries, as measured in terms of GNP per capita, the banks loaned $700-$800 million during the early 1970s. This ties them to what the financial press itself calls 'one of Africa's most ruthless dictators.'[57] Of more concern to bankers, they are tied to a regime that is notoriously corrupt and inefficient.

The corruption has had serious effects on the living standard of the population. As Mobutu, his relatives and Zairian business groups have accumulated fortunes, mass pauperization has occurred with urban wages in 1978 about 15 percent of their 1960 level in real terms. The situation in rural areas is similar.[58] This corruption has led, in turn, to a loss of legitimacy for the regime and thus greater repression of Mobutu's opponents. Going against the trend in the rest of Africa, Mobutu has invited foreigners to return and has provided new investment possibilities and incentives.

In 1975 Zaire began to fall behind in loan payments. The following year, the same Citibank team that was leading the attempt to monitor the Peruvian economy tried to put together a deal with Zaire. As with Peru, the task proved too onerous, and the IMF was again called in. In this case, however, the Fund came in in a much more direct way. Supported by the banks and Western governments, the IMF has taken virtual control of the Zairian economy through management of the Central Bank and the Finance Ministry. The banks regard the Fund mission as the only hope of recovering their investment, but doing so also involves supporting the Mobutu regime.

It is in Chile, however, that the support role of the bankers has been most decisive. As the previous section demonstrated, the banks played an important role in the campaign to overthrow the Allende government; their role in supporting the military junta that replaced Allende is much more dramatic.[59] The difference in the Chilean case, compared with other countries with poor human rights records, is that the Chilean military became an international pariah. For a series of historical reasons (including Chile's impeccable record as a Western-style democracy), it was the one case in which international pressure might have succeeded in overthrowing a government that murdered tens of thousands of its own citizens and put thousands of others in concentration camps. It also threw hundreds of thousands out of work, and lowered wages of the working class as a whole by at least half. Nationalized properties were generally returned to their former owners, and the door was again opened wide to foreign capital. In Chile's case, however, the government went even further, and eliminated most of its historically high tariff barriers. The result has been the destruction of a large part of the domestic industrial sector, the perfect example of an anti-nationalist and anti-progressive regime.

Most governments reduced or eliminated economic assistance to Chile because of the junta's gross human rights violations. Even the United States, after large initial aid, ended its economic and military assistance. The World Bank and the Interamerican Development Bank, after loans that they claimed they had been processing during the Allende years, have also slowed down funds to Chile, although the IMF has provided important financial and moral backing. Private direct investment has been reluctant to come in except for a few mineral projects. The private banks, on the other hand, have been giving loans to Chile at unprecedented rates. As one study of the topic states,

> The tremendous influx of private bank loans since 1976 has enabled the Pinochet regime to ignore international pressure to improve human rights. Repression in Chile can continue precisely because the military junta can rely on private sources of financing rather than governments who have attached rough human rights criteria to their foreign assistance programs.[60]

A graph that appears in the same study shows the dramatic nature of the banks' role in supporting the Pinochet regime when all others refuse to do so (figure 1).

This section on political consequences of private bank loans is relevant to all three of the propositions discussed at the beginning of the paper. The imperialism proposition has been illustrated through case studies on the banks' role in the elimination of Third World regimes that tried to implement nationalistic policies to transfer resources to the control of the Third World and the support for other regimes that were more open to foreign penetration.

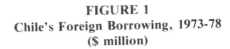

FIGURE 1
Chile's Foreign Borrowing, 1973-78
($ million)

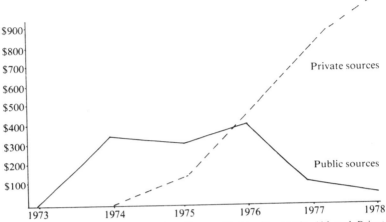

Source: I. Letelier and M. Moffitt, *Human Rights, Economic Aid and Private Banks: The Case of Chile*, p. 8.

Evidence for the sub-imperialism proposition was seen through the economic and political differentiation of certain Third World countries which then became a buffer between center and periphery and helped to dampen demands for a shift in resources from the former to the latter. The banks participated in both the economic and political aspects. The dependency proposition was seen in operation through the elimination of progressive governments that tried to shift income and property between classes within Third World countries and the banks' support for regimes that preferred to reconcentrate property within small privileged groups. Further-more, we tried to show that this third process was the result of cooperation between domestic Third World classes and outside groups in such a way that a larger share of resources would accrue to both.

THE DIALECTICS OF
INTERNATIONAL FINANCE

In the analysis above, a fairly straightforward case has been presented. Private bank loans have exacerbated three kinds of unequal development: between center and periphery, within the periphery, and between classes within peripheral countries. Both economic and political processes have been relevant to these developments. While evidence has been presented to support all three propositions, stopping here leaves a picture that is too simplistic and deterministic. Capitalism is a contradictory system, and the dialectic of the appearance, resolution and reappearance of contradictions must be acknowledged and analyzed. We will finish by looking at some of these contradictions and then asking how they can provide a basis for modifying our three propositions.

A first fact that complicates the analysis made thus far is that, even though the banks have undermined progressive nationalistic regimes and supported anti-nationalist reactionary ones, they have also provided funds to the former. The banks are out to make profits, and if a country looks promising in this respect they may be willing to overlook some of its political characteristics. For example, Cuba and the socialist countries of East Europe have borrowed considerable amounts on the Euromarkets; Vietnam and North Korea have obtained lesser sums; the banks are stumbling over themselves trying to get into the China market; Peru was able to avoid the US government-imposed credit blockade because the banks were more enticed by potential profits from Peruvian oil than turned off by the military's rhetoric and policies. In Chile as well, at the same time they were cutting off trade credits, the banks (unlike the US government) agreed to refinance their part of Chile's foreign debt.

Second, as I have detailed elsewhere, the onslaught of loans to Latin America and other Third World governments enabled the banks to avoid a potential profits crisis in the early 1970s and especially after 1973.[61] While other sectors of the international economy were buried in the morass of recession, the banks were enjoying hefty profit increases. But there were costs. On the one hand, medium-term loans to Third World governments are certainly riskier than short-term loans to blue-chip multinationals. One need not resort to the 'scare scenario' of a few years ago — defaults, bank failures, collapse of the world financial system — to realize that a number of bad loans were made, and the banks may have to write them off. Likewise, they are tied in to rolling over loans for a number of countries that have 'borrowed beyond their means' in conventional terms and accumulated huge debts in the process. The size of these debts is seen by some as increasing Third World countries' power vis-à-vis the banks.[62]

A second cost of the massive turn to Third World clients is that the very success of the venture has brought its own reaction. All banks now want into the market; European and Japanese banks have come in with a vengeance. Competition has increased tremendously in the last few years, and as a result spreads are down to what many bankers (especially the US banks, which tend to have higher costs) consider to be dangerously low. Even some Third World borrowers have obtained loans with spreads around 0.5 percent. It has become a borrower's market in others ways as well. The banks are being forced to refinance at lower rates, to extend maturities and to relinquish some earlier privileges (e.g., many borrowers are now insisting that legal jurisdiction for loan disputes be in their own court systems).

A final contradiction that is worth mentioning (the list is certainly not exhaustive) is the increasing tensions that are being revealed within the international capitalist hierarchy itself as a consequence of these loans. One example is a potential contradiction between multinational banks and multinational industries. The banks, in their eagerness to make sure that borrowers service their loans on time, are strangling the industrial sector in many Third World countries. Of course, this hits hardest at small and medium-size domestic industrialists, but the multinationals are seeing demand and local credit dry up as well. (GM's closing in Argentina is perhaps the most dramatic example.)

Some observers also foresee potential conflicts between banks and raw materials consumers where the banks, in order to guarantee the Third World governments an adequate supply of foreign exchange to service loans, would support commodity agreements. Similarly, the banks might support low tariffs for Third World industrial exports. The latter situation might also pit the banks against the United States and the governments of certain other advanced capitalist countries. In addition there is the hostility toward banks felt by many members of the US Congress — no one in Washington wants to be seen as 'bailing out the banks.' Finally, for all that the banks and the IMF seem to have worked in harmony in many of the cases described in this paper, they are not in complete agreement either. The IMF, for example, has refused to provide the information the banks want in order to lower the risk involved in loans to Third World governments.

What do these contradictions imply for the propositions relating private bank loans to various kinds of unequal development? Generally they would seem to indicate the need for increased sophistication and subtlety while maintaining the notion of political-economic hierarchies between and within countries. The dominant forces cannot be assumed to always get their way, and the autonomy of forces lower on the hierarchy must be taken into account to understand apparent deviations. This does *not* mean, however, that we end up with the currently popular concept of 'interdependence.' Interdependence there may be, but it operates within a hierarchically structured system between extremely unequal partners.[63]

To give some specific examples of needed modifications, the imperialism proposition about center-periphery relations needs to be revised to take account of the growing power dispersion within the Western alliance and the increasing role for European and Japanese corporations including the banks. The implications of the resulting autonomy of Europe and Japan must be analyzed. It is necessary to investigate the extent to which the new competition can help Third World countries seeking favorable terms for loans, but it is also crucial to examine the limits of competition, i.e. the point at which the banks and their allies will unite to prevent moratoria, expropriations and other such activities.

Turning to the sub-imperialism proposition, the concept of autonomy is again important. As a certain group of peripheral states gains economic and political importance, they cannot always be counted on to serve the role they are 'supposed' to play (whether in the Galtung or Wallerstein models). Under what conditions will this autonomy manifest itself, and what form will it take? On the other hand, looking at the semi-peripheral states from another point of view, the loans have almost surely helped them increase their economic capacity. Nevertheless, they have also caused economic problems in the form of large debts and high service payments. What conditions would cause these problems to limit the development of a semi-periphery?

The dependency proposition about unequal development within countries was empirically related to the undermining of progressive governments that had tried to narrow the income gap within countries.[64] The fact that the banks have occasionally supported such governments indicates the necessity to examine the conditions under which this will occur. Under the circumstances are private bankers willing to finance nationalist — and even socialist — regimes? Furthermore, we must be careful not to denigrate governmental autonomy in peripheral as well as semi-peripheral states. The banks may lend their support (political and economic) to governments that advocate regressive economic strategies, but the preferences and activities of influential domestic groups that favor these same strategies must not be overlooked.

In summary, as a next step in fashioning a theoretical framework to deal with the consequences of private loans, we would suggest maintaining the basic propositions of this paper while (1) specifying the conditions under which the predicted outcomes do not occur, and (2) paying close attention to the interrelationships between foreign and domestic groups even when the predicted outcomes do occur. It is this latter task that can provide a clarification of the process involved in the establishment, maintenance and modification of international and domestic hierarchies, and the role of private banks in this process.

NOTES

1. In this paper, we are dealing with loans and leaving aside the role of direct investment. To give an idea of the relative importance of the two, the OECD estimates that, between 1970 and 1978, about 15 percent of new capital inflows to Third World countries came from direct investment while the rest was from loans (private, public bilateral, and public multilateral). Calculated from OECD, *Development Cooperation* (Paris: OECD, 1979), p. 199.

2. Although it is difficult to separate out works dealing exclusively with the three subject areas mentioned in the text, the following are key sources that primarily deal with technical, economic and political topics respectively: A. Angelini et al., *International Lending, Risk, and the Euromarkets* (London: Macmillan, 1979); J. Aronson (ed.), *Debt and the Less Developed Countries* (Boulder, Colo.: Westview Press, 1979); and US Senate, Subcommittee on Foreign Economic Policy of the Foreign Relations Committee, *International Debt, the Banks, and U.S. Foreign Policy* (Washington: US Government Printing Office, 1977). Other major works are P. Wellons, *Borrowing by Developing Countries on the Eurocurrency Market* (Paris:

OECD, 1977); R. Devlin, *International Commercial Banks and their Cross-Border Lending to Governments of Developing Countries: A Study of Peru, 1965-76* (Santiago, Chile: UN Economic Commission for Latin America, 1979); and M. Wionczek (ed.), *LDC External Debt and the World Economy* (Mexico: El Colegio de Mexico, 1978). Many of the above books have extensive bibliographies. The bankers' viewpoint can be found in F. J. Mathies (ed.), *Offshore Lending by U.S. Commercial Banks* (Washington: Bankers Association for Foreign Trade, 1975) and I. Friedman, *The Emerging Role of Private Banks in the Developing World* (New York: Citicorp, 1977). Continuing discussion of the Euromarkets can be found in the following journals: *Euro-money, The Banker, Institutional Investor* and *World Financial Markets; Foreign Affairs* and *Foreign Policy* have also had symposia on the topic (July 1977 and Spring 1978, respectively).

3. B. Stallings, *Latin America and the U.S. Capital Markets, 1915-80* (forthcoming). This project has both theoretical and empirical components, the latter based on a computerized data bank with information on individual loans to all regions of the world. This data bank is the source for all statistics not otherwise referenced in this paper. The above project also makes it clear that private bank financing of Third World countries is not the 'new' phenomenon it is often portrayed to be. US banks were very active in this sense in the 1920s, as were British banks in the nineteenth century.

4. Others have been working on a more general synthesis though no very satisfactory one has emerged thus far. See especially, S. Amin, *Unequal Development* (New York: Monthly Review, 1976).

5. See J. Hobson, *Imperialism* (London: Allen & Unwin, 1938; originally published in 1902); R. Luxemburg, *The Accumulation of Capital* (London: Routledge, 1952; originally published in 1913); and V. I. Lenin, *Imperialism, The Highest Stage of Capitalism* (New York: International Publishers, 1939; originally published in 1917).

6. The best known works of the Monthly Review group are P. Baran, *The Political Economy of Growth* (New York: Monthly Review, 1957); P. Baran and P. Sweezy, *Monopoly Capital* (New York: Monthly Review, 1966); H. Magdoff, *The Age of Imperialism* (New York: Monthly Review, 1969); S. Amin, *The Accumulation of Capital on a World Scale* (New York: Monthly Review, 1974); and A. Emmanuel, *Unequal Exchange, A Study of the Imperialism of Trade* (New York: Monthly Review, 1972).

7. A number of critiques of this type are found in R. Owen and B. Sutcliffe (eds), *Studies in the Theory of Imperialism* (London: Longman, 1972), especially articles by T. Hodgkin and R. Robinson.

8. Lenin, op. cit., p. 65.

9. Baran, op. cit., p. 184.

10. See especially the following articles: P. O'Brien, 'A Critique of Latin American Theories of Dependency,' in I. Oxaal et al., *Beyond the Sociology of Development* (London: Routledge & Kegan Paul, 1975), pp. 2-27; C. Leyes, 'Underdevelopment and Dependency; Critical Notes,' *Journal of Contemporary Asia*, vol. 7, no. 1 (1977), pp. 92-107; and I. Roxborough, 'Dependency Theory in the Sociology of Development: Some Theoretical Problems,' *West African Journal of Sociology and Political Science*, vol. 1, no. 2 (1976), pp. 116-33.

11. T. dos Santos, 'The Structure of Dependence,' *American Economic Review* (May 1970), pp. 23-36. This brief article should not necessarily be taken as represen-

tative of dos Santos's other writings on dependency, most of which only appear in Spanish. See, for example, his *Dependencia y cambio social* (Santiago, Chile: CESO, 1970) and *Lucha de clases y dependencia en América Latina* (Bogota, Colombia: Editorial Oveja Negra, 1970). Andre Gunder Frank's best known work is *Capitalism and Underdevelopment in Latin America* (New York: Monthly Review, 1969).

12. dos Santos, 'The Structure of Dependence,' p. 231.

13. F. H. Cardoso and E. Faletto, *Dependencia y desarrollo en América Latina* (Mexico: Siglo XXI, 1969). An English version was published by the University of California Press in 1979 (see n. 14).

14. F. H. Cardoso and E. Faletto, *Dependency and Development in Latin America* (Berkeley: University of California, 1979), p. 15. This approach is spelled out even more explicitly in the new introduction to the English edition; see especially pp. xv-xvi.

15. J. Galtung, 'Conflict on a Global Scale: Social Imperialism and Sub-Imperialism — Continuities in the Structural Theory of Imperialism,' *World Development*, vol. 4, no. 3 (1976), pp. 153-65. Ruy Mauro Marini, another social scientist who has written on sub-imperialism, seems to have a different concept in mind: his sub-imperialism is close to Cardoso's 'associated dependent development.' See R. M. Marini, 'Brazilian Subimperialism,' *Monthly Review* (February 1972), pp. 14-24.

16. Galtung, op. cit., p. 163 (emphasis in original).

17. I. Wallerstein, 'The Rise and Future Demise of the World Capitalist System,' *Comparative Studies of Society and History*, no. 16 (1974), pp. 387-415. See also his book *The Modern World-System* (New York: Academic Press, 1974).

18. Wallerstein, 'The Rise,' p. 405 (emphasis in original).

19. There are a number of general books about the history and functioning of the Euromarkets. A good recent one, written for a general audience, is M. S. Mendelsohn, *Money on the Move: The Modern International Capital Market* (New York: McGraw-Hill, 1980). For a more technical introduction, see G. McKenzie, *The Economics of the Euro-Currency System* (London: Macmillan, 1976).

20. These definitions are now somewhat outdated since new types of financial instruments are constantly being introduced. An especially important one in these years of high inflation is the floating rate note (FRN), a bond with a floating interest rate. Euroloans are also occasionally given on a fixed-rate basis, and during early 1980 experiments began with floating rate loans where the spread, as well as the LIBOR, is adjusted every six months.

21. For a discussion of these developments, see M. Kuczynski, 'Semi-Developed Countries and the International Business Cycle,' *BOLSA Review* (January 1976), pp. 2-13.

22. According to Morgan Guaranty Trust, *World Financial Markets*, Third World countries went over the 50 percent mark as of 1975 with respect to Euroloans. In 1979 they accounted for 58 percent of total loans. In bonds, on the other hand, Third World borrowers still represented only 8 percent of the total in 1979 (down from 12 percent in 1978).

23. This residual category is basically the Third World with the following important additions: Japan, Australia and New Zealand in the Asian Pacific area, and South Africa in Africa. Asia Pacific without these three countries accounted for 9.0 percent of loans and 1.9 percent of bonds; Africa without South Africa represented 2.3 and 0.1 percent respectively. Advanced Mediterranean countries include Spain,

Portugal, Greece, Israel, Yugoslavia, Cyprus and Turkey. These countries are often listed with the Third World; in the analysis that follows (with the exception of Turkey) they are included as part of the industrialized block.

24. The term 'capitalist countries' is a controversial one. Here it includes all countries except for the Soviet Union, Eastern Europe, Cuba, North Korea and Vietnam. A number of other countries, such as China, would be included, but they had not participated in the Euromarkets as of 1978.

25. These categories are those used by the World Bank with the following exceptions: the 'advanced Mediterranean countries' (except Turkey) are included with 'other industrial countries,' and the OPEC category here includes all OPEC members rather than just the surplus issue of the Bank's quarterly publication *Borrowing in International Capital Markets*.

26. The five are Mexico, Brazil, Venezuela, Algeria and the Philippines.

27. See M. Odjagov, 'Transnational Banking' (New York: United Nations Centre on Transnational Corporations, January 1977, mimeo).

28. The five US banks together accounted for 42 percent of all Third World loans in the 1972-78 period, and the top five European banks for 34 percent of Third World bonds. The most important US bank in terms of bonds was Merrill Lynch with $593 million in comparison to Deutsche Bank's $1.1 billion. It should be added that, in the Euroloan market, US banks have been losing ground rapidly to the Europeans and Japanese since 1978.

29. In these regions, US banks managed more loans than banks from all other countries combined.

30. In terms of bond distribution, 90 percent has gone to the industrial countries compared with 10 percent to the Third World. With respect to loans to the private sector, this breakdown is 66 percent to industrial countries and 34 percent to the Third World.

31. To make the comparison over time, we must assume that the regions had their borrowing distributed over time in similar proportions.

32. For example, the average bond maturity for 1972-78 was 10.5 years, compared with only 6.9 years for loans. The average interest rates were 8.8 and 10.4 percent respectively, so that bonds were preferable even before taking account of the increased problems caused by floating rates.

33. Some might argue that any Third World participation in the private capital market is better than the previous situation, when all of this money went to the advanced capitalist countries. This might be true if private bank funds were supplementing public loans; rather, they have tended to replace them. OECD figures show that foreign aid as a percent of GNP has fallen significantly during the 1970s compared with the 1960s. This is especially the case for the United States, where some government officials have argued that the government should withdraw in favor of private bank loans to the Third World.

34. This point has been specifically addressed in R. Devlin, 'International Commercial Bank Finance and the Economic Development of Poor Countries: Congruence and Conflict,' *CEPAL Review* no. 9 (December 1979).

35. Morgan Guaranty Trust, *World Financial Markets*, various issues. The period covered here is 1970 through mid-1980.

36. Cited in C. Diaz-Alejandro, 'The Post 1971 International Financial System and the Less Developed Countries,' in G. K. Helleiner (ed.), *A World Divided* (Cambridge: University Press, 1976), p. 191.

37. ibid.

38. This difference is less if we look only at the more developed parts of the Third World. For instance, doing the same calculations for Latin America shows interest rates on private loans only about one percent higher than those on World Bank loans, and World Bank maturities about three times those for the private banks. The difference is that Latin America does not have any significant access to the IDA's 'soft' loans (0.75 percent interest and 50 year maturities). Almost all Latin American World Bank loans come from IBRD, whose interest rates approach market levels although maturities are much longer. Combining IBRD 'hard' loans and IDA 'soft' loans probably provides a fairly accurate reflection of terms of public sector loans in general.

39. Calculated from OECD, op. cit., pp. 226 and 239 (for bilateral and multilateral aid) and Morgan Guaranty Trust, op. cit. (for Euroloans).

40. If tied export credits (public and private) are included, this figure drops to one-third.

41. Calculated from *World Bank Atlas* (Washington: World Bank, 1979); averages are weighted by GNP. It could be argued, of course, that countries get loans because they are growing rapidly rather than the other way around. Causation probably runs in both directions, but the contribution of bank loans to growth cannot be overlooked.

42. *Transnational Corporations in World Development: A Re-examination* (New York: UN Centre on Transnational Corporations, 1978).

43. For information on the Group of 77 and the New International Economic Order, see, among proliferating sources, J. Bagwati (ed.), *The New International Economic Order* (Cambridge, Mass.: MIT Press, 1977); E. Laszlo et al., *The Obstacles to the New International Economic Order* (New York: Pergamon, 1980); and A. Fishlow et al., *Rich Nations and Poor Nations in the World Economy* (New York: McGraw-Hill, 1978).

44. *Wall Street Journal* (15 March 1978); see also *New York Times* (1 June 1976).

45. The proposal is from the important Trilateral Commission, whose members include the most important businessmen in the advanced capitalist countries. Alumni include many of the top officials of the Carter administration, including the President himself. The main rapporteur for this particular report was C. Fred Bergsten, former Under-Secretary of the Treasury for International Affairs. See *The Reform of International Institutions*, Triangle Paper no. 11 (1976).

46. Interviews with current and past government officials in New York and Washington, January-August 1978. The existence of a 'cooptation strategy' is confirmed (and criticized) in a recent article by Roger Hansen, an academic with close ties to many top foreign policy officials in the Carter administration: see R. Hansen, 'North-South Policy — What Is the Problem?', *Foreign Affairs*, vol. 58, no. 5 (Summer 1980), esp. pp. 1108-15.

47. On the general role of external forces in the overthrow of Allende, see J. Petras and M. Morley, *The United States and Chile: Imperialism and the Overthrow of the Allende Government* (New York: Monthly Review, 1975).

48. *New Chile* (Berkeley: NACLA, 1973), p. 135.

49. On Peru, see B. Stallings, 'Peru and the U.S. Banks: The Privatization of Financial Relations,' in R. Fagen (ed.), *Capitalism and the State in U.S.-Latin*

American Relations (Stanford: University Press, 1979), pp. 217-53; and Devlin, *International Commercial Banks.*

50. The role of the IMF in bringing about 'adjustment' to balance of payments difficulties in Third World countries has become increasingly controversial of late. Critics as diverse as UNCTAD, the Brandt Commission and London's conservative newsweekly *The Economist* have all called for new strategies, especially an emphasis on medium-term finance rather than a 'shock treatment.' An early critique along these same lines, which gives an idea of the types of conditions involved in Letters of Intent and the usual political/economic consequences, is C. Payer, *The Debt Trap* (New York: Monthly Review, 1975), especially chs. 1 and 2.

51. *New York Times* (5 May 1980). For a detailed view of Jamaica's economic problems and relations with the IMF, see A. Brown, 'Economic Policy and the IMF in Jamaica' (Kingston, Jamaica: Institute of Social and Economic Research, 1980, mimeo). A more accessible source is S. Keith and R. Girling, 'Caribbean Conflict: Jamaica and the US.,' *NACLA Report on the Americas*, vol. XII, no. 3 (May-June 1978), pp. 3-36.

52. Some people consider the fall of the Ecevit government in Turkey in October 1979 to be yet another case of bank and IMF participation in the downfall of a progressive government. There are certain similarities, but the Turkish situation seems more complex than the Latin American examples discussed above. On the one hand, Turkey is considered critical to Western security arrangements and thus has more access to government loans. On the other hand, the former opposition leader in Turkey, Suleyman Demirel, was not trusted by the international financial community and, in fact, was considered by many to be responsible for Turkey's economic problems because of his heavy spending while prime minister in the early 1970s. Nevertheless, after returning to office, he announced an austerity budget and opened the country to foreign investment early in 1980.

53. An analysis of the relationship between authoritarian governments and foreign investment can be found in G. O'Donnell, 'Reflections on the Patterns of Change in the Bureaucratic-Authoritarian State,' *Latin American Research Review*, vol. XIII, no. 1 (1978), pp. 3-38.

54. 'Living with Nationalism: Chase in Latin America,' *NACLA's Latin American and Empire Report*, vol. X, no. 4 (1976), p. 9. For more recent information on Brazil's economy and political conditions, see S. Hewlett, *Cruel Dilemmas of Development: Twentieth Century Brazil* (New York: Basic Books, 1980).

55. See analysis in Wellons, op. cit., pp. 102-17.

56. *New York Times* (31 March 1978).

57. *Euromoney* (February 1979), p. 9.

58. C. Young, 'Zaire: The Unending Crisis,' *Foreign Affairs*, vol. VII, no. 1 (Fall 1978), pp. 175-6. For more detailed discussion of similar topics, see G. Gran (ed.), *Zaire: The Political Economy of Underdevelopment* (New York: Praeger, 1979).

59. On Chile and the banks, see I. Letelier and M. Moffitt, *Human Rights, Economic Aid and Private Banks: The Case of Chile* (Washington: Transnational Institute, 1978). See also S. Griffith-Jones, 'The IMF and Economic Adjustment Policies, Chile 1973-80' (Brighton, Sussex: University of Sussex, 1980, mimeo).

60. Letelier and Moffitt, op. cit., p. 10.

61. Stallings, 'Peru,' p. 249.

62. See, for example, J. Aronson's characterization of the banks and Third World governments as 'mutual hostages': J. Aronson, 'The Politics of Private Bank Lending and Debt Renegotiations,' in Aronson, op. cit., p. 306.

63. Among the best known works in the interdependency literature are R. Cooper, *The Economics of Interdependence* (New York: McGraw-Hill, 1968); E. Morse, 'The Politics of Interdependence,' *International Organization*, vol. 23, no. 2 (Spring 1969); and R. O. Keohane and J. S. Nye, 'World Politics and the International Economic System,' in C. F. Bergsten (ed.), *The Future of the International Economic Order* (Lexington, Mass.: D. C. Heath and Co., 1973). Two prominent authors within the dependency tradition try to distinguish the concepts of dependence and interdependence as follows:

> Almost all contemporary national economic systems are articulated in the international system. Superficial or apologetic analysts, in order to minimize exploitative aspects of the international economy, have merely assumed that 'modern' economies are 'interdependent.' By stating this platitude, they often forget that the important question is what forms that 'interdependency' takes... While some economies become indebted to the financial capital cities of the world, others are creditors. Of course bankers need clients, as much as clients need bankers. But the 'interrelationship' between the two is qualitatively distinct because of the position held by each partner in the structure of the relationship. The same is true for the analysis of 'interdependent' economies in world markets... In order to go ahead with economic expansion, a dependent country has to play the 'interdependency' game, but in a position similar to the client who approaches a banker. Of course, clients usually develop strategies of independence and can try to use the borrowed money in productive ways. But insofar as there are structural border lines, successful attempts are not an automatic output of the game. More often, rules of domination are enforced, and even if the dependent country becomes less poor after the first loan, a second one follows. In most cases, when such an economy flourishes, its roots have been planted by those who hold the lending notes. [Cardoso and Faletto, op. cit., pp. xxi-xxii]

64. If the data were available, it would probably be possible to make a direct, rather than indirect, link between private loans and inequality within Third World countries. That is, it could probably be shown that certain groups and regions derive disproportionate benefits from the loans while other groups and regions are being left behind.

9

FINANCIAL INSTITUTIONS, CREDIT ALLOCATION AND MARGINALIZATION IN THE BRAZILIAN NORTH-EAST: THE BAHIAN CASE

Harry M. Makler
University of Toronto, Canada

INTRODUCTION

Efforts to maintain the rate and pattern of economic development in Brazil have led to financial innovations and new group alliances that have a significant impact on the society and economy. National and international financial market and institutional changes have been designed primarily to mobilize more efficiently domestic and foreign resources to be employed for the attainment of profess-

Author's Note: The first version of this paper was presented at the Symposium on Achieving Social Change: The Working of Social Stratification in Brazil, American Anthropological Association Annual Meeting, San Francisco, 4 December 1975; and a revised version was presented at the conference on the Social and Political Challenges of the New International Economic Order in Comparative Perspective, The Rockefeller Conference and Cultural Center, Villa Serbelloni, Bellagio (Como), Italy, 24-8 April 1979. The French translation has been published in Arnaud Sales (ed.),'Développement national et économie mondialisée', a thematic issue of *Sociologie et Sociétés*, vol. XI, no. 2, October 1979. The generous support of the International Development Research Centre, Canada Council, the Joint Committee of the Social Science Research Council and the American Council of Learned Societies, and the Humanities and Social Sciences Committee, University of Toronto, enabled me to conduct the research for this paper. The Department of Applied Economics, Federal University of Bahia and the Center for Latin American Studies, Stanford University have kindly provided institutional support for my continuing research on this topic. I am also grateful to Andrew Beveridge, Richard Bird, Rondo Cameron, Barry Ames, Antonio Barros de Castro, Emilio F. Moran, Arnaud Sales, Neil Smelser and Charles Wagley for their comments, and especially for the revisions suggested by Wendy Barker.

ed development goals. Financial institutions have been largely overlooked in the literature as a means of effectively allocating resources to desirable classes, regions and sectors of the economy. Among all the developing nations, contemporary Brazil provides an optimum setting to examine the impact of financial institutions on class structure and economic growth. Especially since 1964, Brazil has both responded to international circumstances and has actively played a growth-inducing role by having devised new mechanisms, particularly through its financial institutions, in a conscious attempt to catch up with the more developed nations of the world. We hope to raise, if not answer, some pertinent questions on the impact of such developments on the class structure in the Brazilian North-East, the largest and most rapidly changing region in Latin America, and particularly in Bahia, the target of most state intervention and industrialization in this region.[1]

Financial intermediation — the mobilization and allocation of surplus capital from savers to investors among different activities according to relative rates of return — is both a significant and an informative socioeconomic transaction. Who makes the decisions behind these operations, how these decisions are made, to whom the credit it allocated, and for what purposes — all have a significant impact on social stratification and economic development. We will show how the performance of credit allocation can hasten the development of certain sectors of the Bahian economy that are considered crucial inputs for the realization of the state's development goals. But at the same time these actions hinder the economic growth of 'less dynamic' sectors, and hence certain social classes associated with those sectors, by effectively restricting their access to funds, or by restraining that access so as to discourage certain economic activities.

Since 1964 the Brazilian regime has voiced and actively pursued a 'developmentalist' economic policy. The financial strategies used by the state reveal its intent of re-ordering social structure to facilitate this policy. The state has, in effect, assumed the role of financial intermediary. A great deal of its creditability and legitimacy rests upon fulfilling this political rhetoric. The name of the game is 'efficiency over equality' — modernization at the expense of structural inequalities (high unemployment, a high degree of income concentration and marginalization of traditional family-owned firms). Following such a 'developmentalist' ideology, prosperity is confined to an economic bourgeoisie who comprise only a small percentage of the total population, while the living standards of the majority remain relatively unchanged; for social mobility is severely restricted and political participation of the masses is stifled, the production base for economic development is externally generated and monopolized by the international bourgeoisie, and the repressiveness of the regime remains unchallenged as it points to the high rate of economic growth to make it appear as if everyone was gaining and no one losing.

The nature and source of the investment that fuel such a scheme may well be in direct conflict with the interests of the various marginal groups of the society, but in the final analysis it is *who* controls the 'valve' for the capital flows that will shape and control the economy and perpetuate the contradictions inherent in the system. And the most significant capital flows are controlled from abroad by an international private and public banking network, and internally by a state that bows to the class interests of an industrial bourgeoisie that is tightly linked with international capitalism; hence, the intensification of Brazil's historic dependent relationship on external affiliations.

Despite the state's professed goals of strengthening the private sector, its intervention in the industrial and infrastructure areas has increased dramatically relative to the private sector since 1964. The private sector's role remains subordinate to that of the state in generating and controlling capital resources for economic growth. Having monopolized the most modern and most profitable sectors of the economy, the state has limited the number of enterprises in the private sector, further exacerbating the historical weakness of that sector. The private cannot possibly compete with the relatively efficient performance of the state or with its ability to attract capital resources from international banking networks, which prefer to make long-term loans to the more 'credit-worthy' governments. Public enterprises are often characterized by low risk and high profits, and thus attract shareholders more readily than the private sector. Interest rates reflect these characteristics, and it will be shown how banks use them as devices for efficiently allocating resources to those dynamic industries that yield the most profitable returns. There seems little chance that the private sector can achieve the financial and technological economies of scale needed to succeed in modern industry without access to low-cost long-term financing. On the regional level we will illustrate how certain industries and certain entrepreneurs within the private sector are able to obtain only short-term loans, which are sufficient for working capital (i.e. wage payments), but not for expansion and growth. In effect, one is presented with examples of how banks can effectively 'smother' certain industries.

BACKGROUND

In the Brazilian North-East industry developed in response to the structures created by the formation of specific financial intermediaries rather than the reverse. Well into the 1950s the North-East still had a stagnant primary export economy. Existing industry was of limited scope, was family-owned, and was closely linked either to primary export sectors or to the production of nondurable goods for the local market. Industrial growth did not require extensive financing, nor did the financial sector play a major role in the primary export sector. The exporters either used their own capital or relied on letters of credit from their importers. Some of the largest exporters were either foreign-owned (e.g., SANBRA) or had foreign capital participation (e.g. Cimento Aratu).[2]

Thus, the financial sector tended to restrict its activities and investments to the development of the commercial (particularly the underwriting of imports/exports) and infrastructural spheres. Accordingly, financial needs could be accommodated within a relatively unsophisticated banking network that remained outside agriculture and industry. Because of this a number of practices began which would seriously affect the North-East economy in years to come. First, surplus generated within the North-East was invested to the growth poles in the Center-South of the country in search of greater returns. Second, the national government initiated exchange policies that transferred the surplus from North-East agricultural exporting sectors to the emerging industrial sectors in the Center-South. Together, these movements created an income transfer to the Center-South of more than $413 million during the 1950s, an average of $38 million per year. The government's use of 'parafiscal' instruments to achieve capital accumulation compensated for a banking system that was unable to finance the transition from a primary export to an urban, industrialized economy. This problem became particularly acute during the latter phase of import substitution (1962-64), when large-scale and long-term investments were required.[3]

What is important is not only the fact of involuntary capital outflows — which would have had to be reversed if the North-East economy were to acquire a greater dynamism — but also that they reflected an attempt to compensate for the inability, and perhaps reluctance, of financial institutions in the Center-South to provide the capital necessary for an economy in transition. This problem would at a later date be reproduced in the North-East. However, in this region the problem could not be solved by bypassing financial institutions; instead they became the lever which the government developed and used to lift the North-East out of its stagnation.

Many hold that economic development involves a slow incremental growth of both savings and investment along a simple and unilinear trajectory. In fact it involves the adoption of economic models that may require restructuring of the financial system in order to mobilize surpluses more efficiently, particularly in the transfer of resources to new sectors. However, in the North-East the financial sector had developed primarily to serve the primary export economy. Indeed, some of the banks were even owned by members of the agro-commercial elite, who looked upon growing import substitution industry as threatening their framework.[4]

In the competition for scarce financial resources the nascent industrial sector was thus pushed aside in favor of more conventional projects, such as the expansion of infrastructure by which a growing hinterland could be incorporated into the commercial grip of the major urban centers. The agro-commercial and financial bourgeoisie resisted the new industrial order. This was especially felt by industrialists who were directors of the new durable (especially consumer) goods enterprises.

These new entrepreneurs, in other words, required considerable finance capital, which was scarce in the North-East. Their need was further exacerbated by dependence on foreign technology and an increasing demand for their manufactures by a growing middle class.[5] This greatly expanded need for finance capital occurred in the North-East at a time when the ability of the financial institutions to mobilize such resources was severely hindered by the existence of archaic financial structures and by the general drain of the surplus capital to the more prosperous regions of the country. As individual industrialists were becoming increasingly dependent on the financial sector, the financial sector was increasingly unable to satisfy industrial demands.[6]

The problems encountered in the early periods of north-eastern development left their impact on contemporary financial structure, as is demonstrated by two apparently opposite patterns. In the first place my data indicated that the industrial bourgeoisie was quite dependent on banks. In Bahia, 65 percent of those interviewed used mainly bank credit for the financing of their activities. If we omit those who used non-bank credit and those who did not answer our question, only 29 percent of Bahian industrialists depended primarily on self-financing, and among those private partner participation was even lower.[7] Few said their companies issued shares to raise additional capital. This practice requires the existence of a large middle class with sufficiently large incomes as well as a large number of enterprises both able to generate public confidence and willing to issue shares. While a stock market has been recently established in Brazil (with rather ambiguous success), investment (e.g., purchase of local enterprise stocks) was rare in the North-East. Recognition of this was often voiced by the industrialists; when asked about the possibility of issuing shares, the following replies were typical: 'Unlike America, the stock market has not caught on here'; 'The market is only in São Paulo where the few who invest purchase shares in huge southern companies such as Volkswagen'; or 'There is little sense in issuing shares as the public doesn't buy them.' However, when asked about future financing, a sizeable proportion (34 percent) indicated that if they expanded their enterprise they would prefer to raise capital by issuing shares. The will is there, but the conditions are simply absent.

Only 39 percent of the industrial bourgeoisie conducted frequent commercial relations with banks in the private sector and fewer borrowed capital from these banks. The limited relations with the private banks is due to the latter lacking capital in sufficient quantity and the consequent lack of medium and long-term credits. This was a source of frequent complaints among industrialists.

If we subtract from the private banking sector those banks that do not originate within the North-East, the percentage of credit relations shrinks even further. Only 19 percent of credit relations were with private north-eastern banks. If we take into account the fact that the Banco da Bahia, the largest private bank in the North-East, was recently bought out by a southern bank (Bradesco), this percentage is reduced by more than half.

In short, the private banking sector has been unable to fulfil the demands of the industrial sector, and this has been doubly true of the north-eastern banks. Salvador, the capital of Bahia, was once a major Brazilian banking center, indicating the extent to which its banking sector has been eclipsed.

There are two tendencies at work here. First, the private north-eastern banks are being replaced by private southern and foreign banks, either through the establishment of branch banks or through mergers. In the second place, the entire private banking sector is being displaced by the government banks.[8] Simultaneously, the industrial sector's need for financial resources is growing.

Through its financial institutions (and to a lesser extent the southern banks) the regime is attempting to absorb the role of the older north-eastern banks because of the latter's inability to meet the requirements of a dynamic industrial sector. This involves the creation of national, regional and state development banks, movement into commercial banking activities, and industrialization programs. The programs of the Superintendency for the Development of the Northeast (SUDENE) and the Bank of the Northeast (BNB) serve as examples of this trend. Created in 1959 as an 'integrated comprehensive' regional development program, SUDENE has stimulated mainly industrial development, especially under 'Article 34/18,' a powerful tax credit clause.[9] Another important source of industrial finance is provided by the Bank of the Northeast (BNB). This bank, as part of the regional development program, finances at very favorable interest rates (12 percent annually without inflation adjustment, as compared with 30 or 40 percent in commercial banks) up to a maximum of 50 percent of the additional resources that are required by the original entrepreneurs for their projects.[10] Given the rate of inflation in Brazil, a BNB loan is in reality at negative or zero interest charge. In addition to these industrial incentive programs and financing facilities, each north-eastern state, and in some cases the large municipalities in these states, offers programs to attract new industry.[11] In Pernambuco, for example, there is Banco de Desenvolvimento (BANDEPE); in Bahia, there is a similar agency called the Banco de Desenvolvimento do Estado da Bahia (DESENBANCO).[12]

With the possible exception of the Amazon region, no other area in Brazil has witnessed the establishment of so many official industrialization programs and financial incentives as the North-East. However, this intervention cannot be considered a mere response to industrial demands; government involvement is, in fact, so great that the relation of demand and response are revers-

ed. Government intervention thus became the conscious proponent
of an emerging industrial order. By playing a preponderant role in
the financing of industry, the state is in a position to influence not
only its extent (the actual level of industrial development reached)
but also its nature (the balance between different industries and
their distribution among different categories).

THE BAHIAN INDUSTRIAL BOURGEOISIE
AND ITS RELATIONS WITH
FINANCIAL INSTITUTIONS

Analysis

A survey conducted in 1973 and 1974 with a large representative
sample ($N = 134$) of heads of larger Bahian industries provides the
evidence to examine the questions raised about state control of
north-east industrialization and class structure via financial intermediation.[13]

The geographic origins characterized as: 'native' to the North-
East, 'migrant' from another part of Brazil (overwhelmingly from
the Center South), or 'foreign-born' (foreigner). This categoriza-
tion approximates the emergent stratification system within the industrial class as suggested by the different stages of north-eastern
development in general and that of Bahia in particular. These types
also represent a clustering of specific values of enterprise
characteristics such as industrial sector, family ownership,[14]
technological complexity,[15] enterprise size,[16] corporate affiliation,[17]
foreign capital participation[18] and, among other biographical
characteristics, social class origin of the industrialists.[19] In this
sense the natives represent an earlier period of economic development (or lack of it) associated with the traditional sectors
(foodstuffs, beverages, tobacco, textiles, wood and paper products, printing and graphics), labor-intensive and family-owned
enterprises. Many were from upper socioeconomic origins and had
inherited their enterprises. This group was later displaced (in
relative terms) by more middle class migrant managerial types
associated with the more modern economies of the Center-South.
Also corresponding to this type are the dynamic sectors (durable
consumer goods, petrochemicals, chemicals, electrical machinery,

steel) requiring capital-intensive production processes as well as the larger, more modern, forms of organization (e.g., non-family-owned enterprises, branch plants, etc.)

This 'displacement' occurred in two waves. The first was in the late 1950s. Because of the proximity of Bahia to the Center-South, the construction of the corresponding transportation links, and the formation of the petrochemical complex, this period of industrial growth was of much greater significance and took on more sharply defined characteristics in Bahia than in the North-East as a whole. As such, Bahia was the recipient of more southern capital, of more modern and capital-intensive enterprises — in short, of more migrants. Bahia was rapidly becoming integrated into the national economy as defined by the productive and the market structures. It appears that the extent and suddenness of this transition accounts for the weakness of the native industrial bourgeoisie (in terms of both its ability to adapt economically to the new situation and to manipulate the local power structure) relative to industrialists in other north-eastern states.[20]

The second wave of economic development occurred in the late 1960s and was based in part on the earlier integration of Bahia into the Brazilian economy; that is, the recovery of the Bahian, and for that matter the Pernambucan, economy was in part dependent on the recovery of the Brazilian economy. In this sense the second wave was a continuation of tendencies expressed in the earlier phase. Yet to this must be added the role of government incentives at the level of the financial structure; the creation of new banks, the streamlining of the operations of older banks, as well as the creation of SUDENE and the 34/18 program. The extent of these incentives should not be underestimated. It is possible if one receives the approval of the appropriate government agencies to expand in the North-East almost entirely on the basis of loans, grants and other people's tax credits. Of all the migrants interviewed in Bahia, over half their firms (56 percent) had been established during this second phase, as compared with approximately a third of native and foreign-born enterprises. These recently established migrant firms tend to be in the most modern sector and are the most capital-intensive. The migrants increasingly resemble the above characterization of them. This is so much the case that some observers have begun to complain about artificial economies with minimal links to the traditional economies in terms of either inputs or outputs.[21]

The foreign-born bourgeoisie can be divided into two corresponding categories: (1) the small family-owned industry, and (2) the
modern branch plants of transnationals. The foreign-born
represents a relatively small part of our sample (approximately
1:5); and, correspondingly, this essay will concentrate mainly on the
natives and migrants. These three types, however, will be analyzed
in terms of their enterprise characteristics.

Credit Transactions

As discussed earlier, the majority (nearly 70 percent) of the industrialists relied mainly on bank loans to finance their economic
activities. Few raised capital by issuing shares or debentures,
although many expressed a willingness to do so in the future if they
decided to expand their enterprises. Most credit transactions were
conducted with official banks such as the Bank of Brazil and the
Bank of the North-East and, following these, two or three private
banks, some of which were located in the Center-South of the
country.

We then asked what the content of these transactions was.
Knowledge of the kinds of capital being borrowed and the terms of
the credit would illuminate not only state development policy but,
for our particular purposes, the pattern of discrimination and
marginalization as well. The industrialists who had previously indicated that they had used bank credit were asked to specify the
items for which they borrowed capital over the past year. These
items were then grouped into either a short- or long-term capital
category in order to facilitate the analysis.

Short-term Capital Borrowing

In both Bahia and Pernambuco the greatest borrowing was in terms
of short-term capital.[22] Nearly three-fifths of the industrialists (59
percent) borrowed working capital, and over a third (34 percent)
reported that they had borrowed short-term capital. This suggests
that the average enterprise in these north-east states found it difficult to meet its short-run costs. Indeed, when asked about the two
most important problems confronting their enterprises, the lack of
'capital do giro' (working capital) was often mentioned. There are
a variety of factors that explain this. Perhaps the most important

factor behind this heavy short-term capital borrowing was the lack of long-term or fixed capital on the financial market. The banks, especially the private ones, seemed reluctant to make long-term loans to many north-eastern industries. However, as we began to gather during our interviews, this was more crucial for traditional sectors, particularly the older, family-owned enterprises, whose profits were reduced by strong price controls, severe national competition, inflation and/or the low purchasing power of the population. All these were exacerbated in the North-East.

Focusing more closely on particular industrial types confirms the fact that natives heading traditional sector family enterprises and natives heading dynamic sector non-family-owned enterprises are the heaviest borrowers of short-term capital.[23] One may infer that the former, numerically the most important, group is being squeezed economically as the traditional economy is being displaced. That the proportion of these borrowers was larger in Bahia than Pernambuco (85 percent compared with 72 percent) attests to this group's greater financial difficulties, the greater weakness of its sectors and thus its greater marginalization.[24] As noted earlier, Bahia's economy is more skewed to the national (especially petrochemical) market, while Pernambuco has attracted more investment in consumer goods, continuing a 'commercial' role it has traditionally performed in the region. Its bourgeoisie, then, would be more central, and that is more important to the economy's development.

Natives directing dynamic non-family enterprises are the 'deviant cases' in our study. Many were the Schumpeterian innovating entrepreneurs who took advantage of various government industrialization programs (e.g., SUDENE 34/18) that enabled them to leave former civil service or commercial positions in order to start industrial enterprises. Their heavy short-term borrowing mainly reflects the difficulties they encountered in penetrating a new sector if not industry itself. In both states it should also be noted that, especially among natives in dynamic sectors, the presence of foreign participation in the enterprise is associated with heavy borrowing; this suggests either that these enterprises create foreign alliances because of the economic difficulties they encounter in meeting short-run costs, or that these enterprises are being used by foreign interests to penetrate and take advantage of local financial markets.

Long-term Capital Borrowing

One sees that a greater percentage of natives, compared with migrants and foreign-born, borrow not only more short-term but also more long-term capital. This is particularly the case in Bahia, and again suggests the greater fragility of this group compared with their counterpart in Pernambuco. Other calculations show that these differences are most apparent in the borrowing of capital to finance new installations. Again, the natives who are the heaviest borrowers are those affiliated with the traditional family-owned enterprise and the newer non-family enterprise in dynamic sectors. In Bahia 86 percent of the traditional family and 71 percent of the dynamic non-family enterprises borrowed long-term capital. In Pernambuco, the figures are 61 percent and 33 percent, respectively.

Why would these two types of native enterprises, which can barely meet their short-term costs, wish to incur long-term expenses? Among the traditional family-owned enterprises, the heavy borrowing of long-term capital could be in response to short-run difficulties, and fears that their solvency is being threatened by the emergence of more dynamic sectors. In part, their borrowing can be interpreted as a desperate attempt to alleviate their insecure status by quickly modernizing their plants regardless of the price of the credit. Or it could be argued that, since the traditional family-owned enterprise had better access to finance capital because of its linkages to the banking system, it therefore could obtain long-term loans with favorable credit terms more easily.[25] This does not appear to be the case. Aside from the fact that there were few linkages, there is a weak positive correlation between banking linkage and heavy long-term borrowing. In fact, in Pernambuco where one finds a greater proportion of these natives who reported banking linkages (55 percent compared with 46 percent in Bahia), the proportion who borrowed long-term capital was much lower than in Bahia (61 to 86 percent, respectively). Most importantly, even though the banks with which both these groups of Bahian and Pernambucan natives had linkages were mainly private, the bulk of their long-term loans were secured from official banks.[26]

Apparently the severity of the situation caused even the traditional native industrialists — those who would have the easiest access to funds — to seek official sources of capital. Locked into a vicious circle of capital shortages, high interest charges, inflation and a skittish market, private local banks could not compete with the volume and terms of credit offered by the government banks.[27]

Credit Arrangements: The Bahian Case[28]

One way to determine whether or not a particular industrial group is receiving favorable credit terms for particular types of loans is to examine interest rates — the money paid for borrowing capital. Based on the figures provided by the industrialists, it was possible to calculate an average interest rate paid for each type of loan.[29] While the differences are not that marked, nevertheless, Bahian industrialists on the average paid nearly 17 percent per annum for long-term capital (based on rates reported by 74 percent of those who borrowed this type of capital). The average rate for short-term capital was 20 percent (based on figures reported by 83 percent of the borrowers of this type of capital). These high rates also have been reported by observers of Brazil's monetary policies. For example, Syvrud has noted that interest rates that ranged between 10 and 20 percent in the late 1960s climbed steadily in the 1970s to range between 21 and 58 percent.[30]

The reasons for this fluctuation are worth noting. Until 1964 the state allowed interest rates to seek their market levels and did not actively enforce the limits long established by usury law. The two important exceptions were the official National Economic Development Bank (BNDE) and the Bank of Brazil, which usually adhered to the 12 percent ceiling permitted by the law. However, as interest rates followed prices upward, the state became increasingly concerned about cost-push effects and the tendency of private financial institutions to allocate credit on the basis of 'family connections rather than the customer's ability to pay the price' or the worthiness of a project. Because this was causing serious structural imbalances in the economy, and particularly in the country's emerging regions (e.g the North-East), the government decided to take a more active role in the financial market.[31] Preferential interest rates and subsidized credit were provided to priority sectors and projects primarily through the Bank of Brazil and the BNDE.

Despite evasion or state neglect of the usury law, normal interest rates rarely exceeded the rate of inflation. This meant that most loan transactions carried negative real interest rates. Because of galloping inflation, by 1964 commercial bank loan notes reached a negative 30.1 percent while the Bank of Brazil's loans reached a negative 37.5 percent. Among the consequences of this policy (or lack of policy) was: (1) the growth of a costly financial intermediation system with the proliferation of financial institutions, bank agencies, finance companies and insurance companies; (2) ruthless competition among the banks for the public's deposits, which in turn led to excessive operating and administrative costs; and (3) excessive demand for subsidized loans ('cheap credit') rather than their own resources (or equity), which were usually invested in real estate, other real assets or foreign currency. Industrialists attempted to meet working capital costs from borrowed funds, which lost their value with inflation. A number in our study reported that they spent a good deal of their time in the 'pra, ca' (commercial/financial marketplace), going from bank to bank in an attempt to raise capital at the lowest possible rate. Considering the centralization of decision-making characteristic of north-eastern enterprises, there is little doubt that an industrialist's absence prejudiced his firm's operations.

Between 1964 and 1969, the state used monetary correction and financial subsidies to correct interest rate distortion. However, these policies had little, if any, effect. Despite offering sizeable subsidies to commercial banks — which most accepted — they still earned an average of 30 percent on their loans. The measure proved as ineffectual as the usury law in reducing real interest rates. Therefore in 1970 the state launched a new policy. It eliminated interest rate ceilings for commercial banks, thus leaving them to once again compete with one another, in the hopes that rates would be reduced and that the financial structure would be rationalized.[32] While it seemed that the state was abandoning its intermediation, in reality it was moving more forcibly on another front. It was gradually hegemonizing the entire financial structure of the country, and, in doing so was precluding certain classes from certain lines of credit.

Differentiating among industrialists shows that natives paid somewhat higher interest rates for long-term capital and lower rates for short-term capital, but the opposite was the case for the migrants and foreign-born. The average interest rate paid by natives for long-term loans was 16.6 percent per annum, compared with 15.9 percent paid by migrants. For short-term loans, natives paid 19.3 percent, migrants 20 percent, and foreign-born 21 percent per annum. These calculations suggest that, for long-term capital

— important for industrial expansion — natives did not receive as favorable credit terms as the other industrialists. But whether this is peculiar to local entrepreneurship or to a particular industrial sector, the form of ownership, the size or an enterprise's technological complexity can be more readily determined by considering the proportion that paid lower or higher than average interest for long- and short-term capital. While our conclusions are tentative — because of the limited number of industrialists who reported their interest rates — certain patterns are nevertheless apparent.

If we begin by examining the industrial bourgeoisie in terms of their ownership, we note that family-owned enterprises paid higher than average rates for long-term capital than did non-family enterprises. Generally, the same pattern is found when small enterprises are compared with large, non-affiliated with affiliated (subsidiaries) and, in terms of social class, when industrialists from upper-class origins are compared with those from the middle class. But combining enterprise characteristics enables a clearer understanding of the marginalization process in Bahia.

Let us begin by focusing on family ownership and the industrial sector. As already noted, a greater proportion of family-owned enterprises paid higher interest rates for long-term loans than non-family enterprises. But this is especially the case among family-owned enterprises in dynamic sectors, where practically all the industrialists paid higher than average rates. Moreover, the difference is particularly apparent among natives. While 58 percent of native traditional sector family enterprises paid higher rates, in dynamic family enterprises this increased to 86 percent.

The percentage increase among migrants is not as great. In fact, other calculations indicate that, if only the interest rates for new installation loans — the most cited item in long-term borrowing — are considered, then migrants in dynamic sectors paid lower than average rates while the pattern for natives remains unchanged. What seems to be happening (or has happened) in Bahia is that family-owned enterprises that have ventured into the dynamic sectors are subject to high interest rates which doubtless act as a deterrent to their growth and proliferation in these sectors. However, among those natives heading non-family enterprises, particularly those affiliated with dynamic economies, the opposite is the case. Indeed, the interest rates of this group (native, dynamic, non-family) are lower than that of any other. This suggests that this group is being actively encouraged to expand its activities.

But while certain kinds of native industrialists have been discouraged from modernizing or expanding their plant, their marginalization is not complete. The banks seem to allow them to amble along by granting them more short-term loans at favorable interest rates. This is particularly the case among natives in family-owned enterprises. A greater proportion (78 percent) received short-term loans but fewer of them (36 percent) paid higher than average interest rates. This is even more apparent in traditional sectors and in the case of natives from upper-class origins in these sectors. An owner of a Bahian leather processing company noted that, while the government's regional development bank, the Bank of North-East, 'behaves toward us in a very disagreeable manner, having never sent one person to inspect our installations nor seriously analyze our sector, I cannot complain about the Bank of Brazil, which always provided us with a "yes" or "no" whenever we approached them for a working capital loan.'

What about the other two groups of industrialists, the migrants and the foreign-born? How do they fare in comparison with the natives?

Our findings with respect to short-term borrowing indicate that migrant and foreign-born industrialists generally paid higher than average interest for short-term loans. Most short-term borrowing was from the Bank of Brazil, which in its official role might have been attempting to curb the dynamic sector enterprises' access to cheap credit and thus cause them to liquify their equity or investments.[33] It seems more likely that the Bank of Brazil's policy was to reserve short-term loans for the traditional sector. Indeed, in 1970 the largest proportion of its loans (39 percent) went to foodstuffs, textiles and clothing to help these producers to meet their working capital costs.[34]

However, for long-term borrowing the pattern was the opposite. There were definite indications of bank encouragement for certain migrant industrialists.[35] First, migrants associated with dynamic sectors, large, non-family-owned, technologically complex enterprises tended to pay lower than average rates for long-term capital. Moreover, as indicated earlier, if only figures for new installation borrowing are considered, then migrants with these characteristics readily stand out as the 'most favored' group of industrialists as regards lower cost long-term borrowing. These enterprises were more likely to have connections with the more financially reputable Center-South area foreign corporation. However, it should not be forgotten that the majority of these loans have been negotiated with the national development bank (BNDE). This suggests that the government was actively attempting to encourage the establishment of these types of enterprises in the North-East.

In comparison, migrants who were affiliated with the traditional economies, family-owned enterprises, technologically non-complex, smaller, non-affiliated enterprises and were from upper- or lower-class background paid higher rates for long-term loans. Nor does confining our analysis to new installation borrowing alter these results significantly. Two-thirds of the migrants directing traditional family-owned enterprises paid more than average interest for long-term loans, and in dynamic sectors the proportion is even higher, as it is for natives. However, in contrast to natives, these migrants are not granted a reprieve (are not compensated) in their short-term capital borrowing. In this regard other calculations indicate that the least favored group in terms of short-term capital borrowing were migrant bourgeoisie of large family-owned enterprises affiliated with Center-South corporations.

In effect, migrant-directed family-owned enterprises have faced double discrimination in their long- and short-term borrowing. While the native family-owned enterprises have been 'put out to pasture,' the migrant family enterprise has been completely discouraged, at least in terms of its financial dealings. This group is reminiscent of northern 'carpetbaggers' who infiltrated the southern United States after the Civil War in order to take advantage of devasted real estate, markets and other economies.

Until now we have largely neglected the role of foreign capital in our discussion of credit terms.[36] But we might now pose the question: Does foreign capital participation in north-east industrial enterprises result in more or less favorable interest rates? As in the analysis of other enterprise characteristics, the answer to this question involves focusing on industrial types in conjunction with primarily industrial sector and family ownership.

These figures for native long-term interests rates indicate that the banks appear to discriminate against local entrepreneurs who are associated with foreign capital.[37] This is particularly apparent in dynamic sectors and extends to short-term borrowing as well. In contrast, those natives who operate traditional enterprises with no foreign capital participation obtained favorable interest rates both in their long- and short-term capital loans. For example, only 28 percent paid higher than average rates for short-term loans as compared with 75 percent of the natives in dynamic sectors in whose enterprises foreign capital participated. Data on family ownership provide further insights into this marginalization process. Our data indicate that banks appear to have discriminated most against native family enterprises who have associated with foreign capital. Most have paid higher than average rates not only for long-term loans, but for short-term capital as well. Moreover, there seems to be an actual continuum of discrimination. The most favored groups would be native, non-family-owned, smaller, non-affiliated, non-foreign-funded traditional sector enterprises. The least are native family-owned enterprises in dynamic sectors with foreign capital participation.

Foreign capital allied with family capital is a combination that the financial institutions serving Bahia and Pernambuco seem to be unwilling to endorse. More acceptable alliances are between native family capital in traditional sectors and non-foreign financial capital in traditional sectors and non-foreign financial Center-South companies. But the most favored are those that involve foreign affiliations with non-family ownership, regardless of the geographic origins of the industrialist.

THE MARGINALIZERS: THE BANKS

While we have identified what part of the Bahian industrial bourgeoisie has been marginalized and what part has been endorsed, we have yet to identify the prepetrators of this process, or the marginalizers. To do so we consider the proportion of elites who received long- and short-term capital as well as the principal suppliers. Thus, for example, the national level bank, the Bank of Brazil, was the main source of finance capital for the 'traditional' industry (native entrepreneurship, the upper class and family capitalism), while the southern, regional and the development banks supplied 'modern' industry (the migrant, middle-class and non-family capitalism). But regardless of these principal connections between certain banks and certain industrialists, we now must discover whether the apparent division of labor between the types of capital allocated to specific groups corresponds to a differentiation in terms of interest rates.

The marginalizing role of the banks is especially apparent in the case of natives from upper-class origins directing family-owned enterprises in dynamic sectors, and migrants of family-owned enterprises in traditional sectors (the 'carpetbaggers'). The principal suppliers of credit to these groups were the Banks of Brazil and North-East and, in the case of migrants, private southern banks as well. Upper-class natives were charged higher interest rates for long-term loans by these banks particularly (as other calculations show) if the enterprises were family-owned and were associated with dynamic economies. In fact, noteworthy in this regard is that the few upper-class natives who managed to secure loans from the state and national development banks were all charged higher than average rates. In terms of short-term loans, however, the upper class was treated more favorably by the government. Not only did many secure loans of this type, but the interest rates charged were lower than average. The limited number of non-local bourgeoisie (migrants and foreign-born) allows only a tentative hypothesis, but I would venture that family ownership and industrial sector weigh more heavily on credit allocation than social class. Of course traditional sector, family ownership and upper class are positively correlated.

The case of migrant directors of traditional family-owned enterprises is comparable at least with respect to long-term borrowing. However, as discussed in the previous section, in short-term borrowing not only did the government banks impose high interest rates, but so did local private and southern commercial banks. From this it seems that entrepreneurship from this group is the least welcome in the North-East, perhaps because it would constitute a further threat to the local entrepreneurs who had already been marginalized by dynamic newcomers.

Turning from industrialists who have been marginalized, what of those who have received favorable interest rates from the banks, e.g., the natives heading larger enterprises, or natives in non-family owned companies operating in traditional sectors, or the migrant and foreign-born directors or dynamic non-family enterprises? Which banks provided low-interest loans?

Official banks once again played a prominent role. Notable in this regard was the regional development bank, the Bank of the North-East, which provided most of the long-term lower than average interest loans for natives in larger enterprises, particularly those in traditional sectors. In fact, over 60 percent of their long-term loans were secured from this bank. Similarly, the largest proportion of short-term loans at favorable rates were supplied by the Bank of Brazil to this group.

Underwriting migrants, or at least those affiliated with dynamic sectors, larger enterprises and non-family capital was the BNDE, Brazil's national development bank. In fact, this bank rarely appears as a financial source for natives and never was indicated by foreign-born industrial elites. For their short-term capital this group was furnished loans at favorable rates by southern commercial banks.

There is ample evidence, then, that official banks play an extremely important role not only in financing but also in stratifying Bahian industrial enterprises, more so than the private commercial banks. Particularly noticeable is the Bank of Brazil's sanctioning capability. It completely marginalizes, as in the case of migrants in traditional sectors; it partially marginalizes, as in the case of natives heading family-owned enterprises; and it endorses, as in the case of the large, non-family native enterprise.

The Bank of the North-East also affects north-east industrial stratification in its support of local entrepreneurship, particularly as a supplier of long-term, low interest rate capital. Notable in this regard is its financing of native-directed large, traditional, non-family enterprises. To a lesser extent this bank also furnishes short-term capital, but since it usually did so at higher than average rates its endorsement of a particular group is not as complete as the Bank of Brazil. We suspect that this is partially due to its recent expansion into commercial activities from its earlier role as strictly a development or investment bank.

The other official banks play a smaller role, but nonetheless have been important for certain groups. Bahia's state development bank, Desenbanco, has supported smaller native industrialists by offering favorable rates for long-term credit to technologically complex, non-family-owned enterprises. In this respect I recall that the bank's president, in discussing lending policies, remarked that this bank primarily considered the industrial sector, the 'solidness of the group' (its balance sheet, investments), bank references, 'know-how,' administrative structure and possibilities of success. Continuing, he said:

Desenbanco endorses neither monopolies nor overfractionalization of production in order not to promote idle capacity [capacidade ociosa]. This, I might add, is also the policy of SUDENE. Our areas of priority are chemicals, petrochemicals, metallurgy, mining, agro-industrial enterprises and tourism. The more difficult sectors for us to give financial support are logging, beverages, vegetable and animal oils and furniture. We are leaving family and traditional economies and moving towards an economy of corporations and capital. Here in Brazil, no, in the factory, the owner ['dono'] lives richly and the workers miserably. Because of this the Brazilian government makes them participate in social obligations. This will eventually diminish when their mentality changes. It is disciplinary conditioning (of industry). All industrial enterprises must benefit industry and provide social benefits.

If an enterprise is not successful we try to help it recuperate. This is our policy and in this regard we encourage the entrepreneur to associate or relinquish his stock control to another enterprise. Thus we salvage the debts and make new loans to the new group, preferring to do this after the control has passed to it. If the enterprise doesn't do this, of course we foreclose. [Interview with Artur Ferreira, President of Desenbanco, 22 May 1974.]

The national development bank (BNDE), as we have already noted, primarily supported migrant industrialists, offering low-interest-rate long-term finance to those in large, technologically complex enterprises in dynamic sectors. Since the bank does not lend short-term capital, its endorsement is not as complete as the Bank of Brazil. Nevertheless, many observers consider it potentially the strongest force for bringing Center-South investment to the North-East. But, at least directly, this is not foreign investment. Indeed, our calculations reveal that, next to family capitalism, foreign capital participation was negatively sanctioned by the official banks. Native enterprises who had foreign capital were charged higher than average rates for both long- and short-term capital. However, it is noteworthy that local private banks, such as the Banco Economico, endorsed the native-foreign capital alliance, at least in terms of short-term credit loaned at favorable interest rates. Likewise, there is some support for migrant and foreign capital relations via the BNDE and private southern banks. And, while our cases are few, there is evidence that Desenbanco, consonant with the policies and practices described by its president, endorsed some alliances between foreign capital and migrant and foreign-born managed subsidiaries of Center-South corporations.

SUMMARY AND CONCLUSION

There is little doubt that financial institutions in Brazil through the manipulation of credit are transforming the industrial structure and industrial stratification in Bahia, Pernambuco and elsewhere in the Brazilian North-East. I have shown that some industrialists are being heavily supported and are thus emerging: the migrant and foreign-born managers of mainly large, technologically complex, non-family-owned enterprises in dynamic sectors; others are being marginalized, or 'put out to pasture': native or local industrialists affiliated with traditional, family-owned enterprises; while still others are being completely discouraged or pushed out of the market: natives in family-owned enterprises who have ventured into dynamic sectors, or migrants and foreign-born who established traditional sector enterprises in the state. These are the anomalies, the deviant cases. High interest rates are levied upon them regardless of prior SUDENE endorsement. What is occurring in terms of social stratification is the emergence of a clear and rigid industrial class structure even in this period of flux in Bahia. And while I have not fully discussed the Pernambucan case, a similar stratification has occurred there.

The agents of these changes, or the main perpetrators of these divisions, are the government banks, especially the national bank, the Bank of Brazil, and the regional development bank, the Bank of the North-East. In this regard I noted that the Bank of Brazil performs three roles. Together with the Bank of the North-East it mainly sustains or partially marginalizes, as in the case of natives in family-owned, traditional enterprises; it completely discourages or marginalizes, as in the case of migrants in traditional, family-owned enterprises; and it positively sanctions, as in the case of non-family-affiliated native industrialists. No other government bank performs such a wide variety of roles in the financial sector. The other banks, whether government or private, cater to specific clientele and concentrate in either long- or short-term finance. Again, this signals the clear division of labor and the stratification that characterizes Bahia. In this respect it was noted that the Bank of Brazil is associated with short-term financing of local entrepreneurship, family capitalism and traditional sectors, while the Bank of the North-East mainly provides long-term loans at favorable rates to native entrepreneurs provided that their enterprises are not family-owned. Brazil's national development bank (BNDE) emerges as the backer of a dynamic migrant class, furnishing it with long-term loans at attractive rates, particularly, it seems, if there is a foreign capital connection.

And at the state level the division of labor continues. We saw this in the case of the foreign-born elites. While Bahia's state development bank (Desenbanco) emerges as the primary provider of long-term loans to the larger, non-family, foreign-owned subsidiaries, the state bank (BANEB) is the supplier of long-term capital to the smaller non-affiliated enterprise. Here too the role of the local private banks is visible as the supplier of short-term capital to the few foreign-born who are in traditional sectors and the natives who have opened their enterprises to foreign capital participation.

From another perspective, then, it seems that new class alignments are being forged. At the state level a direct alliance with foreign capital is in the making, and there seem to be some attempts by the local financial bourgeoisie — some of whom are heirs of the agro-commercial oligarchy — to incorporate the foreign-born into their midst. Luciano Martins conceives of this as a new partnership policy, which is 'explicitly aimed at establishing a more equitable balance of power between local interests and foreign capital, without restoring to the classic measures of expropriation or of reserving whole sectors of production exclusively for nationals.'[38]

At the national and regional level the picture is not as clear. While the national development bank (BNDE) endorses foreign capital participation, it is indirect (via migrant intermediaries) and restricted (to non-family enterprises in dynamic sectors). The national bank (the Bank of Brazil) emerges as countering the foreign alliance with the traditional local classes through the application of unfavorable credit terms. Thinking about this configuration more abstractly, one begins to wonder whether this division of labor or high correlation between certain financial institutions and certain industrialists is a conscious strategy on the part of the regime to maintain 'a balanced,' highly rigid class structure in an era of economic fluidity and dynamism. One wonders why the regime, through its banks, simply doesn't close the valve entirely on traditional family enterprises, which they sustain at the margins with periodic injections of short-term capital at favorable rates. The answer is found in part in the 'philosophy' of the regime, when its spokesmen (e.g., the president of Desenbanco) discuss the benefits of 'disciplining' the recalcitrants and resurrecting the failures. While it seems on the one hand that family enterprises are odious to the regime, epitomizing archaism, unwieldly power and influence, disorganization and unfettered capitalism, on the other hand one senses that the regime wishes to reincorporate them as soon as they join the 'economic miracle' and subscribe to the 'national revolution.' Curious in this regard is that 'coronelismo,' once the prime social control mechanism of the agro-commercial oligarchy, has passed to the middle class, Brazil's technocracy, and is now being used against its originators to enforce their subscription to the norms of a 'rationalized' capitalism. Other evidence suggests that the regime's efforts are conscious. The analysis of short-versus long-term credit allocation and credit terms, and the division of labor among the banks, indicate that no one is left out, that there is something for everyone. One need only recall the recent proliferation of official development banks (especially at the state level), SUDENE's modifications designed to appease the claims articulated by traditional economies, the recent movement of local commercial banks into investment activities, and the regime's relatively tolerant (permissive) policy on foreign capital investment. From the analysis of this financial configuration in Bahia, it appears that the regime, while contributing to the rise of new industrial classes, also wants to placate the old. It is as if they were attempting to balance the political structure while dynamizing the economy, imposing 'Ordem' on the traditional groups and offering 'Progresso' to the moderns.

NOTES

1. David E. Goodman and Roberto Cavalcanti de Albuquerque, *Incentivos Industrializacão e Desenvolvimento do Nordeste* (Rio de Janeiro: Instituto de Planejamento Economico e Social, 1974), pp. 284-7. Also see Albert O. Hirschman, 'Industrial Development in the Brazilian Northeast and the Tax Credit Scheme of Article 34/18,' in his *A Bias for Hope* (New Haven: Yale University Press, 1971), pp. 142-5.

2. Clemente Mariani, 'Análise do Problema Económico Baiano,' *O Observador Económico e Financeiro*, 267 (May 1958), p. 19.

3. Mexico was one of the few countries in Latin America where financial institutions and mechanisms were sufficiently developed to cope with the exigencies of rapid development. See Maria Conceição Tavares, 'Financiamento Numa Economica em Desenvolvimento,' *Da Substituição de Importacões ao Capitalismo Financeiro* (Rio de Janeiro: Zahar Editores, 1973), p. 129.

4. Linkages and interdependencies between the banking and the agricultural sectors characterized the North-East during the 1950s. See, for example, Antonio Barros de Castro, *Sete Ensaios Sobre a Economia Brasileira* (São Paulo: Companhia Editora Forense, 1971), vol. II.

5. ibid., pp. 242-4.

6. Tavares, op. cit., pp. 128-30 and esp. 138-9.

7. In a recent study of state and transnational corporation partnerships in Bahia, Luciano Martins also found private partner financial participation 'extremely low' compared with the state. (See his paper, 'La Joint-venture Etat-Firme transnationale-Entrepreneurs locaux au Bresil' in *Sociologie et Sociétés*, XI, 2 (October 1979), pp. 169-90.)

8. This subject is amply discussed by Tavares, op. cit., pp. 223-30.

9. The 34/18 mechanism allows Brazilian corporations to reduce their annual federal income tax liability 50 percent by agreeing to invest in north-eastern projects approved by SUDENE. SUDENE also confers a number of other investment incentives, such as income tax exemptions for ten years, customs duty exemptions on imported machinery and other materials. Detailed definitions and discussions of SUDENE and the Bank of the North-East may be found in Albert O. Hirschman, *Journeys Toward Progress* (Garden City, NY: Anchor-Doubleday, 1965), pp. 126-9; Hirschmann, op. cit.; Goodman and de Alberquerque, op. cit., pp. 195-217; and David E. Goodman et al., 'Fiscal Incentives for the Industrialization of the Northeast of Brazil and The Choice of Techniques,' *Brazilian Economic Studies*, 1 (1975), p. 201-26.

10. Goodman and Albuquerque, op. cit., p. 195.

11. ibid., p. 199.

12. These banks obtain most of their funds from taxes of larger and state-owned enterprises, private (fixed-term) deposits, and national or foreign loans (see, for example, Wilson Suzigan et al., *Financiamento de Projectos Industriais no Brasil* (Rio de Janeiro: Instituto de Planejamento Economico e Social (IPEA), 1972), pp. 166 and 174-80.

13. In 1973 and 1974, a survey of 134 heads of larger manufacturing enterprises was conducted in Bahia similar to a pilot study carried out in Pernambuco in 1970. Similar to this first study in the Brazilian Northeast and one I conducted in Portugal in 1965, the universe consisted of all manufacturing enterprises of 50 or more persons. Since enterprises of this size comprised only a tiny fraction of all industrial enterprises (even in more industrially advanced countries) but employed most (35 percent) of the industrial labor force, their chief executives were considered members of the industrial bourgeoisie.

The sources of our data were detailed, systematic, tandem interviews of approximately three hours, conducted among heads of all enterprises employing 200 or more individuals and among a random sample of those heading enterprises employing 50-199 individuals. Statistical information necessary to draw the sample was gathered from industrial censuses published by Bahia's industrial association (Federacão das Industriais do Estado da Bahia) and records of the national social welfare office (Instituto Nacional da Providencia Social (INPS)). Topics covered during the interview included organizational structure and decision-making, manpower, labor relations, recruitment, interest group affiliations, competition, attitudes toward and relationships with financial institutions (bank, federal investment programs), and government and foreign investment. Also included were questions on the social background, career patterns, values and opinions of the industrialist. (For a more extensive discussion of the sampling survey design and analysis techniques, see my study, *A Elite Industrial Portuguesa* (Lisbon: Calouste Gulbenkian Foundation, 1969), Appendix A.)

14. Family ownership was based on the percentage of shares that a family held in an enterprise. If this percentage constituted the majority (even though it might be 10 percent), the enterprise was considered family-owned, or a family enterprise. The average percentage of owernship was approximately 65. 'Non-family-owned' either had no family capital or if it did this did not comprise the majority of shares.

15. Technological complexity was measured by determining the number of superior and intermediate technicians relative to other enterprises of similar size (based on the number of employees.) Those that were above the mean derived for each size category, either in superior, intermediate or both types of technicians, were considered 'technologically complex' enterprises. Those below the mean were considered technologically non-complex.

16. Enterprise size was measured by the number of employees: small = 50-99 employees, regular = 100-199; medium = 200-499; large = 500-999; giant = 1000 or more employees.

17. Corporate affiliation was divided into two categories: 'non-affiliated' enterprises refer to single establishments that are not juridically affiliated with any other enterprises; 'affiliated' enterprises were juridically affiliated with other enterprises. Although most were subsidiaries of larger Center-South corporations, some were associated with other enterprises, or part of a group.

18. 'Foreign capital' refers to any enterprise in which foreign capital participated regardless of whether this participation constituted the majority of ownership. In fact, only about 15 percent of the enterprises were foreign owned. 'No foreign capital' enterprises were those that had no foreign capital participation.

19. Class origin was measured by combining the occupation of the respondent's father (an objective measure) with the respondent's assessment of his family's economic situation during his youth. A member of the industrial sector who indicated that his father was a large landowner and that his family's economic situation was prosperous was classified as 'upper-class' in origin. Those who described their family's situation as poor and whose fathers were small shopkeepers or minor civil servants were judged to be 'lower-class' in origin. Other geographical characteristics, such as educational attainment of the respondent, his career type (founder, heir, owner-manager or manager), age and nationality, will be examined in a future essay.

20. While in Bahia migrant industrialists tended to bypass the local industrial association (Federação da Industria do Estado da Bahia) and articulate their interests through other associations, some of which were situated in the Center-South, in Pernambuco the local industrial association tended to be stronger because, among other factors, there were fewer competing associations, the state was geographically farther from the Center-South, and the nature and quantity of migrant-directed subsidiary enterprises differed. I intend to compare the industrial interest group structure in both states in another essay. Goodman and Albuquerque, op. cit., pp. 283-7, compare industry in Bahia with Pernambuco.

21. Goodman has noted 'the remarkably limited degree of interdependence' among north-eastern industries in his essays on development in the North-East in the 1960s. The pattern persisted into the 1970s, as he and Albuquerque have reported

(cf. David E. Goodman, 'Industrial Development in the Brazilian Northeast: An Interim Assessment of the Tax Credit Scheme of Article 34/18,' in Riordan Roett (ed.), *Brazil in the Sixties* (Nashville, Tennessee: Vanderbilt University Press, 1972), pp. 245-50; and Goodman and Albuquerque, op. cit., pp. 245-305).

22. Data from a similar study I conducted in Pernambuco (1970) enable some cross-state comparisons for short- and long-term credit transactions, but information on interest rates was not obtained in the Pernambuco study so our analysis thus focuses on the Bahian case.

23. Other calculations show that in Bahia, among the natives heading non-family-owned enterprises in traditional sectors, 53 percent indeed were founders while 18 percent were heirs, 12 percent owner-managers, and 18 percent managers.

24. Goodman and Albuquerque, op. cit., p. 283. Also see D. E. Goodman, 'The Brazilian Economic "Miracle" and Regional Policy: some Evidence from the Urban Northeast,' *Journal of Latin American Studies*, 8, I (May 1976), p. 2.

25. An enterprise and a bank were considered linked if a respondent indicated that (a) he (she) or any executive of his (her) enterprise (or its parent company) was formally connected with any bank (i.e. a director, member of the board); (b) his (her) enterprise (or parent company) possessed more than nominal shares in a bank; or (c) a bank participated in the directorate and/or the ownership of the enterprise.

26. Even within Bahia there was little evidence that linkages explained access to long-term credit. Migrants who were linked to banks also tended to secure their loans from government-owned banks.

27. For details on the movement of the state into banking and financing see, for example, Suzigan et al., op. cit., esp. pp. 41-80 and 92-101.

28. See n. 22 above.

29. One specialist of the Brazilian monetary system notes that 'No banker would ever admit he was charging rates higher than determined by [Brazil's] National Monetary Council.' (See Donald Syvrud, 'Estrutura e Politica de Juros no Brazil — 1960/70,' *Revista Brasileira Do Economia* 26, 1 (Jan-March 1972), p. 121.)

30. As reported by Syvrud, whose figures were based on a study of approximately 50 manufacturers surveyed by the Commercial Association of Rio de Janeiro: Syvrud, op. cit., p. 120.

31. Donald F. Syvrud, *Foundations of Brazilian Economic Growth* (Stanford, California: Hoover Institution Press, 1974), pp. 96 and 104. Most of the subsequent discussion is based on Syvrud's chapter on 'The Impact of Interest Rate Policy,' esp. pp. 100-17.

32. ibid., pp. 111-17.

33. One effect of pre-1964 interest rate policy was to distort the internal financial structure of Brazilian firms. The cost of borrowed capital was low in comparison with equity capital, enabling firms with access to this cheap credit to expand. Equity was invested in real estate and other real assets which did not depreciate in value with inflation. After 1966 interest rates turned from negative to high positive rates, resulting in numerous bankruptcies and impeding stabilization efforts. Donald Syvrud, *Foundations of. . . Growth*, pp. 103-4.

34. Suzigan et al., op. cit., pp. 146-50.

35. Statements about foreign-born industrialists shall be entirely omitted from the analysis at this point, since only five reported their long-term interest rates, largely owing to the concentration of these companies' financial operations or their foreign (parent) company headquarters in the Center-South.

36. Here we are interested only in whether or not foreign capital participated in an enterprise at all: whether an enterprise was foreign-owned is a topic that will be discussed in another paper.

37. It is possible that native enterprises associate with foreign capital in order to obtain sorely needed capital. In this case the government's apparent discrimination would merely reflect the enterprises' insolvency. However, it also should be noted that simply because the enterprise is associated with foreign capital does not seem to lessen its need for short-term capital.

38. Martins, op. cit., p. 2. Also see Peter Evans, 'Multinationals, State-Owned Corporations, and the Transformation of Imperialism: a Brazilian Case Study,' *Economic Development and Cultural Change*, 26, 1 (October, 1977).

IV

POLITICAL AND SOCIAL THEMES

10

THE STATE-TRANSNATIONAL CORPORATION-LOCAL ENTREPRENEURS JOINT VENTURE IN BRAZIL: How to Relax and Enjoy a Forced Marriage

Luciano Martins
University of Paris, France

The emergence of new patterns of relationships between the economic actors who control production and technology at the international level, and those local bourgeoisies and governments that can impose political barriers as a condition to entry into their national markets is one of the trends that is shaping the current reorganization of the capitalist system. By this latter expression we mean the process of its readjustment to a new scale of power among nations and to new forms of competition, economic control and division of work within the context of the internationalization of production. This is the setting in which certain new types of business associations, under the form of joint ventures, must be situated.

From the mid-1960s onwards, a growing number of developing countries, in Latin America and elsewhere, and irrespective of their political regimes, have adopted new legislation aimed at reinforcing their control over foreign capital and/or redefining the role of

Author's Note: This paper was prepared for the International Sociological Association (Research Committee on Economy and Society) conference on 'Social and Political Challenges to the New International Economic Order in Comparative Perspective,' Bellagio, Italy, April 1979. The French version has been published in Arnaud Sales (ed.), 'Développement national et économie mondialisée', a thematic issue of *Sociologie et Sociétés*, vol. XI, no. 2, October 1979. The basic research work was made possible thanks to a grant of the Social Science Research Council.

foreign investors in their economies. One of these policies is directed toward the establishment of new forms of partnership, by encouraging or making mandatory the formation of joint ventures between transnational corporations and local (private and/or public) firms.[1] Although foreign investors have adopted different attitudes to this move (from stern resistance to benign or even easy compliance), the available data show, at least until the mid-1970s, a substantial increase of this particular form of business associations.[2] Independently of how this trend will evolve in the near future (and there is enough room for doubt), it has already induced some marked changes in the patterns of relationship between foreign investors and host countries — although not always in the direction envisaged by the new legislation.

The partnership policy has been presented (and is generally perceived) as a 'new strategy' conceived by local bourgeoisies and governments in order to regain partial control over, or to avoid further denationalization of, their national economies. This strategy is based on two main assumptions. First, the presence of a local partner in the management of affiliates of foreign firms (especially if this partner is the state) will help to curb, more efficiently than through any other form of government control, some of the transnational corporation's current practices (from transfer pricing to pseudotransfer of technology) detrimental to the development of local economies; second, by associating with transnational corporations (TNCs), private local interests will increase their bargaining power and hopefully stop or reverse the marginalization process to which they are submitted. In short, the partnership policy is explicitly aimed at establishing a more equitable balance of power between local interests and foreign capital, without resorting to the classic measures of expropriation or of reserving whole sectors of production exclusively for nationals.[3]

Little has been done to analyze the content of this discourse, and to question the social process behind it.[4] In fact, most of the literature on joint ventures seems to take this discourse at face value, and has preferred to investigate why transnational corporations have been led to accept such forced partnerships, under what circumstances they do so, and what cost/benefits are involved in each case. This type of analysis has certainly contributed to a better understanding of TNCs' strategies and attitudes towards joint ventures with local partners. However, such an approach has two basic limitations if any attempt is made to situate the joint venture phenomenon in a broader context. First, by adopting a cost-benefit approach, limited to the specific business partnership, the social and political environment tend to be ignored; second, since the label 'joint venture' covers a very wide range of situations and modalities of agreements, the approach currently adopted leads almost necessarily to a case-by-case analysis. Both limitations converge to fragment the object of study and to hamper a reflection on the significance of the phenomenon as such.

We will follow a different avenue. We assume here that the joint venture phenomenon, whatever the concrete characteristics it may show, is significant in itself as an expression of the evolutive adjustment of interests: (1) within the context of 'dependent-associated' development, and (2) as part of the reorganization of the capitalist system. We also assume that this significance tends to be even greater when the local partner is the state as entrepreneur. The reason for this is that, in such cases, these new forms of business associations help to 'crystallize,' at the production level, a particular moment of the interaction between two of the major processes that are shaping the capitalist development in a great number of peripheral countries: the internationalization of production, and the changing role of the state. In this connection, the analysis of the joint venture phenomenon, when not limited to its immediate business aspects, can offer a vantage point for the analysis of the dynamics of these two processes, and of foreign investors', public bureaucracies' and local bourgeoisies' adaptive responses. This paper is a summary of a more comprehensive attempt to place the Brazilian joint venture experiment in petrochemicals in this perspective.

THE PROBLÉMATIQUE

To situate the joint venture phenomenon in the context of the reorganization of the capitalist system is, of course, deliberately to recognize its political dimension. In fact, it could not be otherwise: first, because these are not 'voluntary' business associations, but the result of a public policy; second, because one of the partners is the local state; third, because the transnational corporation, through its ability to shape production and demand patterns and its impact on the international division of work, is also a political actor. Accordingly, the 'problématique' that emerges with these new forms of business associations has to be expressed in political terms.

As it is well known, the 'relative advantages' of the transnational corporations vis-à-vis other forms of capitalist enterprise are basically related to their superior ability to mobilize resources in (at least) the following basic domains: access to capital and managerial expertise, control of the flux (and, partially, of the offer) of technological innovations, leading position (often oligopolistic) in different and simultaneous markets, and the intensive use of well-known practices such as product differentiation, transfer pricing and cross-subsidization.[5] The maximization of these advantages, through the cumulative effects obtained by their articulation in a world scale, supposes a centralized system of decision-making, a condition traditionally met by the full ownership and/or control by the parent company of the TNC's subsidiaries around the world. As it is also known, it is the maximization of these advantages, according to the 'global logic' of the corporation, that, first, creates a tendency for subsidiaries' activities and local economic interests to clash and, second, has helped to speed up the internationalization of capitalist production.[6]

Therefore, assuming that a joint venture implies some sharing of the control over the TNC's subsidiaries, and assuming that the different partners have at least some areas of conflictive interests, the issues at stake are: (1) to what extent these new forms of business associations will tend to limit the capability of transnational corporations or, conversely, will tend to increase the countervailing power of local groups; and (2) to what extent the practice of joint ventures tends to restrain or, on the contrary, to reinforce the internationalization process. Although both issues are part of the same problématique, they have to be analytically distinguished: while the first refers to the behavior of individual actors in the process, the second deals with the process as a whole. A proper treatment of these issues, of course, goes far beyond the purposes of this paper; our intention here is simply to define the problématique involved in the joint venture phenomenon and possibly to contribute to the discussion with some elements found in the Brazilian experiment. Before this, the following additional clarification is needed.

The available literature on joint ventures does not consider the second issue, but deals with questions related to the first one. However, this is done in a way that is not very helpful to us. In fact, the approach usually adopted leads almost necessarily to the following conclusion: that the limitation of the transnational corporation's capability in a joint venture is a function of the degree of control that is shared, and of the advantages (conflictive areas) that the transnational corporation has to relinquish as part of the trade-off. Besides being quite obvious, this does not seem to lead us very far. It is evident that a joint venture that does not result from a voluntary association between partners, but is imposed by the political will of the state, implies that the association is designed precisely to make compatible interests and goals that are divergent in their origin. In this sense, the very existence of the association implies (1) that problems both of sharing control and of conflictive areas have been solved prior to its constitution, and (2) that any business limitation resulting from the joint venture is acceptable to the associated partner. (This does not mean, of course, that all conflictive areas have been 'permanently' ironed out.)

The real problems begin when this sort of conclusion stops. For instance, what does 'acceptable' mean to the partners, when the partners are so different in nature as a transnational corporation and a local state? This difficulty cannot be solved just by considering a joint venture as a non-zero-sum game, in which the gains of one partner in a given area have to be compensated for by equivalent gains of the other partner in another area — an approach that usually leads to a cost-benefit analysis. The difficulty is that the cost-benefit analysis tends to reduce the joint venture merely to a relationship between business partners, and, hence, to assume the existence of two things that are quite debatable: first, that the partners' interests and envisaged payoffs are of the same nature, and therefore can be equated or reduced to a common denominator; second, that the partners play the non-zero-sum game following a 'rationality' traceable only to their (supposedly identical) business condition. However, the simple presence of the state as a partner (even through a state firm) is sufficient to indicate that we do not face just a business association, and that the state's interests, envisaged payoffs and rationality are of a different nature than those of the private partner, be it a transnational corporation or a local firm. Of course, the structural ambivalence of state firms, expressed through the fact that they are public firms that also behave as private corporations, gives ample room for discussion. If this ambivalence exists, nothing authorizes the arbitrary elimination of one of its terms (and the stronger one) by reducing the state to a simple business partner.

Our insistence on this point is for the following reason: the tendency to consider the partners of this type of joint venture as abstract actors, 'rationally' playing a business game, subsumes that the behavior of the state as a partner is conditioned by contradictory social processes and is submitted to the constraints of the political environment, including the political constraints produced by the internationalization of production. This is why our approach here will be a different one.

We will proceed as follows. First, we will trace the social actors and interests involved in the policy-making from which the Brazilian joint venture experiment in petrochemicals resulted; second, we will analyze the two main findings (which concern the patterns of control and of financing) resulting from the research we have conducted on the subject; finally, we will briefly discuss these findings in connection with the problématique previously mentioned.

THE POLICY-MAKING PROCESS

The development of the petrochemical industry in Brazil started, in the late 1950s, with the production of plastics and other final products under the control of subsidiaries of the biggest US- and European-based international corporations (Union Carbide, Koppers, Solvay and Rhône Poulenc). Although the state had the monopoly of oil production, refining and import, Petrobras was too concerned with the search for oil to think of initiating any other activity. Besides, the law was not clear as to whether petrochemicals were part of the monopoly or not. This is why, by the end of the 1950s, the Petrobras refinery in São Paulo began to produce and sell petrochemical raw materials (propylene, ethylene and gaz oil) to the subsidiaries of foreign firms, fostering their expansion. These first petrochemicals investments (in the São Paulo/Rio region) experienced a moderate path of growth until the mid-1960s, under the control of foreign firms, except for a few small local entrepreneurs. This moderate growth was sufficient to consolidate the offer of final products, but not to integrate the industry backwards (basic and intermediate products) or to substitute imports to the extent required. It soon became clear that this situation could not be changed without government intervention. On the one hand, transnational corporations, as long as they were able to continue to export to Brazil, and as long as their competitors did not threaten to set up local facilities, were not interested in integrating or expanding the industry in the country. On the other hand, local entrepreneurs were unable to combine financial resources and know-how required for the task.

It was in this (almost classic) situation where the national bourgeoisie 'can't' and transnational corporations 'won't,' that sectors of the public bureaucracy began to move to fill in the gap. Behind the curtains pulled down by the authoritarian regime established in 1964, the state apparatus was, for five consecutive years, the arena of an intricate plot in which different actors tried to make their interests prevail in the definition of a policy for the expansion and control of the petrochemical industry. What follows is a succinct characterization of the actors and of the interests involved in the policy-making.

The basic orientation of the first post-1964 government was stated in no uncertain terms as being in full support of the foreign and national private sector expansion in all branches of the economy; at the same time, the fiscal resources of the state were considerably increased and new regulative agencies were created, in parallel with those existing, to coordinate the industrial policy and to distribute generous tax exemptions and government subsidies to new industrial projects considered as priorities.[7] A very ambiguous situation was thus created. On the one hand, the huge increase of the financial and regulative powers of state agencies and enterprises, along with the authoritarian nature of the regime, made public bureaucracy more and more influential; on the other hand, the official orientation adopted in the high echelons of the government refrained any further expansion of the direct entrepreneurial activities of the state. This apparent paradox — and how public bureaucracy managed to escape this doom of Tantalus — is clearly shown by the policy-making on petrochemicals.

A newly created government council (CDI), integrated by representatives of the main state agencies involved in economic policy-making, was assigned to the task of selecting those industrial projects applicable for government incentives, financing and tax exemptions. The council was composed by task forces ('grupos executivos') in charge of planning the development of different sectors of production, including the chemical sector. In fact, the criteria established by CDI for project approval were perfunctory and extremely liberal. One of the reasons for that was that not a single one of the different value-oriented groups in the bureaucracy could prevail over any other, owing to the collegiate nature of the agency. However, the CDI's 'nihil obstat' was important to the private sector, independently of the fiscal advantages obtained, because it could always be invoked as governmental approval in the case of resistance from other echelons of bureaucracy, or in the case of changes in policy priorities; at the same time, the projects submitted to the CDI gave the different groups in the bureaucracy a 'vue d'ensemble' of private investment decisions in the main sectors of the economy.

It was this sort of information that convinced members of the second echelon of the bureaucracy of both BNDE (the state bank in charge of financing industrial projects) and Petrobras that the private sector, national or foreign, was incapable of, or not interested in, building up an integrated petrochemical industry. They took the initiative of setting up an 'informal' task force to examine alternatives without consulting the hierarchy of their respective agencies. After they had reached a tentative conclusion they then submitted it, in November 1964, to the BNDE Board of Directors, which approved it two months later. The conclusion was: (1) that the development of the petrochemical industry was hampered by the incapacity of Petrobras to allocate resources for investment in basic and intermediary petrochemical products; and (2) that an integrated investment program should be carried out by Petrobras with the financing and 'under the leadership' of BNDE.[8] An 'official' BNDE-Petrobras task force was then created by the directorates of both agencies to specify this investment program. Eighteen integrated projects were selected, representing an investment of US$123 million over a period of seven years. The financing was to be split between Petrobras and BNDE, the latter suggesting that its part should be transformed into equity of the new enterprise to be created. Hence, the expansion of the industry was to be made through a joint venture between state agencies.

Both the exclusion of the private sector and BNDE bureaucracy's desire to have a share of the equity of the new industry gave birth to a complex pattern of crossed alliances between local entrepreneurs, foreign interests and different groups in the bureaucracy. The BNDE Board of Directors split over the issue of state vs. private initiative. The high echelons of Petrobras cooled off, fearing a BNDE bureaucracy drive to transform the bank into an IRI-style holding of the public sector. The private sector intensified its pressure to obtain a clear definition of the government's intentions.

Two executive decrees were issued in July 1965, establishing that priority should be given to private projects and instructing Petrobras to sell (at world market prices) raw materials for national and foreign producers; but these decrees did not exclude a state supportive participation in the business.

Three private investments initiatives were subsequently announced. By the end of 1965 Union Carbide announced the construction of the naptha cracker with a capacity of 120,000 tons a year of ethylene (twice Brazil's consumption), using the Wulff process, 'the most advanced in the world' according to the firm.[9] Five years later, however, this wonderful technology proved that it just did not work, the Union Carbide's allegedly $40 million investment had to be written off, and the firm gave up for a period any significant project of expansion in Brazil. The second initiative originated from the association of two influential local groups (Capuava-Moreira Salles) in joint venture with several transnationals, with an estimated investment of more than $100 million. This Brazilian group later split up and the remaining partner (Capuava), threatened with bankrupty, gave up its share to Petrobras in the early 1970s. The third project was a minor one ($18 million) from a Bonden subsidiary.

Although the Minister of Planning (Roberto Campos) had made his disapproval of BNDE financing a state firm clear, and in spite — or because — of the announced private projects, the negotiations between Petrobras and BNDE bureaucracy were reopened. By mid-1976, BNDE and Petrobras succeeded in ironing out their divergences and agreed on a modified petrochemical program of 12 integrated projects, with an estimated investment of Cr$100 million (about $40 million), to be carried out by Petrobras alone, with BNDE financial backing.

Two subsequent and unrelated events contributed to transform the project on the basis of the II Petrochemical Pole and gave birth to the tripartite joint venture policy. The first is related to the initiative of the Brazilian group mentioned before. This initiative consisted of a project to build a naphtha cracker, in joint venture with Phillips Petroleum, and with a capacity to produce 500,000 tons a year of different basic and intermediary products. This project was conceived in order to integrate forwards downstream products being produced through four affiliated companies in joint ventures with transnational (Huls-Bayer, Solvay, Diamond Shamrock and National Distillers). The appeal to these foreign firms was due to the need to guarantee demand for the basic products, rather than for technological reasons;[10] Phillips Petroleum, by the way, decided later on to abandon the partnership, and this did not constitute an obstacle to the acquisition of technology. At the same time that the Brazilian group was pulling together its foreign partners, it also began to pressure Petrobras to enter the venture. There were at least two reasons for that. First, it was a way of guaranteeing supplies of naphtha (produced by Petrobras); second, it was also a way to reinforce the Brazilian group's position vis-à-vis its foreign partners, through the countervailing alliance that the powerful state firm represented. There were probably two additional motives: (1) in case of financial trouble, and in the best tradition of Brazilian capitalism, the association with Petrobras would make a 'rescue operation' easier — which in fact occurred; (2) Petrobras-BNDE envisaged joint venture could be more easily frozen, liberating the bank's resources for the private sector (the Brazilian group was counting on BNDE to finance its project). However, Petrobras was legally prohibited from entering into associations on a minority basis, moreover in a joint venture that also had foreign partners. And it used this argument to reinforce its resistance to the project.[11] Mainly as a result of the pressure put on government by Capuava, this legal obstacle was removed. In December 1967, an Executive Decree created a Petrobras subsidiary (Petroquisa), which was authorized to enter into joint ventures in petrochemicals with local and foreign firms. The actual participation of Petroquisa in the project with 25 percent of the equity (later on extended to 68 percent, when the Brazilian group pulled out) made obsolete, in practice, the controversial issue on the state vs. private initiative leadership on petrochemicals. In addition, it opened up the path for the institutionalization of three-way format of the joint venture.

The second sequence of events was created by the political pressure exerted by regional (not necessarily entrepreneurial) interests of the Estado of Bahia. Thanks to the initiative of a small but very active Brazilian consulting firm (CLAN), the 'baiano' lobby succeeded in influencing segments of the bureaucracy and in establishing bizarre political alliances within the federal government, to make sure that the II Petrochemical Pole would be located in Bahia — a decision that, by economic wisdom, is highly debatable, to say the least. The 'baiano' lobby backed its action with a feasibility study made by the prestigious Institute Français de Petrole, and managed to convince the then all-powerful Army Intelligence Community that the industrial concentration in São Paulo was a terrible danger — in case of bombardment.[12] Although the basic aim of the lobby was to have a petrochemical complex in Bahia, the action that it developed accelerated the decision-making process and turned out to be an additional political support for Petrobras moving in petrochemicals. Having its position reinforced, Petrobras was able to resist BNDE demands to participate as a shareholder. The major factor that explains Petrobras' drive, however, is the huge increase in its financial capability (both in cruzeiros and in foreign currency) from the late 1960s onwards. In fact, Petrobras did not dare to consult BNDE when Petroquisa was formed, and from the initial 12 projects set up with the bank only two were submitted for financing. As a consequence, Petroquisa alone coordinated its partners for the joint venture and negotiated, also alone, the majority of the contracts of technology.

By July 1970, the government finally drew up the definite guidelines for the establishment of the II Petrochemical Pole in the North-East, under the leadership of Petroquisa and on the three-way joint venture basis. The following year Petroquisa formed a new subsidiary (COPENE) to coordinate all production activities in the region.[13]

It is important to note that the three-way joint venture policy for petrochemicals is not mandatory. When a decision was not reached — and even after — local and foreign firms succeeded in having the CDI approval for a dozen individual projects based on full ownership or voluntary private joint ventures. The Dow-Chemical project is perhaps the most striking example of this. Dow-Chemical although having to face bureaucratic resistance, but also counting on strong political support from the high echelons of government, succeeded (by slicing its original project in different units) in implanting its own petrochemical complex — also in Bahia, simultaneously with Petroquisa, and with a project potentially competitive with the one carried out by the state firm.

From this brief description of moves and counter-moves that contributed to shape the policy-making, two observations should be made. First, the decision to set up the industry on a three-way joint venture basis was not the result of a deliberate government 'new strategy' on how to deal with transnationals (see the Dow-

Chemical example); and if the decision certainly increased the bargaining position of Petrobras and other sectors of the bureaucracy, it was not an ideological expression of classic statism.[14] Rather, the three-way joint venture solution appears as a de facto compromise solution among different interests that were more or less loosely represented. The second observation is that the technological question, always mentioned as a major obstacle to setting up highly complex industries, was never invoked as an issue during the decision-making. In other words, the argument that the joint venture solution was deliberately aimed to curb transnationals and to guarantee access to technology seems to be an ex post rationalization. Concerning technology, by the way, it is known that the market for chemical processes is fairly competitive and that competition plus technological change in this industry 'favor a rapid erosion of the monopolistic position of the original innovator.'[15] An important study on the subject has found, for instance, an average of 17 firms offering processes for each of the 26 petrochemical products surveyed.[16]

What we want to suggest with these two observations is that the joint venture policy (at least in the particular case we have examined) has a meaning that differs from the one usually attributed to it. It is not so much the result of any strong political stand of the government or the consequence of the technological 'must.' Rather, the joint venture phenomenon is the expression of two other things: (1) how the increase of the state entrepreneurial activities in developing economies, even in countries of more relative development, becomes more and more inevitable; and (2) how this state role in the present stage of the internationalization of capitalist production can only be 'legitimized' if played in association with foreign partners. In the extreme, this subverts a common view and, at the same time, helps to qualify local government discourses on joint ventures: the strategic major constraint is not imposed by the state on transnationals, but the other way round. To be more precise, if, on the one hand, the state acquires a greater ability to curb specific practices of this or that individual foreign firm, then, on the other hand, the association of local states with the transnational corporation also provides the latter, qua mainly an actor of the internationalization of capitalist production, a very effective leverage to dilute bureaucracy resistances to this process — and to curb any tendency that could possibly lead to one form or another of 'state capitalism.' The next section will contribute further elements to this interpretation.

PATTERNS OF CONTROL
AND FINANCING

Control and financing (in the sense of capital requirement) are, of course, central issues in any discussion concerning power distribution within industrial organizations, especially if we are dealing with joint ventures. The reasons for this are so evident that any further elaboration risks being redundant. We will only note, in order to put the themes to be discussed in context, that one of the reasons most frequently invoked to explain government motivations in encouraging or making mandatory the practice of joint ventures with transnational corporations is based on the assumption that through this partnership the best of both worlds can be obtained, guaranteeing a constant foreign capital inflow and, at the same time, curbing the negative effects that result from transnational corporation business practices and political 'overpresence.' Therefore, the problems of control and financing, in addition to their intrinsic connection, are also linked, in the joint venture phenomenon, as two complementary goals of the same policy. Therefore, the knowledge of how these two problems have been solved is important to the assessment of a joint venture experiment.

Legislation and practical rules concerning the constitution of joint ventures (as well as most of the discussion on the subject) are focused on the firm's structure of ownership. Nationalization goals, for instance, are set up in terms of percentage equity required for national owning. The basic assumption is that access to ownership and access to control can be equated, or, at least, that the former is a condition for the latter. Of course, no one ignores that the relationship between ownership and control is not a linear one; in fact, even in cases of wholly owned firms, actual control can be exercised by non-shareholders through management contracts or different forms of technological and market dependency. However, such cases generally represent de facto situations, born not out of juridical regulation of property, but out of market constraints. Leaving aside market considerations, it is plausible to assume that equity participation (to the extent that it also gives access to management) opens up the path for the exercise of some degree of control over business operations. Moreover, specific legislation in each country normally establishes the basic rights of shareholders, according to the stock they own. The relationship between these basic rights and the nature and extent of the partners' ability to control business operations is, of course, a function of different factors affecting each partner's bargaining power, either at the moment of the firm's constitution or during the existence of the association. A rather different situation occurs, however, when special rules of control are previously set up and codified in the act of constitution of the firm, irrespective of each partner's equity share. In this respect, the Brazilian experience is an interesting example.

The basic orientation adopted for the Camaçari Petrochemical Pole concerning ownership was that equity should be shared in the ideal proportion of one-third for each category of partners in the joint venture (state, private local and transnationals). A certain flexibility in carrying out this basic rule was allowed, under two conditions: (1) Petroquisa's voting stock should always be superior to the stock of any other individual shareholder; (2) Brazilian interests (through either the state or a local firm, or both) should always have the majority of the voting stock. This orientation has been strictly enforced by Petroquisa for all firms in the Pole. (See Appendix for names of firms, equity control and other characteristics.) Thus, it is reasonable to expect that patterns of management and control of business operations should reflect this pattern of ownership. However, this is not necessarily so.

All joint ventures formed as a result of the three-way system adopted, through mutual agreement, very specific written rules concerning each partner's rights and obligations, binding provisos in relation to management, and definite directives on how certain strategic business decisions must be made. These by-laws ('contratos de acionistas'), along with the contracts of technology, both considered confidential, make the rule on different domains of the life of the enterprise — and show little or no relation at all with the patterns of ownership. Therefore, the special agreements — and not the structure of property — are the key to understanding how these joint ventures operate and to making any assessment of the partnership policy.

We had access to eight contracts of this type, concerning eight firms (out of 18 located at the Camaçari Pole), covering cases in which European, Japanese and US-based corporations were partners. Although some differences among them exist, related more to the specific characteristics of the product than to the foreign partner origin, all of them have a basic format and follow the same rationale. The most important feature, in relation to what we are discussing, concerns veto power on management decisions.

All contracts establish that a certain number of business decisions can be made only by the unanimity of the partners' votes, irrespective of the percentage of their voting stock. This principle applies to any of the corporation's bodies (directorate, board of directors or assemblies of the firm) that have decision-making power. The typical domains in relation to which decisions must be made on an unanimous basis are the following: (1) changes in the company laws ('estatutos'); (2) dissolution of the company; (3) mergers with other firms, or the take-over of other firms by the company; (4) the issue, redemption or conversion of shares, debentures and bonds; (5) participation in other firms; (6) loans on collateral; (7) transactions and contracts of any nature between the company and its shareholders, or firms in which they participate; (8) the acquisition, selling, licensing or relinquishment of patents, trade marks, technical information and production secrets; (9) expansion plans involving operation for which costs might exceed the company's authorized capital by 10 percent; (10) distribution of the company benefits.

These dispositions may assume slightly different forms in each of the contracts examined. Provision (10), for instance, may not always appear; in other cases it takes the form of recommendation that dividends should be distributed at a maximum possible rate; also, the percentage mentioned in provision (9) can be reduced to 5 percent, or the percentage can be indexed according to inflation rates. These agreements also: (1) fix the amounts of investment, working capital and the financial requirement to set up the plant; (2) determine the number of the members in directorate and board of directors to be indicated by each partner; (3) in at least one case, establish rules of secrecy, concerning not only technical information but all information related to the company's activities, which partners and employers must in Brazil obey. (The foreign partner however, is not committed to those rules outside of Brazil.) Also, in one case (in which the partner is a Japanese corporation) divergences and disputes related to the agreement are to be settled through arbitrage, with the qualification that, if the object of the claim is the Japanese partner, arbitrage procedures must be held in Tokyo.

Independently of these variations, the important thing is the agreed principle that decisions related to such a wide range of domains — on which strategy, expansion and even current activities of the firm depend — should be made by unanimity of votes. En clair, this means giving a veto power to any minority shareholder on basic business operations. Since this minority shareholder is the foreign firm, transnational corporations are entitled, at least theoretically, to veto the company expansion, or even its current operations, at any time, with an insignificant part of the stock.

A first interpretation could be that these by-law agreements only reveal the preoccupation of foreign partners with defending their investment, by insuring sufficient arsenal to compensate for their minority position in the association; a similar (optimistic) interpretation could be that the veto power necessarily leads to compromise solutions, and in this sense, rather than an obstacle, it represents an insurance against possible periodical conflicts over management, which would have disruptive effects on business operations. These arguments are often invoked by those who took active part in policy enforcement, although sharp criticism is also voiced in the bureaucracy.[17] This may be partially true. However, to know the extent of this 'truth,' it would be wise to ask: (1) what are the investment risks that minority shareholders are so eager to defend; and (2) what is the counterpart to the veto power offered by minority shareholders in the association? This leads us to the question of financing.

State intervention to build up the Camaçari Pole is not limited to coordination and entrepreneurial activities, but is also extremely important in the financing of the entire project. This is a new orientation, in sharp contrast with the prevailing one of counting on external financing for expansion of sectors that are also under state entrepreneurial responsibility. For instance, the share of external financing (BID, BIRD, etc.) in the expansion of the steel industry accounted for 48 percent of all resources involved during the period 1972-76; in the case of the Camaçari Pole (which represents twice the amount of the steel investment) external resources accounted for only 9.7 percent. This new orientation was apparently adopted in order to make a more intensive use of equipment and services locally produced or available, according to the 'buy national' policy.[18] Locally produced equipment for petrochemicals (which is

TABLE 1
Camaçari Pole: Financial Sources

Sources	Cr$ million*	%	US$ million*
Own resources	14,056,862	41.1	979,571
Government	4,005,750	11.7	279,146
Local partners (FIBASE)	3,104,699	9.1	216,355
Foreign partners	1,166,948	3.4	81,320
Public funds (Finor, others)	5,779,465	16.9	402,750
Financial resources	20,179,553	58.9	1,406,242
BNDE	13,855,220	40.4	965,521
Endorsement/BNDE	2,593,655	7.6	180,743
Other local financing	413,577	1.2	28,821
Other external financing	3,317,101	9.7	231,157
Total	34,236,415	100.0	2,385,813

* Cr$ and US$ of June 1977.

Source: BNDE

not necessarily produced by national firms) accounted in fact for 70 percent in value of total equipment, while in the case of Siderurgy it was only 30 percent.[19]

More important to the understanding of all the implications of the joint venture policy is an examination of the financial contribution of foreign firms and local entrepreneurs to the build up of the Camaçari Pole.

Table 1 provides a consolidated view of amounts and sources of financing, covering 23 firms of the Camaçari Pole in June 1977. The most striking feature is, of course, the extremely low ratio of the private partner participation, both foreign and local. Concerning the latter, the real figure is much lower (probably less than half) of that indicated, since data from local partners and FIBASE (a subsidiary of BNDE) are aggregated. The extent of foreign firms' participation must also be qualified, since in the majority of cases their contribution is made by capitalization of technology. In some cases, the value attributed to technology and know-how is fixed by the by-law agreement; in such cases the difference between this agreed price and the part of capital subscribed by the foreign partner has to be in the form of paid-up capital. When the value of technology is not fixed, however, one could hypothesize that, in the extreme, the price paid for technology will represent one-third of the firm's benefits (the equivalent of the foreign partner's share in the joint venture). There is no need, however, to speculate on the various benefit possibilities that a participation under the form of capitalization of technology may offer for a foreign firm. The data shown in table 1 are sufficient to establish the total discrepancy between the actual investment 'risk' for the private sector (both foreign and local) and the power acquired through the right of vetoing major decisions, i.e. the power to influence development strategies for the entire petrochemical pole.

Unfortunately, statistics on joint ventures (such as those produced by the magnificent Harvard project on US-based transnationals) only provide us with information concerning structures of ownership;[20] therefore, we have to rely only on limited and modest research efforts to have a better (but not statistically significant) view of the joint venture phenomenon. As a consequence, the discussion of some of the questions raised before (such as of the significance of the joint venture phenomenon and the interaction between the entrepreneurial activities of the state and the internationalization of production) has to be either placed on a much higher level of abstraction or limited to specific contexts; but in the latter case, we have to make use of much more complex social and political variables if the discussion is to have significance. Since none of these approaches can be adopted within the limits of this paper (an attempt is being made in those directions elsewhere), we shall restrict ourselves to the following brief concluding remarks.

In the light of what we have seen, the results of Brazilian experiment on joint ventures appear to be meager when compared with the implicit or explicit goals in the partnership policy discourse. First, foreign capital inflow for the industry was insignificant, since the foreign 'inventor' contribution was basically composed of capitalization of technology and Brazilian public funds. Second, if on the one hand it is possible to admit that the state as a partner will probably exercise its police function concerning some of the TNC's business practices (say, transfer pricing), on the other hand, TNCs' ability to influence, from within the firm, the mode of expansion of the whole sector is much more strategically important in comparison with state-acquired control. It is true, however, that in the long run some unexpected side-effects may result. We are referring to the learning process on how to deal with transnationals that the public bureaucracy directly involved in the experiment is passing through. There have already been some signs of this in the modified strategy (mainly concerning process design, detail engineering and, in short, the unpacking of technology) which is being studied to orient policy goals for the III Petrochemical Pole in Rio Grande do Sul. Needless to say, from these possible side-effects we can only expect better subjective conditions for negotiating with transnationals; the parameters for such negotiations are, of course, determined by social and historical structural conditions.

The question that inevitably arises from what we have seen is: why did the state not assume its de facto role as the 'real' entrepreneur by annexing the II Petrochemical Pole to the public sector? As we have seen, on the one hand, local entrepreneurs have failed before (in São Paulo) and their presence in Camaçari is a rather symbolic (although profitable) one; on the other hand, transnational corporations already in the market were not very interested in expanding the business and there is no evidence to assert that they moved in as a result of an 'oligopolistic game.'[21] In other words, this was the classic situation which in the past led the state in Brazil to transform itself into an entrepreneur. To this we must add two other things: first, capital requirements for the petrochemical project were definitely not an obstacle, and the technological problem was not an insurmountable issue: second, sectors of public bureaucracy, as we also have seen, pushed for a state intervention.

Of course, if compared with previous situations, one important political variable is missing: the 'classic' supportive populist-nationalist mobilization for a state take-over. This is true, but it is insufficient as an explanation. If the public bureaucracy could no longer legitimize its role as entrepreneur through populist-nationalist mobilization, it could — as it actually did — legitimize it by simply associating the local private sector to the project, whatever the latter contribution in capital.

The answer to the question is to be found in the social role of the state in the present stage of 'dependent-associated' capitalism. In this connection, the state clearly appears as an integral part of the international chain of capital accumulation. This is the basic reason why only through the association with transnational firms — whatever the forms this association may assume — local bureaucracies can legitimize the entrepreneurial role opened to them in capitalist contexts marked by the historical 'failure' of national bourgeoisies. How these associations are negotiated is a function of the existing correlation of forces in this or that social context — and this is part of the current reorganization of the capitalist system.

APPENDIX

Basic Complex
Implanted Industries: General Characteristics (June 1978)

Company	Equity control	%	Product	Capacity ton/year	Raw-materials	Origin	Process licensor
			Ethylene	388,000			
			Propylene	200,020			
			Butadiene	52,450			
			Butene	79,000			
			ortho — Xylene	40,000			
			para — Xylene	82,600			
			Xylene Mix	19,000			
			Benzene	129,500			
			Toluene	17,000			
Copene-Petroquimica do Nordeste SA	Petroquisa	54.09	LPG	43,000	Naphta	RLAM	The Lummus Company
	Users	45.91	Propane	10,000			
			Hydrogen	13,000	Gas Oil	RLAM	UOP Process Division
			C$_5$ fraction, Pyrolysis	41,000	Natural Gas	RPBa	Nippon Zeon Company
			Heavy Gas Oil, Pyrolysis	28,000			
			Heavy Gasoline	93,000			
			Residues from Pyrolysis				
			De-ethanized Natural Gas	155,000			
				1,705,000 Nm^3/d			
			Electric Power	275 MVA	Fuel Oil	RLAM	—
			Steam	2,000 t/h	Fuel Oil	RLAM	—
			Oxygen	500 t/d	Air	—	Cryoplants
			Nytrogen	266 t/d	Air	—	
			Demineralized Water	2,000 m^3/h	Raw water	Johannes II	Permutit/Techint
			Clarified Water	7,500 m^3/h			
			Fresh Water	60 m^3/h			
			Service Air, Comp.	22,200 Nm^3/h	Air	—	—
			Instrument Air, Comp.	18,000 Nm^3/h	Air	—	—

APPENDIX (continued)

Company	Equity control	%	Product	Capacity ton/year	Raw-materials	Origin	Process licensor
Ceman — Central de Manutenção de Camaçari SA	Copene	99.99	—	—	—	—	—
Ciquine — CIA Petroquimica	Petroquisa Grujapão Camargo Correia	33.31 33.31 33.31	Octanol Butanol Octanol Isobutanol	20,000 3,000 4,400 15,000	Natural Gas Propylene Natural Gas Propylene	RPBa Copene RPBa Copene	Mitsubishi Chemical Ind Mitsubishi Chemical Ind
Ciquine Cia. de Industrias Quimicas do Nordeste	Ciquine Petroq	98.16	Phtalic Anhydride Maleic Anhydride	2,300 6,400	o-xylene Benzene	Copene Copene	Von Heyden Scient Design
Edn Estireno do Nordeste SA	Petroquisa Bakolar Foster Grant	33.33 33.33 33.33	Styrene Polystyrene Toluene	100,000 45,000 6,800	Benzene Ethylene	Copene Copene	Foster Grant Co., Inc. The Badger
Fisiba — Fibras Sinteticas da Bahia	BNDE Mitsubishi Others	43.10 29.32 27.58	Acrylic Fibers	8,000	Acrylonitrile	Foreign*	Sabrin Mitsubishi
Isocianatos do Brasil SA	Petroquisa Du Pont Petroq. Bahia	48.92 15.08 36.00	Toluene diisocyanate (TDI)	22,700	Toluene Chlorine Natural Gas Sulf. Acid Nitric Acid	Copene Salgema/CQR RPBa Sulfab. Nitrofertil	Du Pont
Melamina Ultra SA Industria Quimica	Ultra Group Others	98.00 2.00	Melamine	8,000	Urea/Ammonia	Nitrofertil	Stamicarbon NV
Metanor — Metanol do Nordeste SA	Petroquisa Paskin Peixoto de Castro Group	33.24 33.24 33.24	Methanol	60,000	Natural Gas	RPBa	Imperial Chemical Industries — (ICI)

Company	Partners (%)	Products	Capacity	Raw Materials	Supplier	Technology
Nitrocarbono SA	Petroquisa 26.50, Petroq. Bahia 26.50, Copea 26.50, DSM 20.50	Caprolactam / Ammonium Sulfate	35,000 / 63,000	Benzene / Ammonia	Copene / Nitrofertil	DSM / Stamicarbon
Fertilizantes Nitrogenados do Nordeste SA	Petrobras Fert 79.32, Petroquisa 20.67	Ammonia / Urea	66,000 / 82,500	Natural Gas / Ammonia	RPBa / Own	Foster Wheel / Mitsui Toatsu
Nitrofértil-NE		Ammonia / Urea	300,000 / 264,000	Natural Gas / Ammonia	RPBa / Own	Kellog Co. / Mitsui Toatsu
Oxiteno Nordeste SA Ind. e Com.	Oxiteno SA Ind. e Com. 99.99	Ethylene Oxide / Ethylene Glycols	105,000 / 142,000	Ethylene / Oxygen	Copene / Copene	Scientific Design
Polialden Petroquimica SA	Petroquisa 33.33, Banco Econômico 33.33, Grujapão 33.33	HD Polyethylene	60,000	Ethylene / Propylene / Hydrogen	Copene / Copene / Copene	Mitsubishi Chemical Industries
Politeno Industria e Comercio SA	Petroquisa 30.00, Sumitomo Chem. 20.00, Itap/Suzano/ Nordesquim/C., Itoh 49.99	LD Polyethylene	100,000	Ethylene / Propylene	Copene / Copene	Sumitomo Chemical Company
Polipropileno SA	Petroquisa 30.00, ICI 30.00, Cevekol 20.00, Cia. Suzano 20.00	Polypropylene	47,500	Propylene / Ethylene	Copene / Copene	Imperial Chemical Industries (ICI)
Pronor Produtos Prganicos SA	Petroquisa 33.33, Petroq. Bahia 33.33, Dinamit Nobel 33.33	Dimethyl Terphtalate (DMT)	60,000	p-Xylene / Methanol	Copene / Metanor	Dinamit Nobel AG
Sulfab Cia Sulfoquimica da Bahia	Natron 87.15, Finep 12.83	Hydrosulfuric Acid / Oleum	108,900 / 23,100	Sulfur	Imported	Natron SA
SA White Martins	Union Carbide 34.80, Electric Furnace Co. 15.30, Others 49.90	Oxygen / Nitrogen	14,600	Air	—	Pwn technologic

* will be supplied by ACRINOR in the future

NOTES

1. For an ample survey on recent new legislation concerning transnational corporations, see UN Centre on Transnational Corporations, *National Legislation and Regulations relating to Transnational Corporations* (New York, 1978). For a brief survey of general trends concerning the formation of joint ventures, see Luciano Martins, 'Definição de uma problemática para o estudo de joint-ventures' (Paris, June 1978).

2. During the period 1951-65, the structure of ownership of affiliates of the US-based 180 TNCs studied by the Harvard Project shows the following changes: (1) the percentage of wholly owned firms decreased from 70.0 to 64.0; (2) the majority-owned (50-94%) went from 12.5 to 29.1; (3) the minority-owned (5-49%) increased from 6.5 to 9.6. From 1966 to 1975, however, the tendency is reversed except for the minority-owned. Cf. Joan P. Curham, William H. Davidson and Rajan Suri, *Tracing the Multinationals — A Sourcebook on US-based Enterprises* (Cambridge, Mass.: Ballinger, 1977). Since legislation encouraging or making mandatory the formation of joint ventures is relatively recent, a new increase of the curve might be expected. Besides, US-based corporations have always been more reluctant to enter in associations than European or Japanese-based TNCs. Specifically on joint ventures, see: Wollfang G. Friedmann and George Kalmanoff, *Joint International Business Ventures* (New York: Columbia University Press, 1961); Karen K. Bivens and Enid B. Lovell, *Joint Ventures with Foreign Partners, International Survey of Business Opinion and Experience*, (New York: National Industrial Conference Board, 1966); James W. C. Tomlinson, *The Joint Venture Process in International Business: India and Pakistan*, (Cambridge, Mass.: MIT Press, 1970); International Chamber of Commerce, 'International Joint Business Ventures in Developing Countries,' Report of the Commission on International Investments and Economic Development (December 1968); Wollfang G. Friedmann and Jean-Pierre Beguin, *Joint International Business Ventures in Developing Countries: Case Studies and Analysis of Recent Trends* (New York: Columbia University Press, 1977); Business International, 'Pros and Cons of Joint Ventures Abroad,' Management Monographs, no. 18 (New York, 1964); Theodore H. Moran, *Multinational Corporations and Politics of Dependence* (Princeton: University Press, 1977) and Richard D. Robson, *National Control of Foreign Business Entry: A Survey of 15 Countries* (New York: Praeger, 1976).

3. These are the frequent arguments given by government officials in some Latin American countries (Peru, Brazil and Mexico, for instance). Sometimes these arguments are made explicit in the legislation on joint ventures.

4. Peter Evans's forthcoming work on Brazil is a noble exception, specially chapter V: 'Entrepreneurship and Alliances: State Enterprise and the Process of Industrialization in the Periphery' (unpublished manuscript).

5. The literature on the subject has tremendously increased in the last two years or so. The UN Centre on Transnational Corporations has recently published interesting monographs. Also, of course, Constantine Vaitsos's important works on the subject. See, for instance, his 'Power, Knowledge and Development Policy:

Relations between Transnational Enterprises and Developing Countries,' paper presented at conference on 'Las Empresas Transnacionales y los Paises Receptores,' Mexico, 1973.

6. The best sources for data on US-based TNCs still are the US Senate and the US Tariff Commission reports.

7. From the expansion of the state apparatus in Brazil during this period see Luciano Martins, 'A Expansão Recente do Estado no Brasil: seus problemas e seus atores' (Report/research, IUPERJ-FINEP, Rio, 1977).

8. This was voiced in many memoranda sent by BNDE to Petrobras. For instance, Ofício P. 51/65 from Garrido Torres (BNDE's president) to Gen. Adhemar de Queiroz (Petrobras's president), 18 February 1965.

9. Cf. Evans, op. cit. p. 27.

10. This is very well analyzed by Peter Evans, op. cit., p. 27.

11. Among other reasons. Petrobras apparently feared a brain-drain of its best managers and technicians to the petrochemical industry (interviews, Rio de Janeiro, July-August 1978).

12. Cf. testimony of one prominent member of CLAN (Rômulo de Almeida) in *Jornal do Economista*, vol. III, no. 2 (April/May 1977), p. 9.

13. The basic complex of the North-East Petrochemical Pole was located in Camaçari (Bahia) and presently consists of a group of petrochemical units that are integrated to COPENE's productive system. The latter comprises COPENE's basic units (the raw material plant, the utilities plant and the maintenance plant) and the consumer or user units that transform the raw materials. The raw materials plant supplies oleofins (with a capacity of 640,000 tons per year) and aromatics (170,000 tons per year) to the second-generation industries. By July 1978, there were a total of 18 industries installed in the area of the basic complex, and 8 others were in various stages of installation. The pole represents an estimated total investment of $2.5 billion (data for July 1978).

14. After 1964, the entrepreneurial activities of the state in Brazil have certainly increased. In fact, more public firms have been created (60% of the total) than in the previous 60 years. However, for the first time since the 1930s the role of the state is not legitimized through an ideology of statism. This point is analyzed in Martins, 'A Expansão Recente do Estado no Brasil,' op. cit.

15. The technological issue in relation to petrochemicals and Latin America is well analyzed in the important Mariluz Cortes's PhD dissertation, 'Transfer of Petrochemical Technology to Latin America: A Summary' (manuscript, 1977); quotes are from p. 4.

16. ibid.

17. Interviews, Rio de Janeiro (July-September 1978).

18. Cf. José Tavares Araujo Jr and Vera Maria Dick, 'Governo, Empresas Multinacionais e Empresas Nacionais: o caso da indústria petroquímica,' in *Pesquisa e Planejamento Econômico*, vol. IV, no. 3, Rio de Janeiro (December 1974), pp. 629-54. This is an excellent pioneer study on the petrochemical joint venture experiment in Brazil.

19. ibid. From the share of local equipment in the petrochemical industry see O. V. Perroni, 'Alguns Aspectos Relativos à Transferência de Tecnologia e ao Fortalecimento da Engenharia Nacional no setor Petroquímico no Brasil,' paper presented at Simpósio Internacional Petroquímico, CONICIT, Caracas, May 1976;

also Ronaldo Miragaya, 'A Tecnologia Química no Brasil,' paper presented at Primeiro Congresso Brasileiro de Engenharia Química, São Paulo, 27-9 July 1976.

20. See, for instance, Curham, Davidson and Suri, *Tracing the Multinationals*, op. cit.

21. We tried to test the 'oligopolistic game' hypothesis as one of the explanations for transnational corporations' acceptance of the joint-venture policy. The oligopolistic reaction probably played a role in this acceptance. However, the importance of the government's intervention and subsidies are such that the Camaçari experiment does not provide, in our view, a good case for such a test.

11

WORLD-SYSTEM AND NATIONAL MOVEMENTS IN THE INDUSTRIALIZED COUNTRIES: The Québec-Canada Case

Arnaud Sales
University of Montreal, Canada

> You will appear in the United States of North America, one of the ancient nations — as they were called — a political division of whose purpose we are not quite sure. One of the designs of your expedition will be to determine why the human race at the time split itself into scores of states, rather than having but one government.
>
> Fredric Brown, *Nightmares and Geezenstacks*
> (New York: Bantam Books, 1961, p. 102.)

The twentieth century, through its manifold vicissitudes, has been marked by two great international movements: (1) a movement of globalization and accentuation of interdependence, which has led to talk about a world system, and (2) a movement of recomposition of the political geography of the globe, characterized by the emergence of a multitude of new states, and thus by dismemberment, separation and balkanization.

Author's Note: This is a revised version of a paper delivered at the conference on 'The Social and Political Implications of the New International Economic Order' organized by the Economy and Society Research Committee of the International Sociological Association, Rockefeller Foundation, in Bellagio, Italy, 24-28 April 1979. The original French version has been published in *Sociologie et Sociétés*, special issue on 'Développement national et économie mondialisée', vol. XI, no. 2 (October 1979).

On the one hand, the contemporary world has witnessed the development of vast aggregations endowed with an unprecedented degree of economic, political, administrative, military, scientific and cultural power, which would lead one to think that modernity is closely associated with concentration, integration and internationalization. On the other hand, the appearance of the 'global village' seems to invoke the appearance of little homelands. The dismemberment of the old colonial empires through national liberation struggles has resulted in the formation since 1945 of more than 100 states — a threefold increase. However, the transformation of the political planisphere is not yet complete since, apart from the Third World, a large number of national or regional movements have also arisen in industrialized countries. Some are still embryonic, but others are powerful enough to make frontier systems tremble. Thus, certain large countries like Great Britain, Canada and France could one day find themselves dismembered or at least reorganized with a much weaker centralized economic decision-making capacity.

The legitimacy acquired by the national liberation struggles in the countries of the periphery has not transferred automatically to the national or regional movements (Basque, Scottish, Occitanian, Jura, Flemish or Québécois) that are arising in the industrialized countries. Undoubtedly the cultural particularism of these regions (their folkloric dimensions?) is being recognized: recognition is being given as well to their relative underdevelopment, and even to the existence of a certain domestic colonialism that is both economic and cultural. But the manifestations of these movements and struggles engendered a certain skepticism and even annoyance. However, in the past few years their global significance has emerged from the shadows and from marginal status. France, Canada, Great Britain, Spain, Belgium and Switzerland have sought first to repress, then to contain and finally to negotiate with these national movements which increasingly take the form of organized parties.

One cannot at this time predict the long-term global impact of the 'reviviscence des mouvements nationaux dans les pays industrialises.'[1] But the question of the possible breakup of some great nation-states remains.

Our intention here is obviously not to deal with the manifold facets of this question. We will only try, on the basis of the Québec example in Canada, to show first how the process of globalization can prevent a country from holding its own as an economic unit, and especially as a meaningful unit for solving the problem of stimulating renewed industrial growth and the problem of uneven regional development that occurs under that process; and second, how in such a context a national movement, founded in the first place on the struggle against domination/subordination structures between two nations in the same country, poses the double question of national differentiation and integration as a means of fighting against marginalization.

GLOBALIZATION

The reality of a world-system is not new: Braudel and Wallerstein date its emergence at the end of the fifteenth century. What is new, however, is the present process of integration that characterizes it. Since the end of the 1960s, many researchers have focused their analyses on the establishment of this new global system. They have studied the process of internationalization of capital, the development of multinational firms, trends towards transnationalization, or world capitalism in general (cf. Vernon, 1971; Amin, 1971, 1973; Palloix, 1971, 1973; Stopford and Wells, 1972; Wilkins, 1970, 1974; Barnet and Muller, 1974; Furtado, 1975; Michalet, 1976). The movement of globalization on the world scale has notably been reflected in a process of integration, an increasingly concentrated economic and political power structure and a trend toward transnationalization which has been manifested in various forms. These dimensions all bear on our topic and therefore should be reviewed.

The process of integration occurs on three specific levels. It first occurs at the center of the capitalist system, where increasingly close connections are established among the great national economies through sizable exchanges of capital, products, highly skilled manpower and scientific and technical knowledge. The result is unification, homogenization of economic space (even if vast regions are left unused), and the appearance of domains of decision[2] that increasingly escape the control of the nation-states (Furtado, 1975).

The process of integration is also increasingly achieved between the center and the periphery, the North and the South, on the basis of the unequal development of different countries. For structural reasons,[3] capitalism cannot survive without shifting production to the Third World and thus without leading this labor force into industrial production, integrating it in a new but always dependent way into the world-system (Michalet, 1976). As it will later be seen, this process obviously has a considerable impact on the evolution of the industrial structure of the countries at the center, which must transform low-productivity industrial branches.

The integration of economic space is accompanied by an integration and centralization within the very apparatus that is materializing the transformations just discussed. Multinational companies, in effect, exceed the traditional boundaries of organization in each country, integrate their key activities among the subsidiaries, and thus centralize, at the level of the firm's international administration, the definition of objectives, strategies and policies that once were essentially the responsibility of independent local or national enterprises. The strategy for developing capital is achieved not in a fragmented and autonomous way by each subsidiary, but at the level of the firm as a whole.

The integration of activities that are very dispersed and differentiated geographically is consequently accompanied by the centralization and concentration of property and power on an international scale, as well as at the level of the whole social organization, since the corporation is one of its most fundamental elements in our societies. This centralization, accentuated by the development of information and communications systems, necessarily implies the subordination of the truncated subsidiary enterprises, local subcontracting companies and manpower that can protest on only a very local level — and on a more general level of the national interests, cultures and ways of life — to the multinationals' global system.

Internally, international competition forces concentration through centralization of capital, and the nation-states of the center have had to intervene in nearly every case to facilitate the reorganization and 'rationalization' of entire strategic industrial branches, acting as the catalysts for the formation of an increasingly monopolized structure. This movement obviously reinforces the monopolist fraction of the domestic bourgeoisie which in turn seeks to become international. However, as I have shown in the case of Québec,[4] the fractions of capital become socially incarnate not only with bourgeoisie as a class but also across specific national and ethnic groups (for example, in Québec French and Jews are mostly in the competitive sector, Anglo-Saxons in the monopolistic sector). To the extent that certain of these groups are better represented in the economic and political power structure, it is easy to understand that concentration works to their profit and to the profit of the regions where the principal bases of their power are to be found.

Centralization and integration are in the end accompanied by a trend towards transnationalization for the whole new world-system. On the one hand, it manifests itself in the development of a supranational superstructure that is formally or informally institutionalized in fields such as defence, the economy, politics and finance, but also in the professions, the mass media, information, science and technology (Sunkel and Fuenzalida, 1979). On the other hand, it is also apparent within the multinational firms, which, as already noted, go beyond the traditional national or regional boundaries to establish their strategies, their modes of organization and their implantation. For the oligarchy of the 'global firms,' the independent nation-state is both an obstacle to the optimization of resources on the world scale and an obsolescent category that is poorly adapted to the economic and technical complexity of our universe. On the ideological level, the imperialistic universalism of the big corporation is radically opposed to nationalism, which restrains, regulates or competes with its growth (Barnet and Müller, 1974).

However, it is essential to take into consideration in any analysis the fact that the multinational firms cannot be considered pure transnational institutions because they always maintain a strong national base (Michalet, 1976; De Brunhoff, 1976). In this respect the relations between the multinationals and the nation-state are at the same time conflictual and complementary, and thus necessarily ambiguous. As principal power centers of the dominant social forces in our societies, the dialectic of their relations is extremely important in the shaping of the new global system, since it is underlain by a complex play of social struggles that are at once internal and external. In fact, if one considers the network of relationships that has been woven between domestic capital, foreign capital and state power more generally, it is appropriate to recognize that these relations differ profoundly from one society to another, depending on the level of development, the degree of dependence and also on the kind of the social struggles that at different times unfold with greater or lesser intensity. From this viewpoint, it is extremely important to consider the impact of social movements that may contribute significantly to the definition of these relationships.

THE GLOBALIZATION AND INTEGRATION OF CANADA

Dependent Continental Integration

If we look at the world-system, we can see that the United States still occupies a hegemonic position in the present system even if the EEC and Japan can increasingly present themselves as serious competitors. It is therefore first in relation to the American giant that the integration of the economies of the center is taking place. However, the intensity of this integration varies depending on the country. Among industrialized countries that are middle-range powers, it is Canada that takes the often bitter prize for dependent integration. To grasp the extent of this, it is enough to recall that 58 percent of the assets and 66 percent of the profits of Canada's manufacturing and processing industries are under foreign control; that in the mining industry the proportion of foreign control is 68 percent of the assets and 72 percent of the profits, and that 80 percent of this foreign control is exercised by American multinational companies.

The natural wealth of this immense territory has made Canada the big supplier of basic products in North America, whether in wood, in ores for many metals[5] or, to a certain extent, in oil and natural gas. Given Canada's economic history, it is not very surprising to observe that Canada represents about 50 percent of American direct foreign investments in this sector.

Canadian dependence on American capital is thus considerable. North American continental integration can be seen at many other levels, particularly at the level of commercial exchanges, since three-quarters of Canadian exports go to the United States. However, these are generally raw materials or semi-finished products, while Canada imports many manufactured products. With the new GATT agreements this integration should continue, since 80 percent of Canadian exports will enter the United States completely duty-free. Through these measures, a gradual move is being made toward a North American free trade zone or else a Canada-USA-Mexico common market.

This dependence on the United States is not solely the effect of a dynamic strategy of direct investment by the American multinationals. It is also a matter of induced dependence. Because of its colonial antecedents, the Canadian domestic bourgeoisie has always been characterized by the dominance of (British-type) commercial and banking fractions. The industrial fraction is relatively weak, which in part explains the difficulties of local industrial development and the penetration of direct American investment in industry[6] (Naylor, 1972, 1975; Clement, 1975; Sales, 1979).

The Internationalization of Canadian Capital

Canada's excessive dependence, which restrains 'national' accumulation considerably, since up to $2.5 billion in dividends and interest are repatriated annually, does not prevent Canadian monopoly capital from going international. Moore Corporation, Inco, Massey-Ferguson and Northern Telecom have very important foreign investments. Several indicators show that the movement has intensified during the past few years. The Royal Commission on Corporate Concentration indicated, for example, that up to 1976 Canadian direct investments in foreign countries exceeded direct foreign investments in Canada (foreign companies in most cases finance themselves directly in Canada). The banks have been particularly active in this process since the 1960s. Thus, 'total foreign currency assets and liabilities of the chartered banks increased by 667% and 668% respectively from December 1966 to December 1976[7]...About a quarter of the balance of revenue of the five largest Canadian chartered banks (or 90% of bank assets in Canada) comes from foreign-currency operations...[while] foreign currency assets account for 30 percent of total assets.[8]

Let us also recall that the total number of branches of Canadian chartered banks in foreign countries rose to 497 as of 31 May 1977 (table 1). In his work on the continental integration of economic power Wallace Clement distinguishes two types of Canadian investment in foreign countries. The first type comes essentially from the transport, service and particularly from the banking and financial institutions sector, where the domestic bourgeoisie predominates.

TABLE 1
Branches of Canadian Chartered Banks Outside of Canada
on 31 May 1977

	Number of branches
United Kingdom	28
United States	70
France	8
West Germany	7
Bahamas	52
Barbados	26
Guyana	11
Mexico	4
Central America and South America	26
Dominican Republic	22
Virgin Islands (American and British)	7
Puerto Rico	16
Trinidad and Tobago	33
Jamaica (and Cayman Islands)	93
Other West Indian countries	31
Other European countries	16
Asia (including the Middle East)	42
Australia	5
Total	497

Source: Canadian Bankers' Association. In Royal Commission on Corporate Concentration (1978). The chartered banks are represented by branches, agencies, representative offices and/or branches of subsidiary companies.

It can be considered as 'real' Canadian investment in foreign countries. The second type, described as 'go-between investment,' allows American subsidiaries to control other subsidiaries in the rest of the world through Canada. Thus 36 percent (or $1,820 million ÷ $9,307 million) of Canadian direct investment in foreign countries in 1974 was of the second type (Clement, 1978).

FIGURE 1

Percentage of the Total Domestic Assets and Sales Accounted for by the 100 Largest Non-financial Corporations, Canada and the United States, 1966, 1971 and 1975 (ranked by sales)

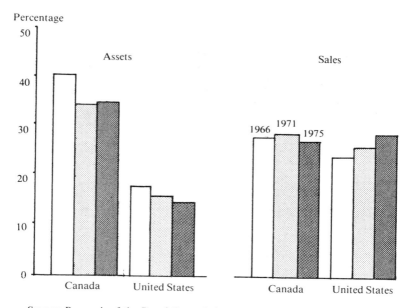

Source: Research of the Royal Commission on Corporate Concentration

The Paradoxes of the Economic Structure

Several paradoxes can further be noted when one examines the relations between the presence of foreign capital, and the concentration and internationalization of local capital. In the first place, it must be indicated that super-concentration is the rule in the Canadian economy. In the banking sector, five big banks share 90 percent of the assets of the sector. In industry, concentration is clearly higher than in the United States, to such an extent that 'aggregate concentration in Canada is roughly twice that of the United States, while the trends in the two countries are virtually the same.'[9]

In the second place, foreign investments do not seem to have had an effect on the level of concentration. On the other hand, the oligopolistic structure of the American or international market has often been transplanted by the investments of the multinationals making up this oligopoly, hence the 'reproduction in miniature' characteristic of many industrial sectors in Canada.[10]

In the third place, super-concentration does not imply that Canadian companies are large enough to confront international competition.[11] Besides, local industrial capital is often found, as we will see a little later, in sectors with low productivity that face increasingly stiff competition. The new tariff structures, the general intensification of foreign competition and the effects of the displacement of labor-intensive industries in the underdeveloped countries are in fact forcing rationalization, which more precisely means an accentuation of concentration. The conclusion of the Royal Commission is clear on this issue:

> In several countries, the largest firms in an industry have been encouraged to merge to increase international competitiveness. If, as seems to be true in many industries, large size is necessary for efficient operations and to compete in international markets, efforts in Canada to reduce corporate concentration by limiting the size of firms will further reduce the competitiveness of Canadian firms in world markets. Equally, if Canadian firms can and do expand to world size, there may well be a significant increase in corporate concentration in Canada.[12]

The Repercussions on Canadian Society

The impact of these movements on Canadian society is obviously considerable. In fact, the increasing integration of Canada into the American economy through capital and markets; the lack of control by Canada over its manufacturing industry and its resources, and thus its relative under-accumulation; the pre-eminence of head office — subsidiary relations over the economic objectives of the country (illustrated again recently by the diversion of important quantities of oil destined for Canada by Exxon NY to the detriment of its subsidiary, Imperial Oil, and moreover to the Eastern Canadian economy); and scientific and technological underdevelopment through monopolization of research outside the country lead to a weakening of national development, since in general the Canadian entity tends increasingly to lose its capacity to transform itself through its own means. Thus, in numerous economic fields as well as political or cultural ones, Canada scarcely manages to play even a role of 'second fiddle to the United States.' But things are going even farther, since these factors, associated with the lack of control over foreign investments[13] and with industrial, commercial and banking superconcentration, favor the emergence of a shattered economy on the regional level.

The lack of control over foreign investment is reflected in the distribution of foreign investment that predominates over Canadian capital in Ontario and Alberta, thus accentuating regional disparities. The effects of super-concentration are reflected in a federal development strategy based on enormous projects linked to energy and its transport, directed by the big concentrated corporations, independently of their nationality, and naturally with state guarantees (Athabaska tar sands, oil and gas pipelines from the Arctic), but without this strategy really taking the regional dimension into account. As for banking, and more broadly financial concentration, it has certainly been harmful to regional development because of the very heavy constraints imposed by this very centralized structure, which always tends financially to asphyxiate small and medium-sized companies whose vocation is most often regional. More broadly, the monetary unification of the Canadian regions, the existence of a unitary central bank instead of a federal system of central bank, imposes a 'unitary style of management' of monetary policy which is much more concerned about the reactions of monopoly capital than about regional particularities.[14] Besides, the centralization of capital has its geographical counterpart, since Toronto tends to bring together the major centers of financial and industrial decision-making to the detriment of Montreal.

One must finally mention the regional impact of the transformation of the relations between the center and the periphery, which threatens whole sections of the economy of many industrialized countries and thus implies a gigantic industrial transformation which often affects very specific regions: Québec is a good example of this, since 25 percent of its labor force is concentrated in the 'soft' sectors: textile, millinery, clothing and furniture. It is there that the regional question enlarged into a national question because the domination-subordination relations established between the two founding nations of Canada is posed in a complex fashion. And indeed, this is not completely due to chance, if manpower-intensive industries, because of the existence of a reserve of cheap labor, settled in Québec.

The Contradictions of
Transnationalization

To the extent that the monopolist bourgeoisie is seeking to extend itself to the international level, nationalist ideology at the level of the central state tends to ebb and to disintegrate because it is then an obstacle to the international strategy of the domestic corporations and foreign subsidiaries that want to expand abroad. To keep the doors open in the foreign country, it is necessary to keep the domestic doors open.

Despite the voluminous Watkins and Gray reports on the harmful effects of foreign investment, the 'screening' agency, in accepting 88 percent of the requests, has let $2.5 billion in assets pass under foreign control in three years. Former Industry Minister Jean Chretien boasted that he had rejected only 10 of the 160 projects that came across his desk. Mel Watkins, on the occasion of the tenth anniversary of his report, recalled that Ottawa has traditionally been on the side of the multinationals against the provinces. For example, when the Saskatchewan government nationalized potash the federal state aligned itself with the multinational cartel in the legal battle before the Supreme Court. The purchase of Asbestos Corporation by Québec will undoubtedly lead to the same type of intervention. One could raise many examples indicating the central government's lack of political will on this question. Thus, in March 1979, members of the federal Parliamentary Commission invited an expansion of foreign banks in Canada to resolve the problem of competition in the banking system.

In fact, the cycle of dependent continental integration in Canada is about to be completed. The Royal Commission on Corporate Concentration, linking the solution of the problem of economic power over Canadian affairs exercised by multinationals and that of the 'rationalization' necessary to take on the world market, concludes that: 'rather than buying back foreign-owned companies, it would be preferable to provide incentives for the merger of both foreign and domestically owned firms in an industry into larger, more efficient units and to use laws that will override any antitrust objection in the United States and other countries.'[15]

As this poorly controlled global integration is perfectly successful in making profits for a small number of power centers, many of which are located on the other side of the border, the disparities between Canadian provinces continue to increase and centrifugal trends are manifest not only in Québec but also in Alberta and British Columbia. Vély Leroy emphasizes that:

against all expectations, the 'balkanization' of the Canadian economy is occurring almost unnoticed. It has been a reality for a long time in many fields. At the beginning of these developments impedimenta of course occur. Thus, the less than perfect mobility of people in an active cause... but in addition there is the awakening of local populations and their aspirations to well-being; also local governments are increasingly concerned about their responsibilities in the economic sphere. Thus we are witnessing the rise of a protectionist current even within common borders, which is exacerbated by government policies, professional codes, legislation, decrees, and hidden duties on imports of merchandise or services from other regions of the country. The tax system itself is not irrelevant to the question.[16]

The Canadian 'grande bourgeoisie,' which is located mainly in central Canada (Ontario and Québec), has always been able to profit from regional imbalances. However, it is strongly opposed to any political fragmentation of Canada. This is why it is playing with a perfect cohesion the card of the Canadian unity which guarantees a large hinterland, where it can easily supply itself and which, up to the present, has hardly imposed any constraints on it. Continental integration without borders would weaken its political power by provincializing it. The executives of the foreign subsidiaries themselves would be submerged in the ordinary upper management of the big American multinationals. In the same manner, any more decentralized reorganization of the present federal system poses the question of the reorganization of economic power in Canada, and thus of the grande bourgeoisie which could see itself facing competition or challenged by 'provincial' states holding much more important economic power than they do today. It is sufficient in this connection to consider the implications of the reorganization of the banking and monetary system, proposed in the White Paper on Sovereignty-Association. This indicates that, if the trend toward political dislocation of industrialized states can from now on be considered as a dimension of the process of globalization, it cannot be considered its mere corollary. As we will see in the case of Québec, the continental grande bourgeoisie has little interest in the transformation of today's Canadian frontiers, since the dislocation would immediately mean reorganization on the regional level and thus the threat of a more statist, more nationalist and more constraining organization of capital. This is true for the internal bourgeoisie but also for the American bourgeoisie in general, which, satisfied with the security of Canada in its present state, has never really been hindered by its borders, which it has often considered to be purely formal, as witnessed by the administrative organization of companies where Canadian activities have often been integrated into their domestic, rather than their international divisions.

This is why, in general, the disaggregation of the large nation-states to the profit of sovereign regional units appears to Western strategists to be injurious to the interests of the established grandes bourgeoisies, and dangerous for the Western political and military security system, which must be interpreted and presented as a dramatically illusory rearguard struggle for social forces and nations that are subordinated to the quest for sovereignty.

NATIONAL MOVEMENTS AND THE BREAK-UP OF LARGE STATES

The trend towards fragmentation is not the product solely of the process of globalization. Indeed, even if the different factors that we have just mentioned lead to a weakening and disarticulation of national development that go beyond the spatial division that capitalist accumulation has always implied,[17] and that thus go beyond unequal development within the nation, the trend towards the splitting or the fragmentation of nation-states is also the 'product' of the particular social struggles of each society considered. In this respect, observation of the shaping of the new world capitalist system cannot be done solely from the perspective of the effects of globalization and integration, independently of the analysis of the trend toward national differentiation manifested in the revival or birth of nationalist movements. This is an extremely complex question which we cannot pretend to deal with in a few paragraphs.

Three comments can nevertheless be made on this subject. The first is that a national movement is obviously not to be reduced to struggles against unequal intra-national development, or solely to the quest for increased power at the regional level; to regionalism. Québec is defined not as a territory — a province — among others, but as a nation. The second deals with the very concepts of nation and of nation-building. The nation is first of all an idea, a representation that the social agents make of the whole that they are constituting from a community of history and culture. Thus the nation pertains first to ideology. However, the analysis of the nation is practically not separable from the analysis of the power that is one of the conditions of its existence. This is why one cannot stop, as several authors have done, at just the ideological dimension of the national fact, which in turn becomes incarnate and material through the process of nation-building and finally through the constitution of a state.

The links that can be established between the nation and power are many. However, their structural specificity manifests itself decisively when one analyzes the relations of domination and subordination that can be established between different national groups: armed occupation, colonization, assimilation. What is new in the protests and national movements within the industrialized states is that they are showing that these types of relations exist within societies that are as apparently well integrated and unified as, for example, French society. The exposure of these structures of domination has become increasingly systematic and precise during the past 15 years:[18] transformation in a minority and marginalization on the level of political power (variations depend on the centralized or decentralized character of the political system); dispossession of (private or public) capital and centers as well as of (managerial and leadership) positions of economic power[19]; over exploitation of the working class; elimination or inferiorization of the language and culture. In this way, a people finds itself generally placed under tutelage and marginalized.

In most cases, the rejection of domination leads to an affirmation of identity that is often first crystallized around language, but which at the same time opens onto struggles against national oppression, the demand for the right to self-determination, and a quest for sovereignty which can go as far as the creation and development of a state.

The prime objective of the project is to transform the collectivity into a sovereign entity. It is the basis of unity in a national movement. However, as the question of 'sovereignty for whom?' is raised almost immediately, one sees more or less radical subsidiary projects for the transformation of society added to the main project, ranging from the communal 'alternative' to 'a civilization disintegrative of natural communities and ethnic personalities' (Quéré, 1978), to the manifold expressions of the socialist way.

This brings us to the third comment. To the extent that a national movement grows stronger and expands, and once the national question ends up occupying the forefront of the political scene in a durable way, Utopia tends to give way to strategy. In this conjuncture, the relations between heterogeneous social forces intensify within the movement itself, while it confronts its adversaries more and more directly (the central state, the grande bourgeoisie that, among other things, 'replans' its assets on the basis of eventual sovereignty, unitary or federalist movements, international 'opinion'). One must also reckon with the particular social stakes of each society and with the struggles of internal forces around both political and economic power.

The outcome of many of these struggles is still very uncertain. Thus, the Occitanian movement, whose first contemporary manifestations date from about 15 years ago, is progressing only slowly and in a dispersed fashion; the Welsh are saying no to devolution, and while 51.6 percent of the Scots voted yes, the number of abstentionists was too high to permit the application of the Scotland Act. In Québec, even if the result of the spring 1980 referendum appears as uncertain as in Scotland, the debate and the alignment and polarization of the social forces have progressed considerably since the Parti Québécois, whose political framework closely encompasses the nationalist movement, took provincial state power. The November 1976 election constitutes a historic step because it decisively opened the crisis of Canadian unity. Thus the nationalist movement is manifesting itself as a central force in Québec society and the quest for a political outcome cannot take place in its absence.

One must therefore spend a little time examining this movement to understand its fundamental orientations. However, given the restricted scope of this paper, we will not enter into a very detailed analysis, which would particularly involve a discussion of the great number of writings that have been done on this question. We will instead limit ourselves to recalling a few elements that are necessary to understand how the 'sovereignty-association' option has been imposed, an option that differs somewhat from a clear independence option because the attempt at dislocation is immediately paired with an integration project: political sovereignty linked indissolubly to a form of economic association to be negotiated with the rest of Canada if the outcome of the referendum is positive.

QUÉBEC/CANADA: THE GAME OF DISLOCATION AND INTEGRATION

The Pro-Independence Alliance and Sovereignty-Association

Because the project for transformation of the collectivity into a sovereign entity takes precedence over any other project of social transformation in the collective action that characterizes national movements, these generally involve heterogeneous social forces. When a party is formed to bring together pro-independence forces, this heterogeneity thus persists, even if the most radical elements do not always join. The history of the Parti Québécois illustrates this characteristic, which, while it makes these political organizations ambiguous, also gives them the strength necessary for popular mobilization in otherwise very diverse forms until the status of a sovereign state is obtained.

The foundation of the Parti Québécois (PQ) dates from 1968. But from the beginning of the 1960s, pro-independence groups of a new type had the objective of liberating the Québec nation:[20] In 1960 the Rassemblement pour l'Indépendance Nationale (RIN), was founded. It began left of center and as a measure of its social radicalization, separated first from its right-wing elements (which formed the Parti Républicain du Québec in 1962), then (in 1964) from its Christian-Democratic elements (Regroupement National, whose goal was to make Québec 'a sovereign and democratic state of the French culture and Christian inspiration') and finally (in 1968) from its 'revolutionary' elements (Front de Libération Populaire, which styled itself as 'pro-independence, socialist and decolonizing'). Aside from the RIN and its offshoots, there were the *Parti pris* and *Socialisme québécois* journals and, of course, the famous Front de Libération du Québec (FLQ). These groups were to play a fundamental role in the shaping of a progressive nationalist ideology though their atomization limited their short-term political effectiveness.

However, nationalist elements were to be found even within the traditional parties, particularly in Québec's Liberal Party. These forces were powerful enough, and they manifested themselves vigorously during the Quiet Revolution, not only with the slogan of 'Masters in our own house,' but also with a whole series of

measures that aimed at making the provincial state into an important agent of development: nationalization of electricity, formation
of the Sociefé Générale de Financement, creation of the Québec
Deposit and Investment Fund and of the state-owned steel company, Sidbec.[21]

It was during the Liberal Party's 1967 congress that the theme of
sovereignty-association surged forth in a major debate, defended
by the former Minister of Natural Resources, René Lévesque. The
congress finally rejected this option, but then René Lévesque, with
a group of other Liberals founded the Mouvement Souveraineté-
Association (MSA).

Its appearance on the political scene completely overturned the independence
movement and eventually the whole political checkerboard of Québec. For the
first time in the history of Québec nationalism, a personality who was
prestigious, charismatic and well-known to the public, was rallying to the idea of
independence. In October 1968, on the eve of the foundation of the Parti
Québécois, which would soon bring together the majority of those who believed
in the independence of Québec, René Lévesque represented the moral guarantee
for this political orientation. He was the only person able to unify the
heterogeneous elements gravitating around this ideal in Québec. A year and a
half later the Parti Québécois, which was at least 55,000 members strong, obtained 23 percent of the vote in the provincial elections of 29 April, 1970. Six years
later, it came to power with 41 percent of the vote.[22]

However, the Parti Québécois did not include all the pro-
independence currents. Its foundation was first of all the result of
the merger of the Mouvement Souveraineté-Association and the
Regroupement National, joined individually by activists from the
RIN, which scuttled itself for this purpose. The socialist left, which
was still embryonic at that time and also somewhat divided on the
national question, remained distinct from the PQ.

Thus, the 'mainstay' of nation-building, to use E. Sicard's expression, was first molded on the sovereignty-association option, a
prudent model of limited sovereignty that activists believed would
obtain the adherence of a majority of the population because, a
priori, this change would not fundamentally overturn its way of
life. And in fact the tensions within the PQ sovereignist alliance did
not emerge on the issue of the 'national' project, but rather on that
of the social project and of democracy within the party. As Vera
Murray clearly demonstrated:

the whole evolution of the PQ was marked by constant tension between the tendency of the 'technocrats' (rallied around René Lévesque) who were concerned above all with economic and governmental efficiency, and the tendency of the 'participationists' (former RIN activitists, but particularly teachers, students, union activists..., who were engaged in their first political involvement), who attached enormous importance to the ideas of participation, mobilization and social reforms.[23]

The impact of these last on the program and structural form of the party, inspired by the constitution of the Communist League of Yugoslavia (Murray, 1978) and consequently favoring a party of activists, played a fundamental role in the winning of popular support, since a high percentage of workers and employees gave their vote to the PQ in 1976. However, the central political choices remain in the hands of the technocratic current, which obviously has considerable weight in the present government, whose 'favorable prejudice to the workers' is, if not non-existent, marginal to its policy, as Gilles Bourque put it.

Reorganization of Social Power
and the Stakes of Sovereignty-Association

Nationalism is not a new phenomenon in Québec; nevertheless, it has been changing since the 1960s and is now different from the traditional nationalism, which was essentially cultural. Nowadays, the national movement sees a tight link between, on the one hand, the economic power and the political power and, on another hand, the future of the French language, French culture and, broadly speaking, the Québec nation.

On the contrary, 'la grande bourgeoisie' and the Canadian state have every interest in containing the Québec question within narrowly linguistic and cultural limits by offering, for example, bilingualism and biculturalism throughout Canada, which, in addition to showing itself impractical outside of Québec, has no appreciable effects, except for some increase of the francophone presence in the federal civil service. This does not mean that the Anglo-Canadian establishment is ready to accept the real settlement of the language question in Québec. The most active resistance to the voting and application of language legislation presented by the government has come, and still comes, from anglophone business circles. In fact, language is intimately linked to the organization of social power, and the national movement raises the question of its reorganization among the social forces. Let us look at an example where economic, political and cultural elements are strongly connected: the question of language at work.

Though 80 percent of the population is French-speaking, the language at work was mainly English in the private companies till 1977, when Bill 101 was enforced ('Charte de la langue française'). English is still the language at work in the upper levels of the hierarchy and in most head offices. The consequences are significant enough: (1) French Canadians in executive or management positions must be bilingual, and a career often implies progressive assimilation into English-speaking culture and community; (2) the majority of new Canadians and immigrants (Italians, Greeks, Portuguese) think that if they speak English it will be easier for them to have a successful career, and so they try their best to identify themselves with the English community into which they want to be integrated; therefore, they strongly resist French; in consequence, they are a threat for the French-speaking group in the long run as they become demographically more important; (3) the occupational structure for highly qualified French-speaking people is also narrower: in particular, French Canadians are strongly under-represented in the executive and management positions in the private sector which is owned mainly by English Canadians or foreigners (particularly American and British, and therefore English-speaking). As a matter of fact, the owners of industrial, financial or commercial companies usually choose top executives among their own national or ethnic group. Therefore the national or ethnic origin, more than the linguistic affiliation, is one of the relatively rigid conditions of gaining an executive or management position.[24] How the ownership of capital is distributed among the national and ethnic groups has a direct impact on the language at work and is in close relation with the control of cultural elements, of the status of the French language, of the status of the people who speak that language, and even with the control of its demographic future. In order to change such a situation linguistic bills may be passed, but the very structure of the ownership of capital still sets important limits to any change. Reinforcing the control of the French Canadians within the economic field, particularly at the level of the ownership of capital, is thus extremely important. Now, as we have emphasized in our work on the industrial bourgeoisie, reinforcing that control implies new and stronger economic powers for the Québec state. That is the reason why the stakes are increasingly economic and less and less cultural. In his inaugural message to the National Assembly in March 1979, René Lévesque indicated this clearly:

> But in our humble opinion, and I'm not telling anyone anything new, any true emancipation will first have to go through the establishment of a new balance of power in the economic field, and through political sovereignty which is the only means for repatriating all the tools necessary for our development. Half of Québec's taxes still feed Ottawa's coffers. This is the half that most directly affects our economy. It gives another government, serving another majority, the margin of strategic maneuver and the major levers of intervention that are terribly lacking in Québec. As soon as possible we must give ourselves the full and autonomous tools of an economic policy that will be entirely at our service, while taking into account the interests we share with our neighbors and the maintenance of the Canadian economic space. This new definition of our relations requires a major transformation of the political structures.[25]

This is why the 'reconstituted federalism' paired with Québec cultural sovereignty, which is proposed by the Task Force on Canadian Unity, while representing, as does sovereignty-association, a third way between the status quo and the complete sovereignty of Québec, is still very far from the proposal of the Parti Québécois. This is particularly so because the main economic powers of the state (monetary and lending policy, commercial policy, industrial strategy, defence, etc.) would remain centralized under the federal government with Québec being unable to intervene directly on an 'equal-to-equal' basis, to use the Parti Québécois' slogan. The settlement of the national question, the apparent dislocation or separation, thus essentially means a major reorganization of economic power within the Canadian economic union. This must be examined more closely.

Québec presently finds itself in a federal-type economic union. The degree of economic integration, despite the imperfections noted earlier, is thus much more important than in the economic and monetary union toward which the Parti Québécois choice bears,

> since to a customs, economic and monetary union is added the dimension of a political association in which a common central government in a direct relationship with the population is charged with questions that concern all of the component units, states or provinces. A sharing of economic powers between a central government and regional or provincial governments is established under the authority of a Constitution.[26]

The overall economic advantages of integration are not negligible, notably because of the economies of scale realized at all the levels of a vast aggregation. But there are also costs.[27] If one can presume, on the basis of a known formula, a balance between advantages and costs that makes economic integration acceptable, one can also presume that these costs of development can be much too heavy if added to them are 'economic dependence, political subordination and national oppression.'[28]

In fact, contention about the positive and negative effects of the federal union on the development of Québec has a prominent place in the national movement's ammunition.[29] We have talked earlier about the 'unitary style of management' of monetary policy. We should discuss here the regional effects of budgetary stabilization policies, and the orientation of federal government spending in Québec, which is directed more toward income maintenance (social measures) than toward employment-generating productive investment, not to speak of manpower policies or the effects on Québec of the Auto Pact. Conversely, one could obviously cite the advantages of a vast market or of temporary federal subsidies for oil imports, but the fact is that the gap between Québec and Ontario is growing considerably, and that these regional inequalities between the two most industrialized provinces in Canada will become dramatically accentuated if labor-intensive industries continue to slump. In effect, as we have already mentioned, sectors with low productivity — furniture, traditional textiles, millinery, clothing and leather goods — which are threatened by new international competition, employ a quarter of Québec's labor force.

Studies dating from 1970 indicate the urgency of a radical transformation of Québec's industrial structure, and new production channels have been identified.[30] However, despite the advantages that a federal union can offer through providing interregional transfers of resources 'for a region facing massive economic adjustments,'[31] the central state and the Canadian grande bourgeoisie appear incapable of resolving both the question of industrial redeployment and that of regional disparities. We have already enumerated the reasons: a Canadian industrial bourgeosie that is considerably weakened by foreign capital; severely reduced capacity in the field of research and development; a high degree of capital concentration; internationalization of Canadian capital and thus displacement of certain activities; a liberal state that, despite the situation of dependence, is loath to ensure a leadership role in the area of industrial development; etc.[32]

For its part, Québec private regional capital, part of which will decline if it does not succeed in its reconversion, cannot hope to take over or try to assert itself as the central agent of development for several reasons. The first concerns its weakness compared with Canadian and American capital. The second concerns its national and ethnic differentiation, which permits cohesion only on limited points and generally on a defensive basis (for example, against direct state intervention in the economy). The third reason concerns the economic and political dependence of Québec regional private capital compared with the hegemonic fractions of the Canadian bourgeoisie. Outside of the cooperative movement, whose mode of control is by definition very specific, this capital cannot define itself globally as external to the Canadian bourgeoisie and thus cannot provide itself with unity and a specific plan. If one restricts oneself to francophone capital, one can obviously identify a series of relatively important power centers, which can be extended if one adds state-owned companies (which are sometimes powerful, like Hydro-Québec, but which are after all few in number). However, one must not forget, as do too many authors who absolutely want to see 'the hand' of a francophone establishment in the national assertion, that only 5 percent of industrial enterprises with more than $50 million in assets in Québec belonged to French-Canadians in 1974, while banks under francophone control represented less than 10 percent of Canadian bank assets. In reality, the weakness of French Canadian capital is an integral part of the national question, since the stakes of control of accumulation underlie this question. Indeed, it is not enough to say, like Gilles Bourque, that the PQ project aims at 'creating maximal favorable conditions for the development of regional Québec capitalism...reserving as much economic and social room as possible for regional Québec capitalism and secondarily for the new petty bourgeoisie.'[33] Indeed, one can not make an abstraction of the fact that the statist orientation of the program implies a struggle against economic dependence, a direct intervention in development that leaves room for debate and for political choices, even if this is not the institution of a socialist society (the many possible faces of which are far from having been discussed for the moment in Québec, given the lack of a mass movement that still has to be built).

In fact, it is the social categories linked to the Québec state apparatus that hope to overcome the problems we have just mentioned, on the basis of a decisive reinforcement of the state's economic power. The struggle for the reorganization of power will, first and foremost, unfold between, on the one hand, the ruling strata of the Québec state apparatus, which as we have seen earlier, is assuming a leadership role in the Parti Québécois through the intermediary of prominent representatives, and, on the other hand, the Canadian grande bourgeoisie, associated with the 'commanding heights' of the federal state. This obviously does not mean, as Louis Maheu has shown in his article,[34] that only these social strata are concerned. But from the perspective of the power structure, these are the social groups that will be most affected by the outcome of the confrontations that are now in progress, with the control and orientation of accumulation in Québec as the stakes.

Sovereignty-association, on the institutional level, first of all challenges the political domination and thus the direct intervention in Québec of a central government that is also in direct relationship with the population through federal elections, which legitimize its policies without regard to their regional significance. Also, because of the decline of Parliament, the strengthening of the executive and the ever-increasing political role of the state bureaucracy, the representation from Québec in Ottawa seems to play a minor role in the defense of the interests of their province. With Québec problems becoming the first if not the exclusive responsibility of the Québec government, its fields of intervention would expand considerably at the same time as its power would increase. Besides, and this is a very important point, sovereignty-association would impose direct representation of top Quebec civil servants in the institutions that would take shape with an economic and monetary union, particularly within the eventual central bank of the Canada-Québec Union of which Vély Leroy speaks.

It is obviously no secret that the economic departments of the federal government have traditionally been monopolized by Anglo-Canadians.[35] This, of course, does not happen without arousing significant frustration. But, in addition, the Québec state finds itself to be the main power center of Québec francophone society. Its development and its programs have played a fundamental role for 20 years in the dynamism and assertion of this society. But despite an increasingly powerful involvement in Québec's economy in the areas of revenues, spending and policies (energy, natural resources, for example), its fields of responsibility and economic power remain relatively residual. In the scheme of power, the stakes of direct representation for top civil servants are thus considerable. In itself, the refusal of the Task Force on Canadian Unity to envisage participation by provincial governments within the main federal economic institutions indicates how crucial these stakes are. The opinion of a Québec civil servant on the economic deficiencies of the report of the Pepin-Robarts Commission, published in the newspaper *Le Devoir*, is unequivocal on this subject:

> Thus, one cannot let the absence of representation of the provincial government within the principal economic institutions go unmentioned. Yet it is in these institutions that economic power is based. It is in these places that policies are decided. And when our representatives are absent, changes automatically come from the same circles, circles that are not ours. In short, we are cut off from the main power, the power of information. While the government of Québec is asking for participation and representation as an equal in these institutions, the Pépin-Robarts Commission is not even suggesting an embryo of representation.[36]

If a true reorganization of the economic power of the state emerges from the current struggles, one should not presume that the Québec state will be satisfied with the mode of intervention in the economy of the present federal state, particularly if the nationalist forces stay in power. The bureaucracy will seek to assert its leadership in the field of development through increasingly direct, one could say 'entrepreneurial,' intervention, particularly in cases where private or cooperative capital proves to be faltering, while incorporating the regional bourgeoisie in its global program. In a capitalist regime and in a dependent society, the national state does not seem to have many possibilities at its disposal. The difference from a situation of total domination is that it can differentiate the support it gives to capital by playing on various economic forces and strategies: strengthening the classic regional bourgeoisie, developing the cooperative sector in the branches of the economy where this is possible, creating and expanding state-owned companies, undertaking joint ventures with foreign capital, eroding the weakest links of foreign capital, renegotiating dependence in the exploitation of natural resources.

The example of the PQ government's present strategy in the natural resources sector is a good illustration of this mode of intervention, which plays particularly on the degree of integration of enterprises and industrial branch plants into Québec as a whole.

> The pulp and paper industry is well integrated into the Québec economy, and buys its equipment in Québec, while the asbestos industry is categorized as 'an industry that refuses to become integrated' and that traditionally maintains the attitude of an occupying force. . . the government's strategy is therefore opposite in these two sectors: in pulp and paper the government has cleared the path for the companies, attacked the problems of costs, reduced risks and proposed a five-year plan based on profitable companies and on an increase in productivity. On the other hand, in the asbestos sector, the government will not hesitate to get involved directly, to take the leadership through the acquisition of Asbestos Corporation, without losing hope of arriving at 'development agreements' with the rest of the industry to process 12 percent of Québec asbestos in Québec within 10 years.[37]

Aside from this, in the context of a debate in the National Assembly on the role of state-owned companies within the strategy for Québec's development, Economic Development Minister Bernard Landry, after declaring that 'foreign domination constitutes a great imbalance in the economy,' affirmed that: 'if a major mining project is going to see the light of day in Québec, there is no question of Québeckers not being involved significantly in share capital and administration. . . . . The state-owned companies will be able to mobilize at the government's request and become a major strategic factor.'[38]

Sovereignty-Association and the Integration to the Center

While it is not known how far the reorganization of state economic power will go, it is not possible on the other hand to imagine the maintenance of the constitutional status quo. The national movement should therefore obtain a strengthening of the economic powers of the Québec state in one form or another, in the short or medium term.

However, and because the continental economic integration will continue during the next negotiations and struggle, we should also question the interaction between the reorganization of Canada-Québec relations and this integration, even if it is still too soon really to answer these questions, given the manifold scenarios imaginable and the changes that will take place in the social balance of power. It is particularly appropriate to examine the hypothesis of Pierre Fournier, who sees sovereignty-association as:

> A medium-term transition strategy, aiming at facilitating the passage towards the North American option, and not as a simple attempt to rearrange Canadian economic power[39]. . . . The 'American option' must be considered as the ultimate objective of the Parti Québécois. It is not a matter of renegotiating the federal pact, but rather of negotiating the terms of dependence directly with the USA. This strategy involves, among other things, the reinforcement of control over the domestic market, the penetration of 'intermediary' branches and an attempt to accentuate the local impact of American capital.[40]

Thus, 'the autonomization and strengthening of Québec econmomic power would lead to one more step in the direction of direct integration into the North American agglomeration.'[41] The double dependence of Québec would then give way to a single direct dependence on the United States. In the very long term, Pierre Fournier considers association with the rest of Canada to be a transitional stage, 'because of the very strong integration and complementary nature of the Ontario and Québec economies. Integration has functioned well to Ontario's advantage; Québec capital is too weak and too little structured to disregard a modus vivendi with Canadian capital and the transition period implied by sovereignty-association.'[42]

As we have shown earlier, dependent continental integration is an extremely strong trend for the Canadian economy, and it is doubtful that Québec can reverse this trend in which it is very much engaged. One can easily imagine as well that an isolated Québec would probably not resist absorption by the United States for very long, and neither would English Canada, which does not have as pronounced a cultural identity. Thus, the refusal of English Canada to associate with a sovereign Québec (which is not very probable, given the interrelations between Québec and Ontario) would lead to the veritable dissolution of Canada as a whole. While this eventuality must be envisaged seriously because of its consequences, it is hard to see, on the other hand, why Québec under a nationalist party would allow itself to be bound hand and foot to the United States. From this perspective, the quest for 'the autonomization and strengthening of Québec economic power,' meaning the quest for greater mastery of the process and product of accumulation, particularly through increased state intervention, contradicts the hypothesis of the strengthening of dependent integration with the United States, even if it does not mean the end of dependence. It is useful to know that, in 1974, 63.1 percent of Québec's international exports went to the United States (80.1 percent of Ontario's). Furthermore, in the same year, 68.9 percent of Québec's unworked, non-edible materials and 44 percent of its non-edible raw materials[43] were shipped to the United States. Therefore, is it so contrary to Québec's interests to seek to renegotiate the terms of this dependence, directly if necessary, while putting a brake on its accentuation, since it has not stopped increasing since 1965?

For Pierre Fournier the PQ option is clearly a North American, if not a 'United States,' option: 'the balance of power will impose a more Canadian solution on the Parti Québécois, but this is not inevitable, and neither is this the objective of the present government.' Would the federal option therefore be strictly 'Canadian' instead of being North American? The facts cited earlier generally show the opposite. Pierre Fournier attributes Machiavellian objectives to the PQ without giving a sufficiently convincing demonstration[44] that these are the objectives of the Parti Québécois, on the one hand, and that other links with the economies of the center will not be established, on the other hand. It is much more probable, in fact, that a new Québec-Canada agglomeration, if it were to come about, would be oriented toward a diversification of its economic links to create a counterweight to American influence. The studies commissioned by the Québec government from Luc-Normand Tellier on 'the possibilities of a rapprochement between Québec, Canada and the Scandinavian countries,' and from Kimon Valaskakis on 'the plausibility of a Québec/Canada/Europe association,' instead indicate that there are many different scenarios and that the choices are still far from being made, since no bargaining table has been established so far. Sooner or later, it will nevertheless be necessary to establish one, and the contemporary history of Québec, through the movement of breakup and integration that is taking place to counter marginalization, will give profound indications of the possible outcome of national movements in the industrialized countries in the late twentieth century.

As a more general conclusion, we can say that, regarding the question of national development, the analysis on the level of the world capitalist system leads to very pessimistic conclusions. In the peripheral countries, it seems now impossible to build up a national economic system. In the core countries the control of domestic economies is becoming more and more difficult. In fact, a very important gap is growing between the political and the economical spheres because most of the capital no longer valorizes itself on a national basis related to the exercise of the sovereignty by the state. In that context, the movements oriented toward a reinforcement of the national sovereignty may appear to be doomed to failure. But at the same time, it is difficult to be completely convinced by the analysis where a transnational system would govern, in a determinist and uniform way, the social relations in any society. The external logic of the multinational corporations cannot always thrust itself on them. It is necessary to reckon with each society's stage of development, with the struggles of the internal social forces over the control of accumulation, and with the role of the states. That is the reason why the analysis of the world-system must give a greater place to these elements and particularly to national movements.

NOTES

1. From the title of an international conference organized by the University of Québec in Montreal on 4, 5 and 6 April 1979.

2. Celso Furtado writes:

Everything happens as if a new dimension had appeared which escapes the forms of action codified by governments on the national or international levels. In short, within the present institutional framework, governments do not have the possibility of coordinating the activity in which a whole agglomeration of powerful agents are engaged in the capitalist system. If coordination exists, it is done in the framework of oligopolies and financial consortia where governments appear through the pressure they exert on such an agent. [Furtado, 1975, p. 490.]

3. Charles-Albert Michalet indicates on this issue that

the major problematical question, with the appearance of the world economy, is no longer that of the realization of value but has become that of creation itself. This does not mean that the new contradiction has ousted the old. . . . But the appearance of a problem on the level of creation, a manifestation of the superaccumulation of capital, has required capitalism to take on new forms for its reproduction. To the extent that the high level of development of the productive forces makes increasing the rates of relative surplus value problematical, the solution is to seek zones where the rate of surplus value is higher. The productive process thus has to be displaced to less developed regions, while obviously being kept under control. [Michalet, 1976, p. 225.]

4. Sales (1979).

5. Canada is the largest world producer of nickel, zinc and asbestos, the second largest of potash, the third of lead and the fourth of copper.

6. The induction of dependence by the Canadian banking bourgeoisie appears in the way it has always welcomed subsidiaries of foreign corporations with open arms to the detriment of local industries.

Multinational enterprises based in the United Kingdom or the United States also have had easy access to large pools of capital, which was available at much lower cost than capital in Canada. When the Canadian subsidiary of a multinational firm chooses to raise its capital in Canada, Canadian financial institutions are more willing to make loans to it than to domestic firms of similar size and often at more attractive rates. [Royal Commission on Corporate Concentration, 1978, p. 193.]

There are today 57 foreign firms among the 100 top companies in Canada, and among the 200 most important industrial firms, 91 are subsidiaries of American enterprises (included in *Fortune* magazine's list of the top 500 companies).

7.

This growth can be attributed to the development of the Eurocurrency system, where Canadian banks compete with foreign banks for large US dollar deposits on the Eurocurrency market. They relend these deposits to residents or non-residents (including foreign banks), or invest them in US dollar-denominated securities. [Royal Commission on Corporate Concentration, 1978, p. 232.]

8. Royal Commission on Corporate Concentration (1978), p. 232.

9. ibid., p. 28.

10. ibid., p. 192.

11. 'The top Canadian firms are larger in relation to the Canadian economy than are the top US firms in relation to the US economy; at the same time, they are absolutely much smaller (these data indicate about one-fifth the average size) than the top US firms' (Royal Commission on Corporate Concentration, 1978, p. 30).

12. ibid., p. 405.

13. On this question see Ray (1975, 1971).

14. Vély Leroy writes on this issue that

> When everything is considered, the current development of monetary policy in Canada still maintains both the spirit and the approach of the 1930s, which moreover have been strengthened by the Second World War and by the excesses of centralization. By this we mean that it participates in a unitary style of management. And since it needs support in the economic and financial spheres to convert the measures upon which it has decided into facts, it is natural that the behavior of the circles of activity that are most receptive to the signals of the central bank will be determinant in the choice of measures to be taken, often in defiance of regional particularities. Yet it is not always true that these necessarily have to be sacrificed. [Leroy, 1978, p. 274.]

15. Royal Commission on Corporate Concentration (1978), p. 208.

16. Leroy (1978), p. 309.

17. On capitalism and the spatial division of labor, see among others Massey (1978).

18. Concerning Québec, one can refer to the article by Bélanger and Saint-Pierre (1978). On a more descriptive level, one cannot ignore the considerable pioneering empirical work of the Royal Commission on Bilingualism and Biculturalism and of the Gendron Commission.

19. On this issue see Sales (1979).

20. On this point, and on the formation and history of the Parti Québécois, one can refer to the excellent synthesizing article by Vera Murray (1978). See also Murray (1976). Also see the interesting analysis by Bourque (9 January 1979), p. 5.

21. On this issue see Fournier (1978).

22. Murray (1978), p. 58.

23. ibid., p. 58.

24. On this issue see A. Sales, 'National and Ethnic Differentiation of the Industrial Bourgeoisie in Quebec,' in Bodgan Denitch (ed.), *National Elites: What they Think, What they Do* (forthcoming).

25. In *Le Devoir* (7 March 1979), p. 11.

26. Task Force on Canadian Unity (1979), p. 72 (French version).

27.

> The cost entailed by integration may be described as essentially social and political. Even when an association has not passed beyond the stage of a customs union, the ability of component units to influence corporate decisions is limited, as is their access to cheaper imports which do not compete directly with regional production, and their ability to promote local employment by means of tariff barriers. Furthermore, any higher degree of economic integration imposes additional constraints on the autonomy of the regional unit. It becomes less able to manage its own economy since it is no longer allowed to restrict the movement of its people, capital or goods, and it must bear the social costs of this increased labor mobility. Moreover, the priorities of the regional unit may be distorted by the existence of common policies which do not sufficiently take into account the distinct regional circumstances. [Task Force on Canadian Unity, 1979, pp. 69-70.]

28. To use the title of the article by Bélanger and Saint-Pierre (1978).

29. Among other things, one can refer to the indictment made by Yves Bérubé, Québec Minister of Lands and Forests and Natural Resources, in which he indicates, for example, that Canadian monetary policy has played against Québec six times in the six most important economic cycles in Canada in the past twenty years. This second tool is instead used by Ottawa to protect Ontario industry...(article by Marie-Agnès Thellier, 'Ottawa utilise mal ses outils,' *Le Devoir* (10 June 1978), p. 11.)

30. Concerning production channels based on natural resources, one can refer to Jauron et al. (1977).

31. Task Force on Canadian Unity (1979), pp. 75-6.

32. For example, note the willingness of the new federal Conservative government to dismantle Petrocan, a state-owned company and the second largest oil company in Canada with $3.35 billion in assets.

33. Bourque (1979).

34. Maheu (1979).

35. The report of the Federal Official Languages Commissioner indicates that in 1978 there were 3 francophones out of 33 top civil servants in the Ministry of Finance. The proportion of francophones rose to 3.6 percent in the Ministry of Consumer and Corporate Affairs, to 11.5 percent in the Ministry of Industry and Commerce, etc. (*Le Devoir*, 21 February 1979, p. 2.)

36. Boucher (1979), p. 5.

37. Interview with Yves Bérubé, Minister of Lands and Forests and Natural Resources, by Marie-Agnès Thellier, in *Le Devoir* (21 June 1979), p. 28.

38. Article by Gilles Gauthier in *La Presse* (19 May 1979), p. E10.

39. Fournier (29 March 1979), p. 5.

40. Fournier (31 March 1979) p. 5.

41. ibid.

42. ibid.

43. GAMMA, under the direction of Kimon Valaskakis, *Prospective socio-économique du Québec*, 1: *Sous-Système extérieur* (3), Rapport Synthèse, Québec (Office de planification et de développement du Quebec, 1977), p. 56.

44. One can also refer to the critique by Luc-Normand Tellier (1979).

REFERENCES

AMIN, S. (1971). *L'Accumulation à l'échelle mondiale* (Paris: Anthropos).

AMIN, S. (1973). *Le Développement inégal* (Paris: Minuit).

BARNET, R. and R. MÜLLER (1974). *Global Reach: The Power of the Multinational Corporations* (New York: Simon and Schuster).

BELANGER, P. R. and C. SAINT-PIERRE (1978). 'Dépendance économique, subordination politique et oppression nationale: le Québec, 1960-1977,' *Sociologie et sociétés*, vol. 10, no. 2 (October).

BOUCHER, J. (1979). 'Les lacunes économiques du rapport Pépin-Robarts,' *Le Devoir* (9 March), p. 5.

BOURQUE, G. (1978). 'Le Parti québécois dans les rapports de classe,' *Politique aujourd'hui*, nos. 7-8.

BOURQUE, G. (1979). 'La nouvelle trahison des clercs,' *Le Devoir* (8 and 9 January), p. 5.

BRAUDEL, F. (1966). *La Méditerranée et le monde méditerranéen à l'époque de Philippe II*, 2 vols. (Paris: Armand Colin).

BRAUDEL, F. (1974). *Capitalism and Material Life, 1400-1800* (London: Fontana-Collins).

DE BRUNHOFF, S. (1976). *Etat et capital: recherches sur la politique économique* (Grenoble: Presses Universitaires de Grenoble et Maspéro).

CHORNEY, H. (1977). 'Regional Underdevelopment and Cultural Decay,' in J. Saul and C. Heron, *Imperialism, Nationalism and Canada* (Toronto: New Hogton Press).

CLEMENT, W. (1975). *The Canadian Corporate Elite* (Toronto: McClelland and Stewart).

CLEMENT, W. (1977). *Continental Corporate Power: Economic Linkages between Canada and the United States* (Toronto: McClelland and Stewart).

CLEMENT, W. (1978). 'Uneven Development: Canada and the World System,' paper presented to the Ninth World Sociology Convention, Economy and Society group, Uppsala, Sweden, 1978. This paper appeared in the *New Zealand and Australia Journal of Sociology*.

DUBET, F. (1976). 'Sur l'analyse sociologique du mouvement occitan,' *Sociologie du travail* (March).

FOURNIER, P. (1978). 'Le Parti québécois et la conjoncture économique au Québec,' *Politique aujourd'hui*, nos. 7-8.

FOURNIER, P. (1979). 'La Souveraineté-association: une stratégie de transition?' *Le Devoir* (29, 30 and 31 March), p. 5.

FURTADO, C. (1975). 'Le Capitalisme post-national,' *Esprit* (April and May).

GAGNON, G. and L. MAHEU (eds) (1978). 'Changement social et rapports de classes,' theme issue of the journal *Sociologie et sociétés*, vol. 10, no. 2 (October).

HALARY, Ch., M. LAGANA, C. SAINT-PIERRE (eds) (1978). 'Québec, de l'indépendance au socialisme,' special issue of *Politique aujourd'hui*, nos. 7-8.

HOLOHAN, W. (1976). 'Le conflit de Larzac: chronique et essai d'analyse,' *Sociologie de travail* (March).

JAURON, Y., N. ALEXANDRE, J.-Y. LAVOIE, L. NADEAU, R. CORBEIL (1977). *Filières de production et développement régional*, Office de planification et de développement du Québec, 'Etudes et recherches.'

LAURIN-FRENETTE, N. (1978). *Production de l'Etat et formes de la nation* (Montréal: Nouvelle Optique).

LEROY, V. (1978). *La Question monétaire en rapport avec le Québec: l'actualité générale du problème sous le régime politique fédéral et les perspectives issues du projet de Souveraineté-association*, report for the Québec Ministry of Intergovernmental Affairs (Québec: Editeur officiel du Québec).

MAHEU, Louis (1979). 'La conjoncture des luttes nationales au Québec: mode d'intervention étatique des classes moyennes et enjeux d'un mouvement social de rupture,' *Sociologie et Société*, vol. XI, no. 2 (October).

MASSEY, D. (1978). 'Regionalism: Some Current Issues,' *Capital and Class*, no. 6 (Autumn).

MICHALET, Ch. A. (1976). *Le Capitalisme mondial* (Paris: PUF).

MURRAY, V. (1976). *Le Parti québécois: de la fondation à la prise de pouvoir* (Montréal: Hurtubise, H.M.H.).

MURRAY, V. (1978). 'Le Parti québécois: les tensions au sein de l'alliance indépendantiste,' *Politique aujourd'hui*, nos. 7-8.

NAYLOR, T. (1972). 'The Rise and Fall of the Third Commercial Empire of Saint Lawrence,' in G. Teeple (ed.), *Capitalism and the National Question in Canada* (Toronto: University Press).

NAYLOR, T. (1975). *The History of Canadian Business, 1867-1914* (Toronto: James Lorimer).

PALLOIX, Ch. (1971). *L'Economie mondiale capitaliste* (Paris: Maspero).

PALLOIX, Ch. (1973). *Les Firmes multinationales et le procès d'internationalisation* (Paris: Maspero).

QUÉRÉ, L. (1978). *Jeux interdits à la frontière* (Paris: Anthropos).

RAY, D. M. (1971) 'The Location of American Subsidiaries in Canada', *Economic Geography*, vol. XLVII, no. 3 (July), pp. 389-400.

RAY, D. M. (1975). 'Regional Economic Development and the location of U.S. Subsidiaries,' paper presented to the Incentives Location and Regional Development Conference organized by the Government of Manitoba, January 1975.

ROYAL COMMISSION ON CORPORATE CONCENTRATION (1978). *Report* (Ottawa: Supply and Services Canada).

SALES, A. (1979). *La Bourgeoisie industrielle au Québec* (Montréal: University Press).

STOPFORD, J. M. and L. T. WELLS (1972). *Managing the Multinational Enterprise* (London: Longman).

SUNKEL, O. and E. FUENZALIDA (1979). 'Transnational Capitalism and National Development,' in J. J. Villamil, *Transnational Capitalism and National Development* (London: Harvester Press).

TASK FORCE ON CANADIAN UNITY (1979). *A Future Together: Observations and Recommendations* (Ottawa: Supply and Services Canada).

TELLIER, L. N. (1979). 'Le Parti québécois ne cherche pas l'intégration au capital américain,' *Le Devoir* (5 April), p. 5.

THELLIER, Marie-Agnès (1978). 'Ottawa utilise mal ses outils,' *Le Devoir*, 10 June, p. 11.

THELLIER, Marie-Agnès (1979). Interview with Yves Bérubé, Minister of Lands and Forests and Natural Resources, *Le Devoir*, 21 June, p. 28.

VALASKAKIS, K. (1978). *L'"Option Europe', analyse de la plausibilité d'une association Québec/Canada/Europe* (Québec: Ministry of Intergovernmental Affairs).

VERNON, R. (1971). *Sovereignty at Bay* (New York: Basic Books).

VERNON, R. (1974). *Les Conséquences économiques et politiques des entreprises multinationales* (Paris: Robert Laffont).

WALLERSTEIN, I. (1974). *The Modern World System* (New York: Academic Press).

WILKINS, M. (1970). *The Emergence of Multinational Enterprise: American Business Abroad from the Colonial Era to 1914* (Cambridge, Mass.: Harvard University Press).

WILKINS, M. (1974). *The Maturing of Multinational Enterprise: American Business Abroad from 1914 to 1970* (Cambridge, Mass.: Harvard University Press).

EPILOGUE

Charles Lindblom
Harvard University,
New Haven, USA

DISAGGREGATING 'CAPITALISM'

In their Introduction to these papers, the editors say of the international economy that 'the unit of analysis on which we focus is the system as a whole, which stands above and cannot be reduced to any of its component parts.' How do they then characterize the 'system'? Passing through historical phases, it is 'first, the transition from feudalism to capitalism; second, the stage of competitive capitalism, third, the stage of imperialism; and fourth, the stage of transnational capitalism.... '

They thus place capitalism and its continuing evolution at the center of the stage. As I understand it, they also tell us — here I develop their point somewhat — that what we must understand is a cluster of closely interlocked institutions, processes and movements called capitalism, and that we shall not understand the international economy if we fail to grasp that this whole is greater than the sum of its parts. For an understanding of the international economic order, it is not enough to understand business enterprises, banks, states, credit, markets, property, armies and diplomats: we must also understand the mutually supporting relations among them, and these are relationships that display important stabilities and continuities, despite the changes that mark each of their four historical stages.

I have recapitulated their points not to disagree with them, but because they establish a point of departure for an epilogue. To understand how the world economy was formed — what forces shaped the contemporary economic world — and to understand the main features of its contemporary structure, 'capitalism' is indeed an indispensable concept. That distinctive, ever-changing yet fundamentally stable powerful combination of forces that we call capitalism has been and still is the great destroyer and creator. Without the key variable 'capitalism,' there is no way to write the history or analyze the contemporary political economy of the world economic order. And if we are to estimate the future, we must take account of the near certainty that the mutually reinforcing institutions that go by the name 'capitalism' will continue to reinforce each other.

Yet for some further questions to which an epilogue might point, 'capitalism' is too big a concept. After asking, as in these papers, 'Where did our world come from and where is it going?' we may wish to go on to ask 'What is to be done?' If so, we turn from explanation and prediction to the kinds of analysis through which we or other persons might gain some degree of control over, some power to shape, a New International Economic Order. For such an analytical task I suggest that we, as scholars, observers or participants in policy-making and other forms of man-made social change, need to disaggregate. We need to take capitalism apart and examine parts of it in the expectation that some of them will be given functions to perform in society independently of capitalism as a whole.

Mine is both a methodological point and a substantive one. Methodologically, I suggest the desirability of disaggregation. Substantively, I suggest that institutions that are part of capitalism in the future can play functions to a significant degree independently of their contribution to that complex called capitalism.

An analogy: as a great destroyer and creator, the automobile has transformed American society. Not its wheels, not its motor, not its brakes — not even the petroleum industry or other connected phenomena — but the auto in all its interdependent aspects with ramifications throughout the social system. Yet if we wish to cope with problems of an automobile society, we had better, in the pursuit of, say, energy conservation, consider grain instead of petroleum fuel, or in the pursuit of, say, clean air, consider cars without internal combustion engines. The auto as key variable in our thinking is displaced by various manipulable disaggregates.

PRIVATE ENTERPRISE VERSUS
THE MARKET SYSTEM

For understanding how to control the emergence of the structure of a New International Economic Order, a critical required disaggregation is to separate, as many analysts do but as many still do not, two institutional components of capitalism: market system and private enterprise system. For any analysis of shaping the new international economic order, their futures should be taken to be separable.

Looking to a future that might be created, it is now widely understood that private corporations and other non-governmental international individual buyers and sellers can be displaced by state agencies. Such a development has of course already occurred in the communist world and to some degree in the West. One can also imagine mixed forms, and they too are already to a degree established. The point is — and it is a familiar one — that international markets do not necessarily require private enterprises.

But as far ahead as we can see, markets, unlike private enterprise, are indispensable to any international economic order. Even the most committed enemy of capitalism will probably have to grant their indispensability. Let us see why.

For organizing or coordinating a group of people too large to permit cooperation simply by direct and cooperative communication among them, three methods are available (though different theorists and other observers will not agree precisely on how they are best formulated).

The first, roughly, is organization through universal or widespread agreement on common rules and norms, so that people autonomously choose to behave in ways that constitute organization and coordination. Common rules and norms appear to account in some large part for the inhibition of many forms of disorderly behavior. For example, they may contribute greatly to social coordination by curbing some forms of deceit that would, if uncurbed, make social coordination impossible. Similarly, they may help curb what would otherwise be troublesome excesses of avaricious behavior in economic life. Their shortcoming, however, is that they effect only broad constraints on behavior, and constraints often incapable of alteration from case to case or from time to time. Thus general rules and norms will not effectively achieve an assignment of a nation's workforce to the many specific tasks that people want performed, an assortment of tasks that constantly changes with new demands, new technologies, and cumulation or depletion of available resources.

For organizing specific tasks, functions and differentiated obligations, for shaping the countless varieties of human behavior that need coordination, and for constantly adapting the patterns of organization and coordination to ever changing circumstances societies must depend, consequently, on a second and a third method of organization and coordination: central control based on at least a limited overview of the variables to be coordinated; and mutual control in which all or many of the persons to be coordinated control each other, though unequally, and adjust to each other.

When on opposite sides of New York's Fifth Avenue, two groups of pedestrians wait for the 'Walk' light and then moved forward toward each other as though to an inescapable conflict, they do not ordinarily collide or injure each other. Central commands could organize their passing each other; the alternative actually employed is eye and body signals that permit each member of each group to slip safely through spaces opened up between members of the oncoming other group. Basketball teams in play are coordinated through a combination of central direction and mutual control. The divisions of General Motors are coordinated through a combination of central control on the one hand, and reciprocal buying and selling on the other. The Soviet workforce is allocated to the nation's various tasks mainly through central coordination; the American workforce, mainly through the mutual controls of the labor market. All of these illustrated controls accomplish a more precise and variable coordination than norms and standing rules of behavior can accomplish.

Of these two available methods of coordination and organization, one of them — central control — is immediately disqualified as a method of international economic organization simply because there exists no central controller or, for as far ahead as we can guess, any possibility of the establishment of one. Hence international economic order and coordination can be accomplished only by mutual control and adjustment among the participants in it (and they may be governmental or private).

The market system is nothing less or more than a system of mutual control and adjustment. It is therefore indispensable unless there exists, or we find, suitable non-market forms of mutual organization and coordination.

To consider the possibility of non-market mutuality, we need first to clarify the meaning of 'market system.' The term clearly embraces a great deal more than the textbook market of atomist perfect competition. Most actual markets depart enormously from the model. They are marked by enterprises of varying size, of which some are extremely large (when compared, for example, with the size of some nation states). In them monopoly, oligopoly and competition are mixed. Some or many prices are set or constrained by government rather than exclusively by the interaction of buyers and sellers. And in some market systems, Yugoslavia most conspicuously, private enterprise is largely displaced by government enterprise. Thus the international market system, though it might at one extreme be composed largely of small businesses trading with each other across national lines, might at the other extreme be composed solely of state trading agencies dealing with each other across national lines.

If the nations of the world traded with each other through discrete bilateral transactions without the use of money and prices, we could speak of coordination through non-market mutual adjustment (although some would call even such a system a market system). But that nations will generally do so, or find any good reason to do so, seems highly improbable. Given their desire to reap the advantages of international trade, they will almost certainly employ the practical efficiencies of some significant degree of multilateralism, of money and credit and prices. New forms of money, credit and prices may be developed; but if nation-states or their citizens offer services and goods to other nations, or to the citizens of other nations in return for quid pro quo, their agreements on terms of their trade or cooperation will constitute prices; their agreements, contracts; and their arrangements for deferred quid pro quos, credit.

Thus the conclusion that an international economic order, old or new, requires mutual control and adjustment leads to the further conclusion that it requires an international market system of one kind. And that is a conclusion we must reach irrespective of the future of capitalism.

Whatever its defects — and they are not to be minimized — the international market system has always been and remains for the guessable future the world's largest — in area and in activities embraced — organizer and coordinator. As an international organizer, nothing compares with it — not NATO, not Comecon, not the UN, not even the Roman Catholic Church.

INTELLECTUAL EVASION

Why have I so laboriously, step by step, advanced to such an obvious conclusion? Because there are several schools of critics of the existing international economic order — including many of the most insightful critics — who seem to twist and turn to escape such a conclusion. Or perhaps it is more correct to say: in order to avoid facing the many powerful implications of the conclusion, which itself cannot be escaped, they do not discuss the market system except as they submerge the market system in capitalism. As a result, their discussion of the New International Economic Order is crippled.

That they twist and turn to escape analyzing the market system independently of what they have to say about capitalism is, I grant, a speculative and controversial proposition. But I find evidence for it in a frequent insufficiently qualified hostility both to the corporation and to the nation-state in their roles in the international economic order. The hostility appears to reflect an assumption that there exists, or might easily be created, alternative major participants in the international economic order — alternatives, that is, to the corporation and the nation-state. The standard or benchmark for evaluation of corporation and state appears to be a hypothetical institution devoid of the strong self-serving partisan motives that govern participants in mutual control and adjustment in the market system. Who might these actors be? The critics appear to have in mind actors more powerful and more broad in membership than regional unions of nation states. It is as though they yearned for, even if knowing the impossibility of, participants in mutual adjustment blessed with the dispassionate high-minded altruism of an idealized central coordinator.

A specific indication of such a state of mind among many critics is their frequent disinclination to weigh the sins of the multinational corporation against the sins of the nation-state in their respective treatments of the Third World. Refusing such a task they choose to condemn the behavior of both, thus either implying alternatives to the partisanship of mutual control and adjustment in the market system, or simply departing into the intellectual world of utopianism.

Other evidence of the critics' desire to escape grappling with the international market system is the very preoccupation with 'capitalism' with which we began. Granting, as I did at the outset, that for many intellectual tasks, including many that the authors of these chapters set for themselves, the usefulness or indispensability of the concept, it seems nevertheless true that in the face of policy choices to be analyzed — choices not between capitalism and some grand alternative but among disaggregates — a preoccupation with capitalism is an escape.

Indeed, such a preoccupation often looks like a form of fatalism, which is itself a form of escape. One can resign himself to the historical and contemporary force of capitalism as a molder of society, thus identifying the enemy, placing blame, yet simultaneously turning away from an analysis of steps that might be taken to soften historical inevitability with a touch of deliberate design of a better international market system. So long as we beat the horse of capitalism — which we can easily justify, since it is not a dead horse — we evade the necessity of designing an alternative beast of machinery to carry the many burdens of economic development.

I can perhaps strengthen the plausibility of my hypothesis — that many critics of the international economic order do not want to turn to analysis of the market system — by suggesting why they do not want to.

Much of the criticism of the international economic order — and much of the best of it — comes from Marxist thought. This intellectual tradition does not sufficiently distinguish between capitalism and market system. But, more than that, the great alternative it offers to capitalism is some form of central administration or planning of the economy. Insofar as Marx and Engels did distinguish market system from capitalism, they looked forward to the extinction of both. A new form of market system, in their eyes, is no acceptable alternative at all to the existing order: only some form of central administration or planning is acceptable. For the analysis of national economies, central administration was immediately accepted as a significant, realistic, intellectually weighty alternative. Earlier thought in political philosophy and actual historical experience in early empires and later nation-states were sufficient to establish central direction of the economy as the great alternative to capitalism and the market system. Thus the standard controversy generated by Marxist critiques of the existing economic order was over the merits of central control versus market system. And the intellectual armament of radical thought was evidence and argument that central direction was superior to the mutual adjustment of the market system. The arguments were strengthened by such broad intellectual traditions as those of the Enlightenment, traditions that held that man's forethought, brain, intelligence could make a better world than could the faltering and erratic hidden hand.

What, then, is this kind of thought to do when it moves from the analysis of the national economic order, for which central control is always an alternative, to the analysis of the international order, for which it is not? On the big issues, radical thought of this kind falls silent. Faced with a situation for which its longstanding rationale for central control is irrelevant, it has little to contribute to the clarification and resolution of the big issues of institutional structure of a New International Economic Order. Its very philosophical or ideological foundations are awry. It lacks a perspective from which to view the range of possible reconstructions of the international economic order. Thus paralyzed, it does not grapple with the fundamental issues of the appropriate place and character of the market system in a New International Economic Order.

SOME ISSUES IN THE DESIGN OF
THE INTERNATIONAL MARKET SYSTEM

In the traditional debate over national market systems, one set of issues concerned the market's possible contribution to or obstruction of liberty and democracy for millions of individual participants in it. In the debate on an international market system, a system in which the participants are mainly governments, regional unions, special-purpose international organizations and corporations, those issues recede. What remain are issues about efficiency and the distribution of gains from such international cooperation as the market might be made to organize.

From diverse intellectual currents — contemporary economic theory, practice and doctrine in industrial administration, new ideas about participatory democracy and worker participation in corporate management, and Maoist thought on mobilizing mass energies — we are coming to perceive that efficiency in social organization stems from at least two quite different sources. One, which has long been appreciated, is efficiency from excellence in the coordination of parts into a whole; thus, efficiency from specialization, division of labor and coordination of the divided specializations; thus also, the efficiencies of balance, as in the theory of balanced economic growth; thus also, the traditional identification in economic theory of efficiency with optimal resource allocation; and thus also, aspirations to raise the level of performance of an economy by 'fine tuning.'

The other is efficiency from a multiplicity of highly stimulated, even if not well coordinated, energies and talents: thus, the Schumpeterian entrepreneur; the advocacy of innovation rather than well-ordered resources allocation; the stress on conflict, flexibility, challenge and initiative rather than on balance or coordination; the gains of decentralization rather than centralization; and the antibureaucratic 'mass line' of Maoist thought.

Markets can, at least in principle, be structured to pursue either of or any one of many mixtures of these two sources of efficiency. Adam Smith found both possibilities in the market system. But the neoclassical tradition in economic theory seems to have stressed resources allocation over the efficiencies of multiple initiatives; and that stress may have carried over into the approach of mainstream economics to the international economic order. A big issue for the future world economic order is how the market might be used to protect and encourage a great multiplicity of growing points in the world; thus to upset, to throw off balance, to undermine the tendency of big organizations, governmental and corporate, to settle into protective stances that are hostile to innovation and growth.

A second great issue, everywhere recognized, is the distribution of the gains from international cooperation, which raises immediately the issue of the international distribution of those resources with which people can enter into international trade. There is no central redistributive authority, the assumption of which or appeal to which is taken for granted in the discussion of resources or income distribution within a national community. How an international redistribution of ownership is to be achieved without such a central redistributive authority is a frustrating question. The hard fact is that it is probably not going to be achieved, except by such exogenous developments as the discovery of oil or other resources in locations now thought to be without them.

Moreover, an international redistribution might be of little consequence without a redistribution of wealth domestically in each nation, for the international transfer might simply put resources in the hands of persons no less wealthy than those from whom the resources were removed. But the required massive internal or domestic redistribution is a highly improbable policy in any country, East, West or South.

It is quite possible that the only major effective method of redistribution of the world's resources, unpalatable as such a conclusion is, is through transfer without transfer of ownership. It may have to take the form, as it has within nations in the past, of processes by which capital is made available to propertyless workers in the form of industrial investment by distant owners. Barring something more attractive in a more distant future, better that we make the most of such a process than wring our hands over its obvious limitations. If so, the international market system should be designed to make the most of international capital movements through all those institutions, including private banks and multinational corporations, that effect just such a transfer of resources. That through repatriation of earnings they in effect charge a high price for making such a transfer, and that they in various ways take economic and political advantage of their position, are to be taken account of in regulating their roles in the New International Order but are not to be taken as justifying an unimaginative truculence about their roles.

WHERE IS THE USSR?

Finally, a striking feature of these essays is the absence from them of the Soviet Union. That the New International Economic Order can be discussed without it is, from some points of view, an astonishing fact. Apparently no ideas of consequence are coming from the Soviet Union. What, then, of action? One would suppose that a great superpower would be an actor in the world economy of such stature that it cannot be disregarded.

It is clear that the Soviet Union is not a major contributor to the building of a New International Economic Order. Nor do any of the contributors to these essays even speculate on pushing it into such a role. As a participant in international trade, it is not a source of major new innovations or directions of movement, not even of those to whom the Third World shows the ambivalence it shows toward the multinational corporations of the West. If the great problems of the Third World are with the West, it is because the Third World's prospects for a New International Economic Order lie in its relations with the West, even if the West is an ungenerous, avaricious and shortsighted partner, intent as much on exploitation as cooperation.

If the Soviet Union is not a source of fruitful thinking or of institutional support for a New International Economic Order, neither, I have argued, is much of the Marxist and some other radical thought in the West and the South. Yet it remains that radical thought is needed to lift our capacities for design above the necessary but inadequate agenda items that occupy us from day to day in the debate on the new economic order. That is a tall order: fundamental thinking about major alternatives unencumbered by some of the great 'idées fixes' of much contemporary critical thought.

NOTES ON CONTRIBUTORS

Volker Bornschier is assistant professor at the University of Zurich, Switzerland. His most recent book is *Multinationale Konzerne, Wirtschaftspolitik und nationale Entwicklung im Weltsystem* (1980).

Fernando Cardoso is director of the Centre for Analysis and Planning (CEBRAP) in São Paulo, Brazil. He has published widely in edited books and journals, and is the author of several books in Spanish on sociology and politics in Latin America.

Christopher Chase-Dunn is assistant professor of social relations at Johns Hopkins University, Baltimore. He is currently studying the process of urbanization in the context of the capitalist world-economy.

Charles Lindblom is Sterling professor of economics and political science at Yale University and is a past director of the Yale University Institution for Social and Policy Studies. He has published numerous articles on political planning, administration, and economics, and is the author of *Politics and Markets: The World's Political-Economic Systems* (1977) and *The Policy-Making Process* (2nd ed. 1980).

Harry M. Makler is associate professor of sociology at the University of Toronto. His special interests are the sociology of development, of financial institutions, and the impact of class structure on Latin American and Latin European nations. He has published books and articles on Portugal and Brazil and his most recent book is *Contemporary Portugal: Antecedents to the Revolution* (1979).

Alberto Martinelli is professor of sociology at the University of Milan, Italy. He has authored articles on economic theory, multinationals, labour unions, and business and politics.

Luciano Martins is a researcher at the Centre National de la Recherche Scientifique, Paris. Previously he was visiting professor at the University of Brasilia and Tinker visiting professor at the University of Columbia, New York.

Charles-Albert Michalet is professor of economics and director of the Research Centre on Multinational Corporations at Paris-Nanterre University. Before that he was a senior officer with the United States Center on Transnational Corporations.

Arnaud Sales is associate professor in the department of sociology at the University of Montreal, Canada. He is the author of *La bourgeoisie industrielle au Quebec* (1979) and edited 'Développement national et économie mondialisée', a special issue of *Sociologie et Sociétés* (1979).

Neil J. Smelser is university professor of sociology at the University of California, Berkeley. Among his publications are *Social Change in the Industrial Revolution* (1959), *The Sociology of Economic Life* (1962, 1975) and *Comparative Methods in the Social Sciences* (1976).

Barbara Stallings is assistant professor of political science at the University of Wisconsin-Madison. She is the author of *Class Conflict and Economic Development in Chile* (1978) and *Economic Dependence in Africa and Latin America* (1972).

Constantine Vaitsos is professor of political economy at Athens University and professorial fellow at the Institute of Development Studies at Sussex University, UK. He is co-editor of the Macmillan series Studies in the Integration of Western Europe.